The Complete
HOME DECORATOR

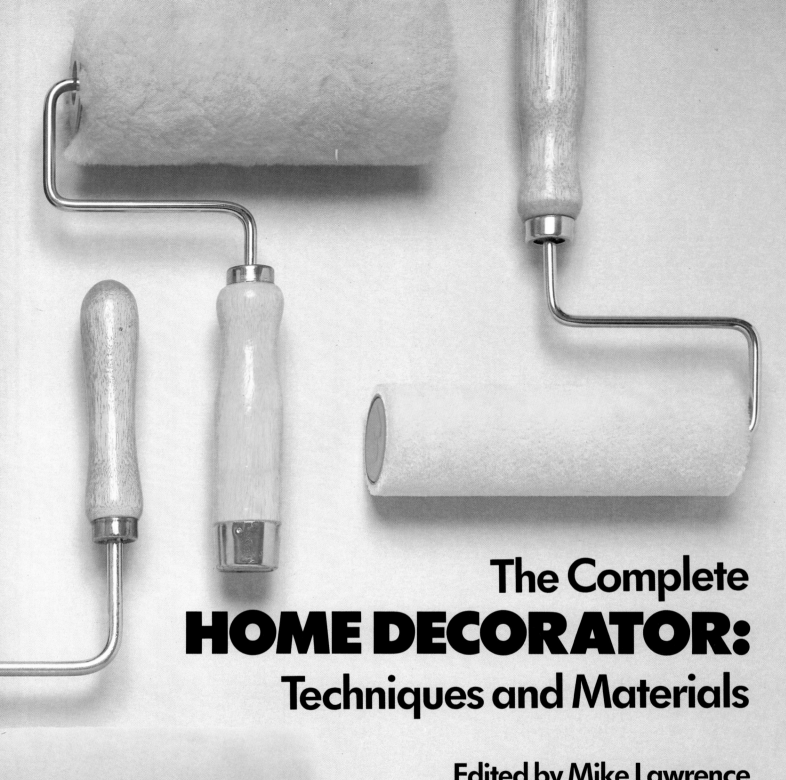

The Complete
HOME DECORATOR:
Techniques and Materials

Edited by Mike Lawrence

Macdonald Illustrated

A Macdonald Illustrated **Book.**

This edition published 1985 by
Orbis Publishing Limited, London
under licence from
Whinfrey Strachan Limited
315 Oxford Street
London W1R 1AJ

Reprinted 1990 by
Macdonald & Co (Publishers) Ltd
Orbit House,
1 New Fetter Lane,
London EC4A 1AR

A member of Maxwell Macmillan Pergamon Publishing Corporation.

Printed in Yugoslavia

ISBN: 0-356-19121-4

Acknowledgements
Photographers: Jon Bouchier, Simon Butcher, Paul Forrester,
Jem Grischotti, Keith Morris, Karen Norquay, Ian O'Leary,
Roger Tuff, Whinfrey Strachan.

Artists: Roger Courthold Associates, Nick Farmer, Val Hill,
Trevor Lawrence, Mike Saunders, Ian Stephen, Craig Warwick,
Brian Watson.

CONTENTS

CHAPTER 1

USING PAINT AND VARNISH

Whether you're painting your woodwork or using varnish and stain to enhance its natural grain pattern, thorough preparation is as important as careful application.
There's skill involved in painting walls and ceilings too – and you can create attractive three-dimensional effects using the latest textured paints.

PAINTING WOOD

Painting is the most popular way of decorating and protecting much of the wood in our homes. As with so many do-it-yourself jobs, getting a good finish depends on your skill. Here's how to paint wood perfectly.

Wood is used extensively in every part of our homes — from roof trusses to skirting boards. Structural timber is usually left rough and unfinished, while joinery — windows, doors, staircases, architraves and so on — is usually decorated in some way. Wood has just one drawback; as a natural material it's prone to deterioration and even decay unless it's protected. Painting wood is one way of combining decoration and

protection, and the popularity of paint is a testimony to its effectiveness. Properly applied and well looked after, it gives wood a highly attractive appearance and also provides excellent protection against dampness, dirt, mould, insect attack, and general wear and tear.

Of course, paint isn't the only finish you can choose for wood. If its colour and grain pattern are worth displaying, you can use

PREPARING WOOD FOR PAINT

1 *Before you can apply the paint you must fill any cracks or holes with wood filler (applied with a filling knife) and leave to dry.*

2 *Sand down the filled areas using medium-grade glasspaper. Wrap the abrasive around a sanding block or wood offcut so it's easier to use.*

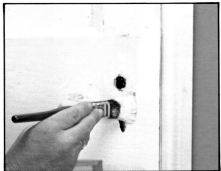

3 *Where paint has been chipped off, sand down the area and apply an ordinary wood primer to the bare wood using a small paintbrush.*

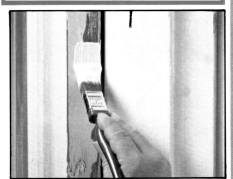

4 *When the surface of the wood is smooth, apply undercoat (as the maker recommends) and leave to dry before you put on the top coat.*

Ready Reference

PAINT TYPES
Paints for wood can be:
● **solvent-based gloss** (the 'oil' paints of the days before the advent of synthetic resins), which can be used indoors or outdoors
● **solvent-based satin** (also called eggshell or silk), intended for indoor use.

Both are fairly slow-drying, have a strong smell and have to be cleaned from equipment with white spirit, paraffin (kerosene) or proprietary solvent.

● **water-based satin and gloss** (emulsions) don't give a finish as hardwearing as that of a solvent-based paint but are quicker drying and have less smell. Clean equipment with hot or cold water and soap or washing-up liquid.

Non-drip paints (thixotropic or jelly paints, as they're also known) are available in both solvent-based and emulsion forms.

PREPARING PAINT

1 *Remove the lid from the paint can using the edge of a knife as a lever – don't use a screwdriver or you'll damage the lip of the lid.*

2 *Stir the paint (if recommended by the maker) using an offcut of wood, with a turning, lifting motion, or use an electric drill attachment.*

3 *Decant some paint into a paint kettle, which you'll find easier to carry than a heavy can. Top up the kettle from the can as you work.*

4 *To load the brush, dip the bristles into the paint to one-third of their length and wipe off excess on a string tied across the kettle rim.*

oils, stains or varnishes to enhance the overall effect and protect the surface. But as most of the wood used in our houses is chosen more for performance and price rather than looks, bland and uninteresting softwoods are generally the order of the day for everything from windows and door frames to staircases, skirting boards and door architraves. And painting them offers a number of distinct advantages.

Firstly, paint covers a multitude of sins — knots and other blemishes in the wood surface, poorly-made joints patched up with filler, dents and scratches caused by the rough and tumble of everyday life — and does it in almost every colour of the spectrum. Secondly, paint provides a surface that's hard-wearing and easy to keep clean — an important point for many interior surfaces in the home. And thirdly, paint is easy to apply ... and to keep on applying. In fact, redecorating existing paintwork accounts for the greater part of all paint bought.

What woods can be painted?

In theory you can paint any wood under the sun. In practice, paint (solvent-based or emulsion, see *Ready Reference*), is usually applied only to softwoods — spruce (whitewood), European redwood (deal), pine and the like — and to man-made boards such as plywood, blockboard, hardboard and chipboard. Hardwoods and boards finished with hardwood veneers can be painted, but are usually given a clear or tinted finish to enhance their attractive colour and grain pattern.

Paint systems

If you're decorating new wood, there's more to it than putting on a coat of your chosen paint. It would just soak in where the wood was porous and give a very uneven colour — certainly without the smooth gloss finish expected. It wouldn't stick to the wood very well, nor would it form the continuous surface film needed for full protection. All in all, not very satisfactory. So what is needed is a paint system which consists of built-up layers, each one designed to serve a particular purpose.

The first in the system is a primer (sometimes called a primer/sealer) which stops the paint soaking into porous areas and provides a good key between the bare wood and the paint film. Next, you want another 'layer' — the undercoat — to help build up the paint film and at the same time to obliterate the colour of the primer, so that the top coat which you apply last of all is perfectly smooth and uniform in colour. With some paints — emulsions and non-drip glosses — an undercoat is not always used and instead several coats of primer or two

HOW TO APPLY PAINT

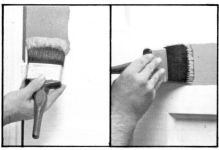

1 *Apply the paint along the grain; with non-drip paint (left) you can apply a thicker coat in one go without further spreading (brushing out).*

4 *Now you must 'lay off' the paint with very light brush strokes along the grain to give a smooth finish that's free from brush marks.*

top coats are applied with the same result.

The general rule to obey when choosing primer, undercoat and top coat is to stick with the same base types in one paint system, particularly out of doors and on surfaces subjected to heavy wear and tear (staircases and skirting boards, for example). On other indoor woodwork you can combine primers and top coats of different types.

If the wood you are painting has been treated with a preservative to prevent decay (likely only on exterior woodwork) an ordinary primer won't take well. Instead use an aluminium wood primer — not to be confused with aluminium paint — which is recommended for use on all hardwoods too. Oily woods such as teak must be degreased with white spirit and allowed to dry before the primer is applied.

As far as man-made boards are concerned, chipboard is best primed with a solvent-based wood primer to seal its comparatively porous surface. Hardboard is even more porous, and here a stabilising primer (a product more usually used on absorbent or powdery masonry surfaces) is the best product to use. Plywood and blockboard should be primed as for softwood. There's one other

2 *Still working with the grain and without reloading the brush, paint another strip alongside the first one and blend the two together.*

3 *Reload the brush and apply strokes back and forth across the grain over the area you've just painted to ensure full, even coverage.*

5 *Paint an area adjoining the first in the same way, blending the two sections together by about 50mm (2in) and laying off as before.*

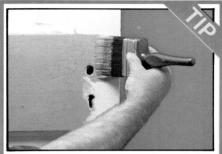

6 *Brush towards edges, not parallel with them or onto them, as the paint will be scraped onto the adjacent face, forming a ridge.*

WHAT CAN GO WRONG WITH PAINT

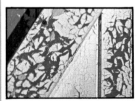

Left: Lifting and flaking occurs if paint is applied over a surface that is damp or powdery.

Right: Crazing is caused when paint is applied over a previous coat that was not completely dry.

Left: Blistering occurs when damp or resin is trapped beneath the paint film and is drawn out by heat.

Right: Cratering results from rain or condensation droplets falling onto the wet paint surface.

Left: Running, sagging or 'curtaining' happens when paint is applied too thickly on vertical surfaces.

Right: Wrinkling or shrivelling can occur on horizontal surfaces if paint is applied too thickly.

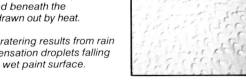

Ready Reference

HOW MUCH PAINT?

Large areas – in all cases coverage per litre depends on the wood's porosity and the painter's technique:
Wood primer 9-15 sq metres (95-160 sq ft)
Aluminium primer 16 sq metres (170 sq ft)
Primer/undercoat 11 sq metres (120 sq ft)
Undercoat 11 sq metres (120 sq ft)
Runny gloss or satin 17 sq metres (180 sq ft)
Non-drip gloss or satin 13 sq metres (140 sq ft)
Runny emulsions 15 sq metres (160 sq ft)
Non-drip emulsions 12 sq metres (130 sq ft)

Small areas – add up all the lengths of wood to be painted. One sq metre is equivalent to:
● 16m (52 ft) of glazing bars
● 10-13m (33-43 ft) of window frame
● 6m (20 ft) of sill
● 10m (33 ft) of narrow skirting
● 3-6m (10-20 ft) of deep skirting

CHOOSING BRUSHES

The best brushes have a generous filling of long bristles and are an even, tapered shape. Cheaper brushes have short, thin bristles and big wooden filler strips to pack them out. The ideal sizes for wood are:
● 25mm (1in) or 50mm (2in) for panel doors, skirtings
● 50mm (2in) or 75mm (3in) for flush doors, skirting, large areas
● 25mm (1in) cutting-in brush for window glazing bars
● 12mm (½in), 25mm (1in) or cheap paintbox brush for spot priming, applying knotting

Alternative to brushes
Paint pads are more widely used on walls than on woodwork, but the crevice or sash paint pad will do the same job as a cutting-in brush. It should be cleaned with white spirit or hot water and washing-up liquid (paint solvents might dissolve the adhesive between the mohair pile and foam).

TIP: PREPARING A BRUSH

Before using a new (or stored) brush work the bristles against the palm of your hand to remove dust and loose hairs.

thing you need to know. If the wood you want to paint has knots in it you should brush a special sealer called knotting over them to stop the resin oozing up through the paint film and spoiling its looks. If the knots are 'live' — exuding sticky yellowish resin — use a blow-torch to draw out the resin and scrape it off before applying knotting.

Paint on paint

You'll often want to paint wood that has already been painted. How you tackle this depends on the state of the existing paintwork. If it's flaking off and is in generally poor condition, you will have to remove the entire paint system — primer, undercoat and top coat — by burning off with a blow-torch,

applying a chemical paint stripper or rubbing with an abrasive. You then treat the stripped wood as already described for new wood.

Where the paintwork is in good condition, you simply have to clean it and sand it down lightly to provide a key for the new paint and to remove any small bits that got stuck in the surface when it was last painted. Then you can apply fresh top coat over the surface; the paint system is already there. You may, of course, need two top coats if you add a light colour to a dark one to stop the colour beneath from showing through.

If the paintwork is basically sound but needs localised attention, you can scrape or sand these damaged areas back to bare wood and 'spot-treat' them with primer and

undercoat to bring the patch up to the level of the surrounding paintwork, ready for a final top coat over the entire surface.

Painting large areas

Though the same principle applies to wood as it does to any other large surface area — ie, you divide it into manageable sections and complete one before moving on to another — if you're using an oil-based gloss paint you have to make sure that the completed area hasn't dried to such an extent that you cannot blend in the new. On the rare occasion that you might want to paint a whole wall of wood you should make the section no wider than a couple of brush widths and work from ceiling to floor.

With emulsions there isn't the same problem for although they are quick drying the nature of the paint is such that brush marks don't show.

You might think that a wide brush is the best for a large area but the constant flexing action of the wrist in moving the brush up and down will tire you out fast. Holding a brush is an art in itself and aches are the first indication that you're doing it wrongly. A thin brush should be held by the handle like a pencil, while a wider brush should be held with the fingers and thumb gripping the brush just above the bristles.

You'll find a variety of paint brushes on sale — some are designed to be 'throwaway' (good if you only have one or two jobs to do), others will stand you in good stead for years. But remember before using a new brush to brush the bristles back and forth against the palm of your hand — this is called 'flirting' and will dislodge any dust or loose hairs that could spoil your paintwork.

It is wise to decant the paint to save you moving a heavy can from place to place — a paint kettle which resembles a small bucket is made for the purpose. Plastic ones are easier to keep clean than metal ones.

Never be tempted to dip the bristles too far into the paint and always scrape off excess from both sides. Paint has the habit of building up inside the brush and if this happens on overhead work, you risk it running down the handle and onto your arm.

Painting small areas

These tend to be the fiddly woodwork on windows, around doors and lengths of stairs or skirting boards — and the hardest bit about all of them is working out how much paint you'll need (see *Ready Reference*).

Special shaped or narrow brushes can make painting these areas easier — for example, they prevent you 'straddling' angles in wood (like you find on mouldings) which damages the bristles in the middle of the brush. With windows and panelled doors you should also follow an order of working to

ORDER OF PAINTING

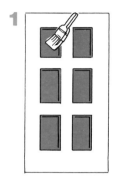 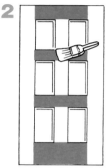 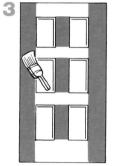

Panel doors: *tackle any mouldings first, then the recessed panels, horizontal members, vertical members and lastly the edges.*

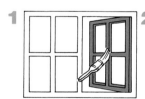 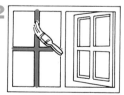 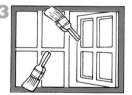

Casement windows: *start with any glazing bars, then paint the opening casement itself (the hinge edge is the only one which should match the inside); lastly paint the frame.*

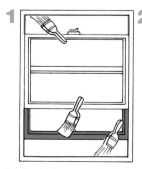 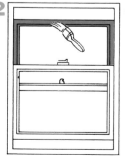 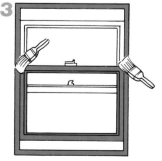

Sash windows: *paint the inside top and bottom and a little way up and down the sides of the frame first. Then paint the bottom of the outer sash. Move the sashes and do the rest of the outer sash, the inner sash and finally the frame.*

avoid causing overlap marks on the parts you've already painted.

Fiddly or not, they are the jobs you have to do first if you are putting up wallcoverings (if you're painting a room, the walls should be done before the woodwork) so that the drops can be placed against finished edges. If you want to touch up the paint without changing the wallpaper, it's best to use a paint shield.

Getting ready to paint

Ideally, before painting doors and windows you should remove all the 'furniture' — handles, fingerplates, keyholes, hooks etc — so you can move the brush freely without interruption. You should also take time to read the manufacturer's instructions on the can. If, for example, they tell you to stir the paint, then stir it for this is the only way of distributing the particles which have settled.

If you open a can of non-drip paint and find a layer of solvent on the top, you should stir it in, then leave it to become jelly-like again before painting.

All your brushes should be dry — this is something to remember if you are painting over several days and have put them to soak overnight in white spirit or a proprietary brush cleaner. If you don't get rid of all the traces of the liquid it will mess up your paint-

work. They should be rinsed, then brushed on newspaper till the strokes leave no sign.

Cleaning up

When you've finished painting clean your brushes thoroughly, concentrating on the roots where paint accumulates and will harden. They should be hung up, bristles down, till dry, then wrapped in aluminium foil for storage. Don't ever store them damp for they can be ruined by mildew.

If there's only a small amount of paint left, you can either decant it for storage into a dark glass screw-topped jar so you can use it to touch up damaged spots — it's important to choose a suitable sized jar so there's very little air space. Air and dust are both potential paint spoilers and there are two ways to keep them out if you're storing the can. Either put a circle of aluminium foil over the paint surface before putting the lid on securely, or — and this is the best way if the lid is distorted — put on the lid and then invert the can to spread the paint round the inner rim to form an airtight seal. Set it back the right way for storage.

If despite these safeguards a skin forms on the paint (usually over months of storage) you have to cut round the edge of it with a sharp knife and carefully lift it off.

Ready Reference

PRIMING WOOD

Primers can be solvent- or water-based. Outdoors, use the former (plus a solvent-based undercoat); indoors, you can use either, but water-based primer dries more quickly. If in any doubt as to which primer goes with which undercoat, consult your local supplier.
Other primers include:
● stabilising primer, for hardboard which is very porous
● wood primer, for wood that's been treated with a preservative, and for hardwoods.

TIP: STRAINING PAINT

Paint that has been stored badly can become bitty, and should be strained into a paint kettle before use. Secure nylon stocking over the kettle rim with string or an elastic band, and pour the paint through into the kettle.

CLEANING BRUSHES

To ensure the long life of brushes:
● remove excess paint from the bristles with the back of a knife
● wash out solvent-based paint in white spirit followed by soapy, then clean water – the soap restores flexibility and softens the brush
● wash out non-drip paint in a hot water/ washing-up liquid solution then rinse in clean cold water
● hang up brushes, bristles down, to dry (drill a hole in the handle to take a nail)
● at the end of a job a build-up of paint can be difficult to remove; soak the brush in a proprietary brush cleaner
● if leaving brushes overnight before continuing a paint job, suspend them in a jam-jar containing white spirit (drill a hole near the ferrule to take a nail) but remove all traces of spirit next day

TIP: STORING BRUSHES

During a short break wrap brushes in plastic cling-film to keep air off and the paint in the brush wet.

PAINTING WINDOWS

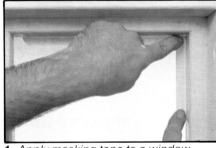

1 *Apply masking tape to a window pane to prevent paint getting onto the glass – leave 3mm (1/8in) of glass exposed so the paint forms a seal.*

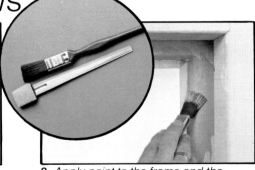

2 *Apply paint to the frame and the glazing bars using a small brush, or (inset) a cutting-in brush or a sash paint pad.*

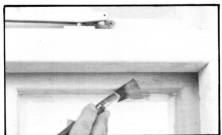

3 *Apply the paint along the grain; remove the tape when the paint is almost dry – if it dries completely you might peel it off with the tape.*

4 *An alternative way of keeping paint off the glass is to use a paint shield or offcut of plywood but, again, leave a paint margin on the glass.*

PAINTING WALLS AND CEILINGS

The quickest and cheapest way to transform a room is to paint the walls and ceiling. But, for a successful result, you have to prepare the surfaces properly and use the correct painting techniques.

Paint is the most popular material used to protect and decorate walls and ceilings in the home. Whereas many people hesitate before hanging wallpaper or sticking more permanent wall and ceiling coverings in place, few would worry about wielding a paint brush for the first time.

One of the chief advantages of painting a room is that it doesn't take much time; large areas can be given two or even three coats of emulsion paint in a day. The paints now available are hardwearing and totally unlike earlier distemper and water paints. They are easy to apply by brush, roller or pad and can be safely washed at frequent intervals to keep them looking fresh.

Any drawbacks are usually caused by faults in the wall or ceiling surface, rather than by the paints. A standard paint alone cannot cover up defects in the same way that some other wallcoverings can, so a surface which is to be painted usually needs more careful preparation than one which is to be papered.

The majority of walls and ceilings are plastered and this type of surface, when in sound condition, is ideal as a base for emulsion and other paints. But it is not the only surface finish you are likely to come across.

Previous occupiers of the house may well have covered the walls with a decorative paper and even painted on top of that. At the very worst there may be several layers of paper and paint, making it very difficult to achieve a smooth paint surface. In this situation it is invariably better to strip the surface completely down to the plaster and to start again from scratch.

This does not mean that no paper should be overpainted. Certain types such as plain white relief wallcoverings and woodchips are intended to be so treated, and actually look 'softer' after one or two redecorations. In short, most wall or ceiling surfaces you are likely to encounter will be paintable. All you have to do is select the right paint for the job and get the surface into as good a condition as possible.

Choosing paints

Vinyl emulsion paints are the most commonly used types of paint for painting walls and ceilings. They are easy to apply and come in a wide range of colours. You will usually have a choice of three finishes: matt, silk, or gloss.

There are also textured paints which are increasing in popularity, particularly for ceiling use. These are vinyl emulsion paints with added 'body' so they can be applied more thickly and then given a decorative textured finish.

Oil-based eggshell paints can be used where a more durable surface is needed or where you want to use the same colour on both walls and woodwork. Resin-based gloss paint is used occasionally also on walls and ceilings, particularly in humid rooms like kitchens and bathrooms.

You should choose paint carefully. The fact that one make is half the price of another may indicate that it has only half the covering power and you would therefore need to apply two coats of the cheaper paint. Also, if you're using white paint, you may find that one brand is noticeably 'whiter' than another.

Tools and equipment

Few specialised tools are needed for wall and ceiling paintwork. If you are content to work with only a brush you will require two sizes: one larger one for the bulk of the work, and a smaller brush for working into corners. It is worth decanting quantities of paint into a paint kettle which is easier to carry around than large heavy cans.

Rollers make the job of painting large areas of wall or ceiling much quicker and also help to achieve a better finish. But you will still need a small brush for working into corners and for dealing with coving, cornices etc.

To prepare a new fibre roller for painting, soak it in soapy water for 2 to 3 hours to get rid of any loose bits of fibre, then roll it out on the wall to dry it off. One point to remember: if you intend using silk vinyl emulsion paint, it's best not to use a roller as this tends to show up as a stippled effect on the silk surface.

Large paint pads will also enable you to cover big expanses of wall or ceiling very quickly. You can use a brush or a small paint pad for work in corners.

Apart from these paint application tools you'll need a variety of other items for preparing the surfaces so they're ready for the paint. The walls must be cleaned, so you'll need washing-down equipment: sponges, cloths, detergent, and a bucket or two of water.

You'll need filler for cracks and a filling knife about 75mm (3in) wide. When any filler is dry it will need to be sanded down, so have some glasspaper ready for wrapping round a cork sanding block. A scraper will also be needed if old wallpaper has to be stripped from the walls.

Finally, because of the height of the walls and ceiling, you'll need access equipment, such as a stepladder, to enable you to reach them safely and comfortably.

Preparing the surface

No painting will be successful until the

Dulux Russet over Dulux Cameo

PAINTING THE CEILING WITH A ROLLER

1 Use a brush to paint a strip about 50mm wide round the outside edge of the ceiling; a roller cannot reach right into angles or corners.

2 Pour paint into the roller tray; don't put in too much at a time or you risk overloading the roller and splashing paint out of the tray.

3 Dip the roller in and pull it back so there is paint at the shallow end of the tray. Push the roller back and forth in the paint at the shallow end.

4 Run the roller over the ceiling so there is a band of paint next to the strip of paint you have brushed along the edge of the ceiling.

5 Reverse the roller's direction so you join up the two strips of paint into one band. Then finish off by running the roller over the band.

6 Now start the next section by running the roller alongside the completed band. Work your way round the ceiling in bands.

Ready Reference

LINING WALL SURFACES

You can use lining paper to do the same job for paint as it does for wallpapers, covering minor cracks and defects on the wall or ceiling and providing a smooth surface for painting.

TIP: SEAL STRONG COLOURS

Wallcoverings with strong colourings, and particularly those tinted with metallic inks, will almost certainly show through the new paint. To prevent this they should be stripped off, or sealed with special aluminium spirit-based sealer.

FILLING HAIRLINE CRACKS

You may not be able to push enough filler into hairline cracks to ensure a good bond:
● it is often better to open the crack up further with the edge of an old chisel or screwdriver so the filler can penetrate more deeply and key better to both sides of the crack
● when using a textured vinyl paint there is no need to fill hairline cracks, but cracks wider than 1mm ($^1/_{32}$in) should be filled.

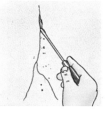

DEALING WITH FITTINGS

Protect electrical fittings so paint or water can't enter them during cleaning and decorating:
● ideally, power to these fittings should be cut off and the fittings removed
● if items cannot be removed, use masking tape to protect them.

SELECTING PAINTS

When choosing paints, remember that:
● emulsion paints are quicker to apply, dry more quickly and lack the smell of resin- or oil-based paints. They are also cheaper and can be easily cleaned off painting equipment with water
● non-drip paints are best for ceilings and cover more thickly than runny ones, cutting down on the number of coats
● a silk or gloss finish will tend to highlight surface irregularities more than a matt finish
● textured paints are suitable for use on surfaces which are in poor condition since they will cover defects which a standard emulsion paint cannot.

PAINTING THE WALL WITH A BRUSH

1 *Use a small brush to cut in at the wall and ceiling join and in corners. With a larger brush paint the wall in bands. First, brush across the wall.*

2 *Move the brush across the wall in the opposite direction. The bands of paint should be about 1m wide and you should be working downwards.*

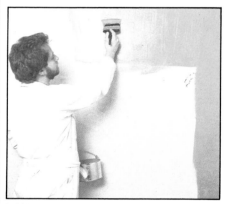

3 *When you are working at the top of the wall your next strokes should be downwards to complete the area you have covered with crossways strokes.*

4 *At the bottom two-thirds of the wall continue working in crossways strokes, but this time finish off each section by brushing upwards.*

USING PAINT PADS

1 *Thin the paint a little (with water for emulsions, turps for oil-based ones). Cut in with a small brush or pad and use a larger pad to paint in bands.*

2 *For precise work you can use a small pad like this. Ensure that you cover areas you don't want painted with masking tape.*

surface beneath has been properly prepared. Unless wallpaper is of a type intended for painting it is usually better to strip it off, and walls which have been stripped of their previous wallcoverings need a thorough washing to remove all traces of old paste. Make sure the floor is protected against debris by covering it with a dust sheet or sheets of old newspaper. Emulsion-painted walls also need washing to remove surface dirt. In both cases, use warm water with a little household detergent added. Then rinse with clean water.

If you decide to leave the wallpaper on the walls you will have to wash it down before you paint. Take care to avoid overwetting the paper, particularly at joins. When the surface is dry, check the seams; if any have lifted, stick them down with a ready-mixed paste.

Ceilings should be washed in small areas at a time and rinsed thoroughly before you move onto another section systematically.

If the surfaces are left in perfect condition, they can be painted as soon as they are dry.

It's possible that walls or ceilings may have been painted with distemper, which may only become apparent after you have removed the existing wallcovering. Unless it is the washable type, you will have to remove it completely since emulsion paint will not adhere well to it. Use hot water, detergent and a scrubbing brush to soften and get rid of the coating; this is hard work, but you could use a steam stripper to speed up the process.

With all the surface cleaned, the next job is to fill any cracks and repair defects such a as indentations caused perhaps by knocks or the blade of a carelessly handled wallpaper scraper (see *Ready Reference*).

Whenever a filler has been used it should be sanded down flush with the wall surface,

once dry, and the resulting dust should be brushed away.

If the plaster is in bad condition and obviously covered in cracks you should consider covering it completely with liningpaper, woodchip or other relief wallcovering before painting it. The paper will provide a good base for redecoration, and will save a great deal of preparation time. However, this can only be done if the plaster itself is still bonded securely to the wall. If it is coming away in chunks or sounds hollow behind the cracks, then the wall should be replastered.

Cracks which have developed round door and window frames are best filled with a flexible sealant, which will be unaffected by movement of the frames. Acrylic-based sealants are available for this purpose and they can be easily overpainted.

After all the preparation work has been

PAINTING PROCEDURE

Paint the ceiling first in 1m-wide bands (1 & 2). Paint round a ceiling rose (3), then complete the rest of that band (4). On walls work downwards (1). At a window, paint along the top band (2) and repeat the process at the bottom (3). Work from right to left unless you are left-handed.

completed, have a good clear-up in the room so that when you begin painting you do not stir up dust and have to work around numerous bits and pieces scattered over the floor space.

Re-lay dust sheets and set up your access equipment before even opening the first can of paint. Make sure your brushes or rollers are clean and ready for use.

Painting sequences
If possible, do all your painting in daylight hours. Artificial light is less easy to work by and can lead to small areas being missed.

Painting is always done from the highest point downwards, so ceilings are the first areas to be tackled. The whole ceiling will be painted in bands across the room no wider than you can easily reach without stretching on your stepladder or platform. This generally means that at any one time you will probably be painting a band no wider than 1m and less than 2m long unless you are using scaffolding boards to support you.

You start at the edges first and then work into the main body of the room.

Linking one section to another is seldom difficult with emulsion paint and is simply a matter of blending the paint from the new section back into the previous one.

Walls are treated similarly, starting at the top and working downwards in sections about 1m wide, cutting in at the ceiling and at return walls.

Painting tips
The number of coats required will depend on the previous colour and condition of the surface and the type of paint. If another coat has to be applied, be sure that the previous one is fully dry first. With modern vinyl emulsion paint it may be that because the paint is water-based it will cause the paper underneath to swell and bubble; however, you shouldn't worry about this because as the water in the paint dries out the paper and paste behind the paint surface will begin to flatten again.

If the paper is badly hung with a lack of adhesive at the edge, seams may lift as the paint dries. They will have to be stuck down in the same way as if they had lifted during washing. Careful preparation would prevent this problem anyway.

APPLYING TEXTURED FINISHES

Textured finishes which you can paint on walls or ceilings are an inexpensive way of covering up poor surfaces. They also give you the chance to exercise your ingenuity in creating relief patterns on them.

Textured wall and ceiling finishes can provide a relatively quick form of decoration. You don't, for example, need to apply more than one coat. And, unlike relief wall-coverings (another type of product commonly used to obtain a textured wall or ceiling surface), you don't have to go through the process of pasting, soaking, cutting, hanging and trimming; you simply spread the finishes on the surface with a paint brush or roller.

One of the advantages of using a 'texture' on walls is that it will tend to mask the effect of any general unevenness in the surface. Similarly, ready-mixed textures are often marketed specifically as a solution to the problem of improving the appearance of old ceilings. They are very suitable for this and can save a lot of tedious repair work.

However, there is no need to think of textures just as a cover-up. You may simply prefer a textured surface to a flat, smooth one. If you use patterning tools, the range of textured effects you can achieve is practically endless, depending only on your skill and imagination.

Choosing textured finishes

One of the factors which will influence your choice of finish is, obviously, how much you are prepared to pay. The traditional compound which you buy in powder form to mix with water is the cheapest type, but, like ordinary plaster, is rather porous and needs to be painted over. Even so, the cost of coverage, including over-painting, is very reasonable. Ready-mixed types are rather more expensive but you don't normally need to paint over them, and some brands offer a reasonable range of colours.

The traditional powder type, thickly painted on a wall or ceiling, has a slow setting time, which makes it ideal for creating a decorative impression with a patterning tool. Ready-mixed products can also be given a textured finish in the same way as the powdery type, but doing so will tend to vary the thickness of the finish so that overpainting might be necessary. (If you just paint them on without carrying out any follow-up patterning treatment, you will be left with a random textured

effect.) Some of the textured products suitable for exterior use can also be patterned with tools; check the manufacturer's instructions for guidance here.

Tools and equipment

Apart from the texture finish itself, and paint if you're going to overpaint, you will need a brush or roller to apply the finish. The most suitable type of brush is a 200mm (8in) distemper brush. The type of roller you use will affect the pattern created and special rollers are available to create certain effects (see step-by-step photographs). Sometimes you paint the material on first with an ordinary roller (or a brush) and then work it over with a patterning roller; follow the manufacturer's instructions for the type of roller you will need.

If you are dealing with a ceiling you will need some form of access equipment; two stepladders with a plank resting between them will usually suffice. Textured finishes, especially when applied with a roller tend to spray and spatter about, so it's best to have goggles and a mask to protect your eyes and mouth when you are looking up; also, don't forget to protect your hair. In addition, whether you're painting walls or ceiling, you'll need a dust sheet or some other form of protective covering for the floor.

You may also require a plumb bob and line (see *Ready Reference*) and any equipment required for filling cracks or joints such as a caulking tool, jointing tape knife, filling knife, filler and so on.

Where you intend to texture the surface after painting on the finish you will also need your patterning tool(s). These can be proprietary or home-made; you can even use equipment which was chiefly designed for other purposes which you may decide will create the pattern you want. Apart from patterning rollers, the proprietary tools available include combs (some of which can give special effects within the combed patterns such as 'rose' and 'flower'), stipple brushes and pads and special 'swirl' brushes. You can also buy a tool called a 'lacer' to dull any sharp ridges; however a plastic straight edge or the blade of a filling knife is a suitable alternative.

Preparing the surface

Textured finishes can be applied to bare or painted surfaces but the surface must be sound and, in some cases, treated. You should not, for example, think of textured finishes as a means of covering up walls which really need replastering or a ceiling which should be replaced.

All porous surfaces should first be treated

SEALING JOINTS

1 *To seal a joint between boards, first use a caulking tool to apply cellulose filler (or a thicker mix of texture compound) along it.*

2 *Use a special taping knife to press a length of jointing tape into the filler so it's securely embedded and free of air bubbles.*

3 *Spread on another layer of filling material, again using the caulking tool, but this time so the filler covers the jointing tape.*

4 *Use a damp sponge to wipe away surplus filler and to feather the edges so the joint surface becomes flush with the plasterboard.*

Ready Reference

PROPRIETARY TOOLS TO USE
You can buy various tools designed for patterning textured finishes. They include combs, patterned rollers, various types of brushes and a 'lacing' tool for smoothing high points.

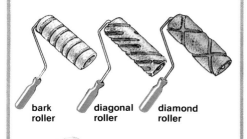

bark roller   diagonal roller   diamond roller

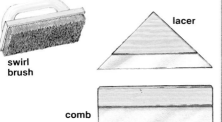

swirl brush   lacer   comb

MAKE YOUR OWN COMB
You can make a comb with a wooden handle and a rigid plastic blade (cut, for example, from an old ice-cream carton). Cut your own designs out of the plastic.

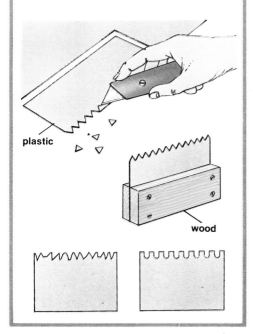

plastic   wood

with a stabilising primer recommended by the manufacturer of the finish so that the setting of the texture material is not spoilt by suction. Surfaces requiring such treatment include brick, render, concrete, plaster and some types of wallboards.

Texture finishes can be used to hide very fine hairline cracks and are usually marketed for their flexible ability to cope with normal movement so cracks don't reopen. However, none of them can cover cracks or joints of more than 1.5mm (1/16in) with any guarantee that these will remain covered up. You will have to caulk the cracks or joints with texture compound (perhaps thickened with a little ordinary filler). Ideally, joints between boards of any kind should also have a layer of jointing tape over them between layers of whatever types of filler you are using (see step-by-step photographs). Make sure you feather the edges of the filling material so there is no

noticeable ridge when the texture covers it.

Painted surfaces should be clean, sound and sanded lightly to provide a key for the finish. Distemper and low-quality emulsion paint may not hold the texture; test by pressing adhesive tape on a small area first and remove any painted surface that has a tendency to delaminate when the tape is peeled off. If the surface has been painted in a dark colour it's best to paint over it in a light colour first before you apply the texture.

You will have to remove wallpaper or light tiles such as polystyrene tiles. You can, however, safely apply a textured finish over ceramic tiles provided they are clean, the gaps are filled and they are primed with a coat of PVA adhesive, diluted according to the manufacturer's instructions.

Do check that lath-and-plaster ceilings are strong enough to support the extra weight of the textured coating. If they are

MAKING TEXTURED PATTERNS

Textured materials can be applied by brush or roller. If you are applying this type of finish to walls it's best, if possible, to work in an upwards direction to minimise the amount of material which gets sprayed over you and the floor. Apply the finish to the wall in bands and apply it thickly so the texture will stand out. You can roll it on with an ordinary foam roller (see left) which will give a stipple effect and then leave the surface to dry as it is. Alternatively, you may prefer to go ahead and use other tools to create other kinds of textured effects.

showing any signs of sagging, lift a floorboard in the room or loft above and check that the laths are still nailed firmly to the joists, and the plaster is well keyed to the laths.

Where there are fixing nails or screws which will be embedded in the texture material, you should paint them over with gloss paint to prevent them from rusting.

You will have to prime wood-faced wallboards if they are absorbent and it's best to treat wood-effect plastic boards with PVA adhesive in the same way as ceramic tiles. In the case of thin wallboards there is a risk that movement will cause the texture material to crack, so test them for flexibility and remove them if necessary.

Applying textured finishes

It's best to apply a textured finish thickly; remember you will only be applying one coat and the thicker the coat the more protection it will provide for the wall or ceiling surface. Also, if you intend using a patterning tool, working on a deep, even coat of texture will give the best results. Apply the finish in bands across the room until the entire wall or ceiling is covered.

Exterior textures are normally applied with a natural bristle brush, though on smooth surfaces where you want a coarser texture you can use a foam roller. Whenever possible, you should work in the shade. If you are painting near drainpipes, you should tape newspaper round the pipes to protect the area you wish to avoid painting. Similarly, use masking tape to protect window frames (outdoors and inside) and also window reveals, light fittings, ventilator grilles and so on. If it does get on any of the areas, wipe it off with a damp rag immediately.

Using patterning tools

The drying time for textured finishes varies from 12 to 24 hours, though the working time for patterning can be much lower, depending on atmospheric conditions. You will normally have at least 4 hours to complete your patterning, but it would make sense to complete one wall or ceiling at a time as far as possible. If in doubt, study the manufacturer's instructions for the particular product you are using.

A random pattern will usually be quicker to achieve than a regular one where you will have to take care in matching up the pattern. In the latter case, it may be better to spread the texture on in strips and pattern each strip as you go rather than covering the whole wall or ceiling and then patterning it.

Finishing off

After patterning, it is normal practice to 'lace' the pattern (to dull any sharp ridges) just as the material begins to dry. Even after it has dried you may still need to remove sharp points; use the blade of a filling knife to knock them back, or, if you want to go to the trouble, wrap fine glasspaper round a sanding block and sand them down. If you don't remove sharp ridges and points, the surface may cut someone who leans against it or brittle parts may break off.

Textured finishes can usually be covered with either an emulsion or oil-based paint but check the manufacturer's recommendations.

Cleaning and maintenance

Most texture finishes are designed to last, which is just as well as it's a messy, time-consuming and difficult job to remove them. Maintenance will normally consist of redecorating them with a coat of paint when they show signs of wear or hard-to-remove dirt or stains. Surfaces should be kept clean: to do so, apply warm soapy water with a paint brush to loosen dirt and dust.

3 *A specially designed, grooved 'bark' effect roller is being run over the textured material to produce a bark pattern on a wall surface.*

6 *This diamond pattern was formed by a purpose-designed roller. With a regular pattern like this you should check that the pattern rows match.*

1 *A straightforward and at the same time striking effect can be produced by running a purpose-designed diagonal roller up and down across the surface.*

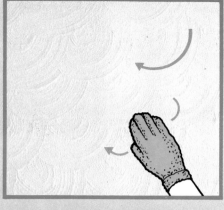

2 *A wide variety of tools, proprietary or otherwise, can be used to form patterns on texture materials; here a coarse nylon mitt produced a swirled effect.*

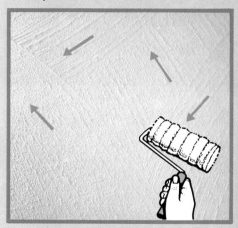

4 *Here a 'bark' effect roller was again used but this time in a random sweeping motion to create a curved criss-cross variation of the basic pattern.*

5 *The fine stipple effect (left) was made using an ordinary foam roller; the coarser stipple (right) by dabbing with a sponge wrapped in plastic.*

7 *Another design: the background pattern was produced by running a 'bark' roller over the surface; a sponge was then used to make circles on this.*

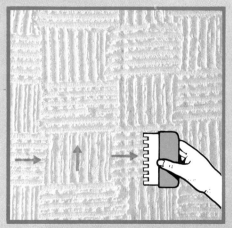

8 *This criss-cross pattern of alternate facing 'squares' could be created using a comb but here a serrated scraper was used instead.*

Ready Reference

TYPES OF FINISH

There are various types of textured finishes available. They include:
● the traditional type, which is a powder compound, generally available only in white, which you mix with water; it needs to be painted afterwards
● textured 'paints', which are ready-mixed products containing similar light aggregates and binders to the traditional type but also plasticised like modern paints; they come in a range of colours and usually don't have to be painted over (though you can if you wish)
● textured paints and coverings suitable for exterior use.

HOW FAR WILL THEY GO?

Powder compounds will cover about 2.5sq m per kg (12sq ft per lb) of unmixed powder and are available in 5, 10, 12½ and 25kg bags. Ready-mix materials will cover 2 to 2.5sq m (22 to 27sq ft) per litre and are supplied in 5, 10 and 12½ litre tubs.

BEWARE ASBESTOS

Traditional compound powder textures sometimes contain asbestos (check the manufacturer's instructions); such types should be mixed in well-ventilated conditions to protect you against a potential health risk.

THE RIGHT TEMPERATURE

Texture finishes can be affected by extremes in temperature so:
● don't apply ready-mix products to a ceiling which incorporates a heating system
● don't carry out application when the temperature is below 5°C or above 40°C or when the temperature is likely to exceed these limits before the material is dry.
  You can apply a traditional compound type of texture over 'hot' surfaces such as heated ceilings and chimney breasts, but you should first seal the surface with a good quality alkali-resisting primer.
  Don't apply either type in freezing conditions.

CREATING REGULAR PATTERNS

If you are creating a regular pattern which requires matching, use a plumb bob and line to mark guidelines on the walls (or to snap chalked lines on the ceiling); paint and pattern in bands between the straight lines.

TIP: REMOVE MASKING QUICKLY

If you have used tape or newspaper to protect window frames, pipes or fittings, remove it before the texture dries; it may be difficult to remove later when the texture has set.

STRIPPING WOOD

Wood has a natural beauty, but it's often a beauty concealed by layers and layers of paint. Doors, window frames, even skirting boards and architraves can all become attractive features in themselves when stripped back to reveal the wood. Even if you prefer to repaint, using the right techniques to strip off the old will give the best possible surface on which to work.

Stripping wood of old paint or layers of ancient varnish isn't the easiest of jobs. It's usually only done because you're after a natural finish, or because the painted surface has degenerated to such an extent that further coats of paint simply can't produce a smooth finish. Either way, once wood has been stripped back to its natural state, it then has to be sealed again – to protect it from moisture which can cause cracking, warping and ultimately decay. Both varnishes and paints act as sealants, giving a durable finish. But which one you choose might depend on the wood itself – and you won't know what that's like until you've stripped it. If you're unsure of its quality, it's advisable to strip a test area first.

Some of the timber used in houses is of a grade that was never intended for a clear finish – large ugly knots, cracks, splits or even an unattractive grain are some of the signs. In cases like this it is probably better to treat the problems (eg, applying 'knotting' – a special liquid sealer – to make the knots tight and prevent them 'bleeding', filling cracks and splits to give a flush surface) and then paint to seal.

If you are set on having the wood on show and don't want to paint it – because it wouldn't fit in with a colour scheme or make the feature you want – you can give it a better appearance and extra protection with stain or coloured varnish.

Stripping with abrasives

For dry stripping there are several different kinds of powered sanders available, all of which use abrasive papers of some kind to strip the surface off wood. On large areas such as floors it is best to use a purpose-made power sander which you can hire. A drill with a sanding attachment, however, is useful for getting small areas smooth after paint has been removed by other methods.

One such attachment is a 'disc sander' and is quite tricky to use effectively without scoring the wood surface. Hold it at a slight angle to the wood and present only half the disc to the surface. Work in short bursts and keep the disc moving over the surface – if it stays too long in one place it can damage the wood.

A 'drum sander' attachment has a belt of abrasive paper stuck round the edge of a cylinder of foam, and if used along the grain only is rather easier to handle than a disc

USING SCRAPERS

1 *A triangular shavehook needs two hands when paint is thick. Hold the blade at an angle to the wood so it doesn't cause gouges.*

2 *A combination shavehook has round, straight and pointed edges to help remove paint and varnish from mouldings round windows and doors.*

3 *A special hook scraper has a sharp replaceable blade suitable both for scraping paint off flat surfaces and for getting into awkward crevices.*

sander. Whichever type is chosen, a fine grade abrasive should be used for finishing stripped wood.

Orbital sanders (which are also known as finishing sanders) usually come as self-powered tools – although attachments are available for some drills. These have a much milder action and as long as the spread of wood isn't interrupted by mouldings they smooth well and are useful for rubbing down between coats. These sanders are rectangular and should be moved over the surface in line with the grain. Make sure you choose the right type of sander, depending on the work in hand.

For sanding by hand – hard work, but much better for finishing – there are many grades of glasspaper from the coarse to the very fine. On flat surfaces it's best to wrap the paper round a small block of wood. As an alternative to glasspaper, there's also steel wool, which is most useful when you're trying to smooth down an intricate moulding. Always sand backwards and forwards *with the grain of the wood,* not across it. Scratches across the grain will always be highlighted by a clear finish. To remove remaining bits of paint use medium grade glasspaper; for finishing, a fine grade is better. Renew the glasspaper frequently as the paint will clog the surface,

although a useful tip is to try cleaning clogged paper with a wire brush. It'll work once or twice, but after that the abrasive surface is usually lost. Alternatively pull the sheet backwards and forwards, abrasive side uppermost, over a table edge to dislodge paint particles.

A useful tool for cleaning paint from corners and mouldings is a hand scraper with replaceable blades. These 'hook' scrapers are also used for 'smoothing' and often need two-hands – they slightly raise the surface of a clear run of wood, giving an attractive finish under a clear seal. Use with the grain.

Heat stripping

Heat stripping is the quickest way to remove paint or varnish, but it needs a lot of expertise if you are to avoid charring the wood. So it is best reserved for stripping out of doors where a less-than-perfect surface will be less noticeable. A gas blow-torch is used along with metal scrapers to lift the finish off the wood while it's still warm. Blow-torches with gas canister attachments are light to use and a flame spreader nozzle makes the job easier (it can be bought separately).

Where there's no glass, it's a two-handed operation. Light the blow-torch and hold it a

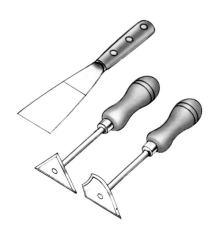
HEAT STRIPPING

1 *Play the blow-torch onto the paint and when it begins to bubble, start to scrape. Protect floor and sills with a sheet of non-flammable material.*

2 *When stripping paint near windows one hand must hold protection for glass. When paint hardens again, return the flame to the area.*

3 *Working overhead can be tricky if using a blow-torch. Protect your hands with gloves, your eyes with safety goggles and cover surfaces below.*

4 *To strip paint overhead, remove torch (be careful where it points), blow out flames and scrape quickly. As the paint loses heat it hardens.*

little way from the surface. Move it back and forth, going nearer and withdrawing, till the paint starts to wrinkle and blister. Now begin to scrape – be careful where you point the flame at this stage or you may damage other surfaces. As soon as the paint is hard to move return the flame to the area. Wear gloves to save your hands from being burnt by the falling paint, and cover areas below where you are working with a sheet of non-flammable material to catch the scrapings. In awkward areas, especially overhead, you should wear protective goggles for safety's sake.

Chemical stripping

Chemical strippers are probably the easiest way to strip wood. Available in liquid, gel and paste forms, their methods of application and removal vary, so always remember to read the manufacturer's instructions before you begin. Though all of them will remove paint and varnish, if you are dealing with a large area of wood they can work out to be very expensive – they're also very messy.

Liquid and gel strippers, decanted if necessary into a more convenient-sized container (read the instructions as to whether it can be heavy gauge plastic or should be glass or metal), are stippled onto the surface with a brush and left till the paint bubbles before scraping. Usually these strippers will work through only 1 layer of paint at a time so several applications can be necessary. If stripping a chair or table, stand the legs in old paint cans or jam jars so that any stripper which runs down the legs can be recycled. Artists brushes rather than paint brushes are useful when applying these strippers to mouldings or beading in windows and No 2 steel wool is useful for removing it.

After liquids or gels have been used, the surface must be cleaned down with white spirit or water (it depends on the stripper used) to remove any trace of chemical and must be left till completely dry before any stain or seal is applied.

Pastes are mostly water soluble and manufacturers stress important conditions for using them safely (eg, not in direct sun, in well ventilated rooms, the wearing of protective gloves, etc). Bought in tubs ready-mixed or in powder form to be made up, they are spread in thick (3-6mm) layers over the wood which must then be covered with strips of polythene (good way of using up plastic carrier bags) or a special 'blanket' (supplied with the tub) which adheres – when you press it – to the paste. They have to be left for between 2 and 8 hours after which the paste can be scrubbed off (with a firm brush) or washed down. Frequent changes of water are needed; follow manufacturer's advice about additives (eg, vinegar). Pastes are particularly effective with extraordinarily stubborn paint or varnish in very awkward places (eg, windows, bannisters etc); or where using a scraper might damage old wood. Some pastes are unsuitable for certain types of wood and can stain it – so read instructions carefully. Washing down should not be done, for example, with valuable furniture for this can raise the grain of the wood.

Bleaching

If the wood is discoloured once stripped (either from the stripper used or from some other source) you can try and achieve an overall colour with bleach – the household type, used diluted 1:3 with water to begin with and more concentrated if necessary, or better still a proprietary wood bleach.

Clean the surface of the stripped wood with paint thinner and steel wool and leave for 15 minutes to dry. Cover areas you don't want bleached with polythene, then brush bleach on generously. Work it into the wood *with the grain* using medium steel wool.

Leave for 2-4 minutes, then wipe off with rags. Leave to dry (up to 5 hours) before sanding after which you can finish the surface as desired.

CHEMICAL STRIPPING

1 *Liquid strippers are stippled onto wood with a brush. First pour the liquid into a smaller container — but remember it will dissolve light plastic.*

2 *When paint is bubbling use a scraper to remove it. Work upwards and be careful not to gouge the wood with the blade.*

3 *Several applications of liquid may be needed as chemicals often only eat through one layer at a time. Use gloves to protect your hands.*

4 *After all paint has been stripped off, wipe the wood down with white spirit or water so that the chemicals are neutralised.*

TIP

5 *A good way to deal with mouldings is to apply a thick layer of stripping paste. This needs to be covered while it works, but is very effective.*

6 *After leaving for the specified time (can be several hours) wash the paste off with sponge or a scrubbing brush, changing the water often.*

COLOURING WOOD

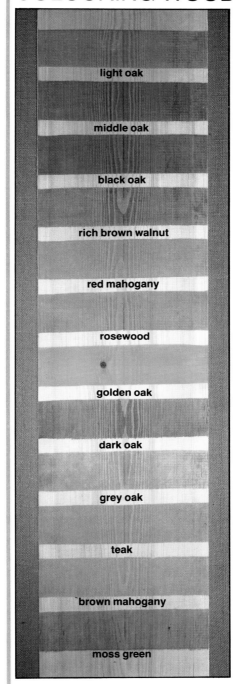

light oak

middle oak

black oak

rich brown walnut

red mahogany

rosewood

golden oak

dark oak

grey oak

teak

brown mahogany

moss green

On a plank of freshly planed wood the colours of different stains highlight the grain attractively (results will differ according to the age and condition of the wood). Stains don't seal and so they need a finishing coat of clear varnish — either gloss, satin or matt.

There are several different ways of altering the look of stripped wood.

● *Wood stains* are based on water, white spirit, alcohol, lacquer thinner or oil. Named after the wood whose colour they resemble, these penetrate the wood permanently. To give an even staining, the trick is to apply several thin coats — work from top to bottom on vertical surfaces to prevent drips and overlap marks. Use a pad (not a brush) made with cotton wool wrapped in a lint-free cloth and work backwards and forwards along the grain. When completely dry, seal with a clear varnish that is compatible with the stain. If applying more than one sealing coat, rub down the surface each time with fine glasspaper.

● *Coloured varnishes* both seal and 'stain' the wood surface and are removeable. They are also named after natural timber and are applied like ordinary clear varnish to sanded-smooth wood. You just go on applying the coats till you get the colour you want — rubbing down between each. Varnishes are oil (interior and exterior grades), spirit (not suitable for outdoors) or polyurethane based. Polyurethane varnishes can also be non-wood colours (such as red and green) and are especially useful if you want inexpensive wooden furniture to fit in with a colour scheme.

When using varnishes remember:
○ Never use a cellulose filler for it will always remain as a white mark. Choose a wood filler of similar colour to the stripped wood.

○ They have to be applied to perfectly smooth surfaces with all dust, grit and paint particles removed — wipe down with white spirit first, then leave to dry.

○ Don't attempt to apply them in dusty or windy conditions — the merest speck will spoil the finish and to be truly effective, stripped and sealed wood has to be beautifully smooth to the touch. A spray will give a more even finish than a brush.

● *Stained oils* both colour and seal. They are particularly suited to wood exposed to the elements (eg, outside doors and window sills) or wood that isn't in very good condition. Choose from a range of natural timber colours and apply several coats to give the wood 'depth'.

STAINING AND VARNISHING WOOD

If you want to decorate and protect the woodwork around your home without obliterating its grain pattern with paint, wood stains and varnishes offer a wide choice of finishes. Here's how to get the best results.

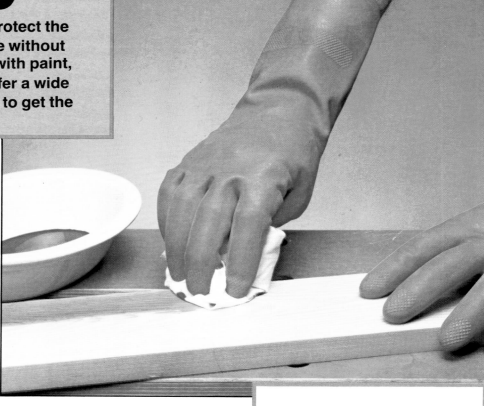

When it comes to giving wood a clear finish, you can choose from a variety of traditional and modern materials, including oils, wax, French polish and different types of varnish. Some are suitable for exterior use, others for interior use only. The degree of skill you need to apply them varies; some are quite simple to use, whereas others, like French polish, require special techniques acquired only by patient practice. The type of wood may affect your choice of finish; for example, open-textured woods like teak, iroko and afrormosia are best treated with an oil finish – they don't take varnishes well.

You may decide to change the colour of the wood before you finish it. You can use a varnish which incorporates a colour or apply a wood stain and then coat the wood with clear varnish or another clear finish.

If you don't wish to change the colour of the wood, but want to restore it to its natural colour – for example, where the wood has been slightly darkened by the action of a paint stripper – you can use a proprietary colour restorer.

Types of varnish and stains

Clear varnishes are like paint without the pigment. They contain a resin carried in a drying oil or spirit and it is the resin which gives a hard protective finish to wood. Traditionally, the resins used were like copal, natural and obtained from various tropical trees, but in modern varnishes they are synthetic, for example alkyd or polyurethane.

While other varnishes are available, by far the easiest to obtain and most widely used are those containing polyurethane resin. Polyurethane varnish is available in gloss, satin or matt finishes and for interior or exterior use. A non-drip variety is particularly suitable for vertical surfaces, ceilings and hard-to-get-at areas.

There are polyurethane varnishes which have added pigments and are known as coloured sealers. It's quicker to use one of these rather than to apply a wood-stain followed by a clear finish but you won't get the same depth of colour, and if the coloured varnish chips in use, timber of a different colour will show through.

Wood stains are colouring pigments suspended in water, oil or spirits. Some come ready-mixed; others in powder form to be mixed up. Oil-based stains tend to be more difficult to obtain and are not as widely used as the other two types.

Preparing the surface

Before staining, bleaching, varnishing or using other types of finish you should ensure that the surface is clean, dry, smooth and free from any old paint or varnish.

To smooth down a flat surface you can use glasspaper wrapped around a sanding block. On small curves and fiddly bits wrap small strips of abrasive round a pencil. For larger curves use a sanding glove which you can make yourself (see *Ready Reference*).

A powered sander is a boon on large surfaces; use an orbital sander rather than the disc type which is tricky to use without causing scratches across the grain.

Besides getting rid of shallow scratches, sanding will also get rid of cigarette burns and similar marks on the wood surface. However, make sure you don't sand for too long in one place or you will leave a depression that will show up after finishing.

Large cracks and dents can be filled with wax (from a crayon of a suitable colour, for instance) or with a proprietary wood

Ready Reference

KNOW YOUR STAINS
● water-based stains penetrate the wood more deeply than other types and are therefore suitable for use on wood which will be subject to hard wear
● oil stains are easier to apply without blotching than water-based ones and, since they dry quite slowly, any overlaps are less likely to show
● spirit stains are available in a wide range of colours. They dry quickly so you have to work at speed; but this also means you can apply the varnish sooner
● don't use a polyurethane varnish over oil stains or a chemical reaction will spoil the finish.

CHECKING COMPATIBILITY
Always check that the stain and finish you intend using are compatible. Buying both from the same manufacturer should ensure this. If you are in any doubt, stain and varnish a small test area first.

filler. But since stains don't hide fillers in the same way as paint would, you may decide not to carry out such treatment and to leave the blemishes for an authentic 'old wood' look. If you do decide to use a filler, don't try to smooth it flat as you apply it with the knife or you'll risk spreading it round – it tends to show up in the nearby grain if it is rubbed in when wet.

Finally, you should make sure the surface is dust-free by wiping it with a clean, dry cloth or a fine brush. It's a good idea, too, to wipe it with a cloth soaked in turpentine to remove any greasy fingermarks you may have left while preparing the surface.

Bleaching wood
One of the snags with staining wood is that you cannot make the surface lighter; you can only make it darker. A light-coloured stain on a darkish piece of wood just won't work. The way round this problem is to bleach the wood before you start sealing it – and for this proprietary wood bleaches are available at most hardware stores.

Some bleaches are applied in one stage and others in two stages. The wood is washed with a neutralizing agent afterwards so the bleach doesn't carry on working when the finish is applied. Follow the manufacturer's instructions when applying the bleach, particularly concerning the time you should allow for each stage of the treatment. Usually, bleach is applied with a sponge or brush; make sure you use a white fibre brush or the dye in the brush may come out onto the wood.

Staining wood
You can apply the stain with a brush or a folded lint-free rag. Aim to get the colour you want in one coat; a second coat can be applied if needed to get a darker finish, but too many coats will result in the stain lying on the surface, lengthening the time it takes for the subsequent coat of varnish to dry and even preventing it from bonding properly to the surface. With water-based types, if overlaps show when the first coat dries you can add about 20 per cent more water to a mixed-up solution of stain and apply a second coat over the whole surface, brushing it out well.

After the stain has dried (usually about 24 hours after application), you should rub the surface thoroughly with a dry cloth to remove excess stain.

Filling the grain
It's not necessary to fill the grain of softwoods, but for a good finish on open-grained hardwoods like oak, mahogany and walnut you will have to apply a grain filler

BLEACHING WOOD

1 In a two-stage bleaching process, apply the first solution liberally and leave it to work for the recommended time – usually 10 to 20 minutes.

2 Brush on the second solution, leaving it to work. If the wood is very dark or stained, reapply both solutions. If a crust forms, wipe it off with a damp rag.

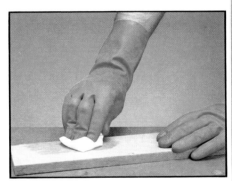

3 Wash the wood with a solution of acetic acid (white vinegar) and water to neutralise the bleach. Allow it to dry completely before staining it.

STAINING WOOD

1 Shake the can well and then pour the stain into a dish wide enough for you to dip in a cloth pad. Avoid plastic dishes; some stains may attack them.

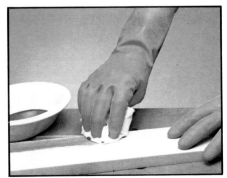

2 Apply the stain liberally using a cloth pad. If you apply it too sparingly you run the risk of getting light and dark areas instead of even coverage.

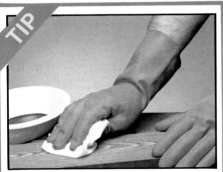

TIP

3 For greater grain contrast, wipe over each strip with a rag after allowing a minute or so for penetration. Leave to dry for 24 hours before varnishing.

VARNISHING WOOD

1 After you've made sure the surface is clean and dry, use a clean cloth pad to apply the first coat. Rub it well into the wood along the grain.

2 Leave the first coat to dry and then brush on the next coat. Make sure the brush is really clean, with no paint particles or loose bristles to mar the finish.

3 When brushing, it is important to work with the grain and brush out fully. On a narrow surface like a shelf upright, first apply the varnish in one stroke.

4 Then work the brush out towards the edges of the upright, working first to one edge and then to the other, using gentle but firm strokes.

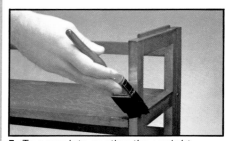

5 To complete coating the upright, again move the brush in one upward stroke. This technique will ensure that there are no ugly 'runs' at the edges.

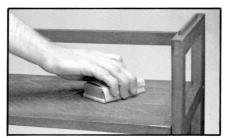

6 Leave each coat to dry for the recommended time (approx 12 hours) before re-coating. Rub down between coats with flour-grade glass paper.

to the wood surface before using varnish.

There are various proprietary fillers available in either a paste or liquid form; choose one to match the wood or stain you are using. Follow the manufacturer's instructions for applying it; normally, you work the filler over the wood with a brush or cloth, wipe off the excess and then sand the surface lightly down with fine glasspaper.

Varnishing wood

Polyurethane varnish is easy to apply; you simply brush it on, taking care to work with the grain of the wood. Follow the manufacturer's instructions as to the number of coats you should apply and the time

allowed between each coat – at least 12 hours. You should sand down the surface lightly with flour-grade glasspaper between coats to provide a key for the next coat, and remove any dust that's accumulated during application with a damp cloth.

As with paints, it's advisable to stir the contents of any can of varnish that's been stored for a while. This ensures an even distribution of the solvents so that the varnish dries evenly when it is applied. Although the varnish will be touch-dry in about 4 hours, it may take as long as 7 days before the surface reaches full hardness – so avoid standing anything on the newly-decorated surface for a week or so.

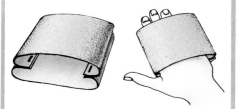
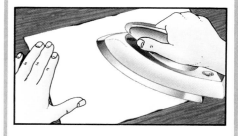

CHAPTER 2

PAPERHANGING

Modern wallcoverings and adhesives have made paperhanging
a far less difficult job than it used to be, but every home has
its awkward corners and you need to know how to approach
these if you're going to get good results.
The techniques are the same whatever type of wallpaper you're
hanging – even if you're tackling a ceiling.

PAPERING WALLS
the basics

No other wall covering can quite so dramatically alter the look and feeling of a room as wallpaper. Correctly hung paper makes the walls sharp and fresh, and to achieve this finish there are important things to know. What do you do if the walls are out of true? Where's the best place to start? How do you prevent bubbles and creases? The answers are here.

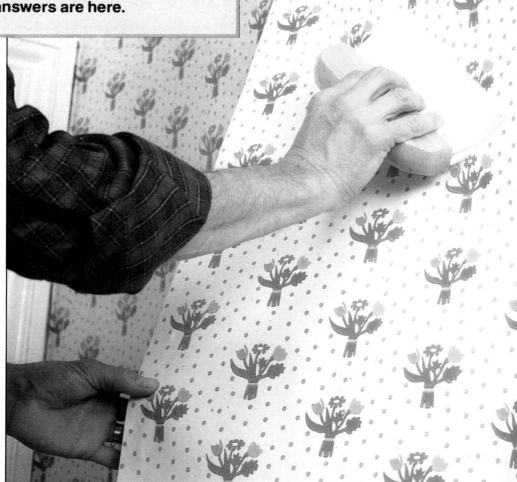

Wallpapering isn't so much an art, it's more a matter of attention to detail. And perhaps the first mistake that's made by many people is expecting too much of their walls. Rarely are walls perfectly flat, perfectly vertical and at right angles to each other. So the first and most crucial part of hanging wallpaper is to prepare the walls properly. Obviously you can't change their basic character – if they're not entirely flat or vertical, you're stuck with them – but you can make sure that the surface is suitably prepared so that the new paper will stick.

This means that any old wallpaper really should come off before you do anything else. Papering on top of old wall coverings won't *always* lead to disaster, but it will quite often simply because the new adhesive will tend to loosen the old. The result will be bubbles at best and peeling at worst.

Adhesives
Always use the correct adhesive for the wallcovering and follow the manufacturers instructions for mixing. Using the wrong paste can result in the paper not sticking, mould growth or discoloration of the paper.

A cellulose-based adhesive is used for all standard wallcoverings. There are two types, ordinary and heavy-duty which relates to the weight of the paper being hung. Heavy-duty pastes are for heavyweight wallcoverings. Certain brands of paste are suitable for all types of wallcoverings – less water being used for mixing when hanging heavy papers.

Since vinyls and washable wallcoverings are impervious, mould could attack the paste unless it contains a fungicide. Fungicidal paste is also needed if the wall has previously been treated against mould or if there is any sign of damp.

Some wallcoverings (like polyethylene foam, some hessians and foils) require a specially thick adhesive which is pasted onto the wall. Follow manufacturers' instructions.

Ready-pasted papers are exactly that and require no extra adhesive – although it's useful to have a tube of latex glue handy for finishing off corners and joints which mightn't

have stuck. (The same applies to all washable wallpapers).

Glue *size* (a watered down adhesive) is brushed over the walls before papering to seal them and prevent the paste from soaking in to the wall. It also ensures all-over adhesion and makes sliding the paper into place easier.

Although size can be bought, most wallpaper pastes will make size when mixed with the amount of water stated in the instructions.

If you buy a proprietary size and the wallcovering you are using needs an adhesive containing fungicide, make sure that the size you buy also contains a

fungicide. Use an old brush to apply and a damp cloth to clean off any that runs on to paintwork. It can be difficult to remove after it has dried. Sizing can be done several days or an hour before.

Where to begin
The traditional rule is to start next to the window and work away from it, but that is really a hangover from the days when paper was overlapped and shadows showed up joins. Today, papers butt up, so light isn't the problem. But as inaccuracies can occur with slight loss of pattern, you have to be able to make this as inconspicuous as possible. In

an average room, the corner nearest the door is the best starting point. Any loss of pattern will then end up behind you as you enter the room. In a room with a chimney breast, hang the first drop in the centre and work outwards from both sides of the drop.

Problem areas in a house (recesses, arches, stairwells) are dealt with later in this chapter.

Measuring and cutting

Measure the height of the wall you want to paper using a steel tape measure and cut a piece of paper from the roll to this length, allowing an extra 50mm (2in) top and bottom for trimming. This allowance is needed for pattern matching, and to ensure a neat finish at skirting board and ceiling.

Lay the first drop — that's the name given to each length of paper — pattern side up on the table and unroll the paper from which the

second drop is to be cut next to it. Move this along until the patterns match, then cut the second drop using the other end of the first as a guide. Subsequent lengths of paper are cut in exactly the same way, with each matching the drop that preceded it.

Remember some wallpapers have patterns that are a straight match across the width, while others have what is called a drop pattern that rises as it extends across the width. With drop match papers the second length will begin half a pattern repeat further along the roll. Length 3 will match length 1, length 4 will match length 2 and so on.

For things to run smoothly, you should establish a work routine when paper hanging. Cut all the wall drops first (so you only have to measure once) and cut bits for papering above windows and doors as you come to them. If you paste say 3 drops, the first will have had its required soaking time

HOW TO CUT AND PASTE

1 *Mark the pasting table with lines at 150mm (6in) and 300mm (1ft) intervals. Measure wall drop and use guidelines to cut your first length.*

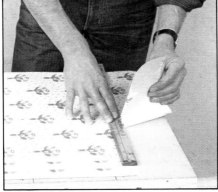

2 *Use the first length as a guide for the other drops, matching the pattern carefully. Tear off the waste against a wooden rule.*

3 *Lay all the drops pattern down, overhanging the far edge of the table. Pull the first drop to the near edge and paste it from centre to edges.*

4 *Fold pasted end, paste the rest and fold in. Now fold up the whole drop and leave it to soak. The top of the longer fold always goes to the top of the wall.*

Ready Reference

STRIPPING OLD WALLPAPER

Never hang new coverings over existing wallpaper – the old may lift and bring the new with it.

Ordinary wallpaper:
● use hot water with washing-up liquid or proprietary wallpaper stripper to soak the surface
● scrape off old paper in strips with broad-bladed scraper, re-soaking stubborn areas; wash surface down to remove bits

Washable or painted wallpaper:
● always score surface coating with serrated scraper before soaking and scraping
● for large areas a steam stripper (from hire shops) is a real time-saver

Vinyl wallcovering:
● lift corner of vinyl coating at skirting board level and peel away from backing paper by pulling steadily up and away
● then soak and scrape off backing paper

WHERE TO START

Room with a chimney breast: start at its centre and work outward to each end of the chimney wall, then on down the two side walls towards the door. Any loss of pattern will be least noticed in the short lengths hung over the door.

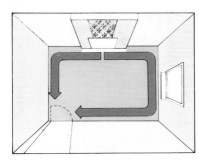

Room without a chimney breast: start at one corner of the room – ideally near the door – and work around continuously until you return to your starting point.

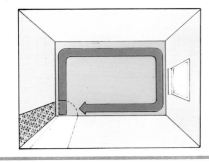

PAPER HANGING TECHNIQUES

1 Place chosen pattern on ceiling line with waste above. Align side edge with vertical and turn waste onto adjacent wall. Brush up to ceiling first, then corners and edges, and then down. Open out short fold last.

2 Mark cutting line for waste at ceiling and skirting board with a pencil — ends of scissors won't fit creases neatly and can give a thick line which causes you to cut the paper inaccurately and will give an uneven look at ceiling and skirting.

3 To cut waste, pull short length of paper away from wall so pencil line catches the light. Cut using full length of blades — hurried, short cuts can make the edges jagged. Brush paper back on wall so that it is perfectly flat.

4 Reduce waste on adjacent wall to 6mm (¼in) to lessen bulk when paper overlaps from other direction.

5 Continue along wall matching the pattern horizontally. Press drop onto wall so long edges butt.

6 As each drop is hung, brush up first, then to edges and finally down to remove any trapped air.

7 To turn a corner, measure between hung paper and corner at the top, middle and bottom of wall. Add 6mm (¼in) to widest width, then use this measurement to cut the pasted and folded drop into two. Set aside offcut for new wall.

8 Hang drop to complete wall, brushing the waste round the corner. Find the new vertical and mark the line the width of offcut from the corner. Check this measurement at the top, middle and bottom of wall. If the same, hang offcut.

9 If corner is out of true, offcut and wall measurements will differ. To disguise pattern loss, hang the offcut so waste laps onto completed wall. Brush into corner, run pencil down crease line and cut waste.

(with medium weight paper) by the time the third is pasted and folded and is ready to be hung. With heavy papers paste, fold and soak 6 drops at a time as extra soaking time is needed.

Avoiding bubbles
The purpose behind soaking time (apart from making paper supple enough to handle) is to give it time to expand to its natural limit. On the width this can be 6mm-12mm (¼in-½in) and the average wall-size drop will gain 24mm (1in) on the length – this explains why you have more to cut as waste than you started with.

If you haven't given paper the time it needs, it will expand on the walls – but its spread will be contained by adjoining drops and so you get bubbles in the central part.

Soak medium weight papers for 3-4 minutes, heavy weights for about 10. Ready-pasted papers don't need too long a soaking, but to ensure they get wet all over, roll drops loosely and press into water till they are completely covered.

Pasting and soaking
Position the paper with its top edge at the right-hand end of the table (or at the other end if you're left handed). Paste it carefully to ensure that all parts, the edges especially, are well covered. Work from the centre out-wards in herring-bone style using the width of the brush to cover the drop in sweeps, first to the nearest edge, then the other – excess paste here will go onto second drop, not the table. Cover two-thirds of the drop, then fold the top edge in so paste is to paste. Move the drop along the table and paste the remainder, folding bottom edge in paste to paste. Because the first folded part is longer than the other, this will remind you which is the

top. Fold the drop up and put aside to soak while you paste the others.

This technique will give you a manageable parcel of paper to hang no matter what length the drop – but always remember to make the first fold longer – this is the one offered to the ceiling line. If in doubt mark the top edge lightly with a pencil cross.

Hanging pasted paper
Wallpaper must be hung absolutely vertical if it is to look right, so always work to a vertical line (see *Ready Reference*).

Position your step ladder as close as possible to where you want to work, and climb it with the first length of paper under or over your arm. Open out the long fold and offer the top edge up, placing the pattern as you want it at the ceiling with waste above. Align the side edge of the drop with your vertical guide line, allowing the other side edge to turn onto the adjacent wall if starting at a corner. Smooth the paper onto the wall with the paperhanging brush, using the bristle ends to form a crease between wall and ceiling, and at corners. When brushing paper into place, always work up first then to the join, then to the side edge, then down. This will remove trapped air.

As soon as the paper is holding in place, work down the wall, brushing the rest of the drop in position, opening out the bottom fold when you reach it. Again use the bristle ends to form a good crease where paper meets the skirting board.

The next step is to trim off the waste paper at the top and bottom. Run a lead pencil along the crease between the ceiling or skirting and the wall — the blades or points of scissors wil make a line that's too thick for accurate cutting. Gently peel paper away from the wall and cut carefully along the line with your scissors. Finally brush the paper back in place.

Hanging the second drop is done as the

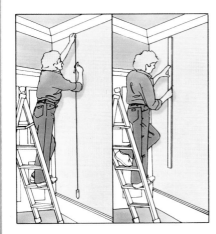
Estimator

Most wallpaper is sold in rolls 10.05m (11yds) long and 530mm (21in) wide. Calculate rolls needed by measuring perimeter of the room and height from skirting board to ceiling.

WALLS	Distance around the room (doors and windows included)										
Height from skirting	10m 33'	11m 36'	12m 39'	13m 43'	14m 46'	15m 49'	16m 52'	17m 56'	18m 59'	19m 62'	20m 66'
2.15–2.30m (7'–7'6")	5	5	5	6	6	7	7	8	8	9	9
2.30–2.45m (7'6"–8')	5	5	6	6	7	7	8	8	9	9	10
2.45–2.60m (8'–8'6")	5	6	6	7	7	8	9	9	10	10	11

The number of rolls needed can be greatly affected by the frequency of pattern repeat. With a large pattern repeat, buy an extra roll.

first except that you have to butt it up against the edge of the first length, matching the pattern across the two. The secret here is not to try and do it all in one go. Get the paper onto the wall at the right place at the ceiling join but just a little way away from the first length. Now press against the paper with the palms of your hands and slide it into place. Using well-soaked paper on a wall that's been sized makes this easy, but if you're using a thin wallpaper press gently as it could tear. Butt the paper up after pattern matching and brush into place.

When trimming waste from drops other than the first, cut from where the lengths butt to ensure even ceiling and skirting lines.

Hanging ready-pasted wallpaper

With these you won't need pasting table, bucket and pasting brush but you will need a special light plastic trough made for the purpose. Put it below where the first drop is to be hung and fill with water – covering the floor with layers of newspaper will soak up accidental spillages. Don't try to lift the trough; slide it along the floor as the work progresses.

Cut each drop so patterns are matching, then roll the first one loosely from the bottom up with the pattern inside. Place it in the trough and press it down so water can reach all the parts covered with paste. Leave for the required soaking time (check manufacturers' instructions but, it's usually between 30 seconds and 2 minutes), then pick the drop up by the two top corners and take it to the ceiling line. Press onto the wall using an absorbent sponge to mop up and push out air bubbles. Press firmly on the edges with the sponge or a seam roller, then trim waste.

COPING WITH WALL FITTINGS ... AND CREASES

Few walls present a perfectly clear surface for paperhanging. Almost all will contain such small obstacles as light switches and power points, while some may carry wall-mounted fittings such as curtain tracks and adjustable shelving. Small obstacles can be papered round with some careful trimming, but larger obstacles are best taken down from the wall and replaced when you have finished decorating. That way you will get a really professional finish.

Creases can also spoil the look of your work. If they occur, take steps to remove them before the paste dries. Here's how.

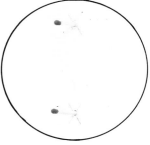

1 *Use matchsticks, pushed head out into wall plugs, to show where wall fittings have been taken down.*

2 *Brush paper firmly over match heads so they pierce it. With hanging complete remove matches and replace fittings.*

1 *To cut round light switches, mark centre of plate, insert scissor tips and cut out towards plate corners.*

2 *Crease tongues of paper against edges of plate, lift away from wall, trim along line and brush back into place.*

3 *With washable and vinyl papers push a strip of rigid plastic against plate edges and trim with a sharp knife.*

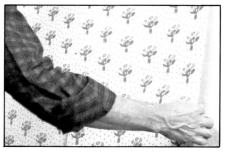

1 *Creases are a common fault where the wall is out of true or if you haven't brushed the paper out properly.*

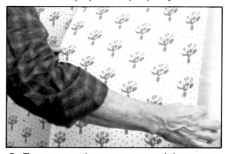

2 *To remove the crease, peel the paper from the wall to a point above the crease – to the ceiling if necessary.*

3 *Brush the paper back into position – across towards the butt join, then to the other edge and down to the bottom.*

PAPERING A STAIRWELL

Even if the walls are flat, papering a stairwell presents problems. The awkward angles, height of the walls and long lengths of wallcovering make for special difficulties of access and handling, but you'll find that these can be overcome.

Hanging wallpaper in an ordinary room is not too difficult. But with stairwells there are awkward corners and long lengths to cope with.

Gaining access

The chief problem in wallpapering a stairwell is that of gaining access to the walls you are papering. This is because of the height of the walls and the awkward angles involved.

It is essential to have a safe working platform and to set this up in the right way to suit the layout of the stairwell and the way the stairs rise. You can hire special platforms for decorating the stair/hall area, or use the components of a tower platform. Alternatively, you can use ladders and steps linked with scaffold boards (see page 35).

A particularly useful item of equipment is a hop-up, a small platform which you can make yourself (see *Ready Reference*).

Preparation

Before you start decorating, remove the handrail and any other wall-mounted obstacles so you can get at the wall. Then prepare the walls properly so the new wallcovering will stick. Always remove any old wallcovering; some will peel off, although with most types you will have to soak and scrape them off.

Once the walls are stripped, you can work out where to begin hanging. You should position the longest drop of wallcovering first, and to establish where this will be, measure the height of each wall in the stairwell. (You will need a long tape and someone to help you when you are measuring the wall in a stairwell.) Then, starting as close as possible to this point but about 50mm away from any obstacles – such as a door or window opening – take a roll of the wallcovering you are going to use and move it along the wall to estimate where succeeding widths will fall. If, according to your calculations, there will be a join between lengths within 50mm of an external corner (at another window opening, for example), change your starting point slightly and measure again so you avoid this. Then mark off where this first drop will be hung.

When you have established where you will hang the first drop, use a plumbline to work out a true vertical at this point. Coat the line with chalk, pin it to the top of the wall and allow it to hang. Then, at the skirting, hold the plumb bob with one hand, pluck the string with the other and let it snap back against the wall to leave a vertical chalk line on the wall. Alternatively, instead of coating the plumb line with chalk, fix it in place, allowing it to hang down, and then place a long straight timber batten so the edge is exactly against the line, and use the batten as your guide to draw a true vertical line down the wall. Remember to plumb a new line every time you turn a corner.

Hanging the wallcovering

The decorating sequence is the same as for any other area – see the techniques already covered. If the wall is bare plaster, start by applying size to the wall to prevent the paste soaking in. Then measure and cut the wallcovering to length, remembering to allow for the angle of the skirting board if applicable, paste it and allow it to soak. If you are using a ready-pasted wallcovering, place your water trough in the hall or on the landing, not on the stairs where you are likely to knock it over. Wallcoverings hung by the

PREPARATION

1 To prepare the wall surface you will have to remove the existing wallcovering. In this case it is vinyl which is easy to remove; it is simply peeled off.

2 Before you remove lining paper it's worth cutting along the paper at ceiling level or you may find you tear off the ceiling paper with the lining paper.

3 When working at a high level make sure that the ladders and scaffold boards you are working from are firmly secured and well supported to ensure safety.

4 To remove paper from the wall when preparing to hang a new wallcovering, soak it thoroughly with a damp sponge. Leave for a while, then soak again.

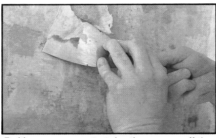

5 Use a scraper to take the paper off the wall and scrape off old flaking paint at the same time. Wash the wall down to remove any remaining bits.

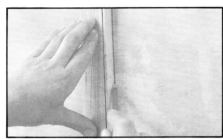

6 When you have established where you will hang the first length, use a plumbline to make sure you get a true vertical and mark a pencil line on the wall.

HANGING THE WALLCOVERING

1 Place the first drop up against the wall, using the line you have drawn as a guideline to get it straight. Get someone to help you hold the long drop.

2 Use a soft-bristled wallpaper-hanging brush to smooth the covering into place. Leave an overlap at the top and bottom for trimming when the drop is fixed.

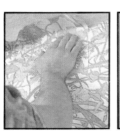

3 Hang subsequent lengths of wallcovering so they butt join and so the pattern matches. Trim each piece; a scraper will help as a guide.

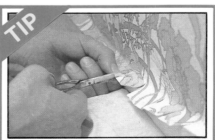

4 Where there is a curve cut into the overlap so the paper will fit round the curve easily without puckering.

5 You can then trim off the overlap in the same way as at a door surround, using a scraper to help guide the knife as you trim along the bottom edge.

6 For convenient paper hanging you will have to remove a wall handrail. This can be replaced when the wallcovering is fixed and the adhesive completely dry.

SAFE WORKING PLATFORMS

1 stairs with quarter landing

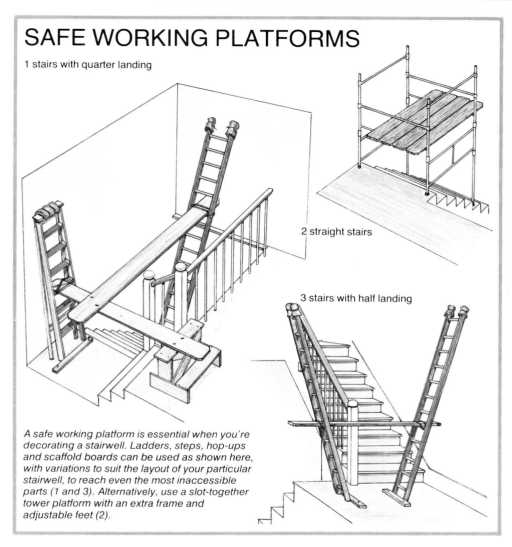

2 straight stairs

3 stairs with half landing

A safe working platform is essential when you're decorating a stairwell. Ladders, steps, hop-ups and scaffold boards can be used as shown here, with variations to suit the layout of your particular stairwell, to reach even the most inaccessible parts (1 and 3). Alternatively, use a slot-together tower platform with an extra frame and adjustable feet (2).

Ready Reference

CARRYING LONG LENGTHS

To make it easier to carry a long length of wallcovering, fold it in concertinas and then drape it over your arm.

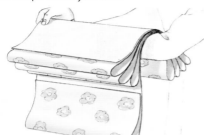

BEWARE ANGLED SKIRTING

When measuring up remember that lengths meeting the stairs skirting must be measured along their longer edge, not their shorter one.

EQUAL SOAKING TIME

To minimise the risk of stretching
● allow the same amount of soaking time between pasting and hanging on each length
● if you do find the paper has stretched, match the pattern as best you can at eye level, where bad matching would be most noticeable.

YOU'LL NEED HELP

It's best not to try hanging long lengths of paper by yourself; the weight of the paper may cause it to stretch or tear. Get someone to take the weight and unfold the paper as you work down the wall.

TIP: TRIM NARROW PIECES DRY

Where long narrow strips are needed, measure up and trim the drop approximately to size before pasting. This is easier to handle than having large waste pieces covered in paste flapping around.

OVERLAPS WITH VINYL

Vinyl will not stick to vinyl where you are using ordinary paste. If an overlap is unavoidable use a special vinyl overlap adhesive.

---

paste-the-wall technique are particularly easy to hang in stairwells, because you are handling lengths of dry wallcovering.

Because the lengths of paper for the wall at the side of the stairs will all be of a different size – caused by the rise of the stairs – it is better to cut and paste one length at a time, unlike straightforward rooms where you can cut and paste several lengths at a time.

Hang the first and longest length of wallpaper, using the vertical line you have marked on the wall as a guideline to get it straight. Then work round the stairwell from this length, making sure the pattern matches as you go along.

If your staircase is curved at the bottom the wallcovering is likely to pucker as it fits around the curve. To prevent this, you can snip into the overlap at the foot of the wall at intervals so the paper is more flexible in its fit.

Coping with long drops

A problem unique to stairwells is the length of paper you are handling – often as much as

4.5m (15ft) long. Apply paste liberally so it is less likely to dry out before you have fixed the bottom of the length. (It's worth keeping a small amount of adhesive ready to apply where the adhesive has dried out before the wallcovering is fixed.) Fold the pasted paper in concertinas (see *Ready Reference*) and then gather up the folds and drape the folded-up length over your arm to carry it.

Because the weight of the paper may cause it to stretch or tear as you are hanging it, try to get someone to help you take the weight. Where there is no one available to help, you will have to sit on your scaffold board, or other form of support, and allow the bottom of the drop to unfold gently to skirting board level. Then you can take the top up to the ceiling and start brushing it into the correct place.

Remember too, that when you are trimming along the bottom of a length of wallcovering that meets the staircase skirting, you will be trimming at an angle rather than horizontally as at the foot of a wall in a room.

PAPERING AWKWARD AREAS

The techniques for papering round tricky areas like corners and reveals are quite basic. But care and patience is required if you are going to get really professional results from your paperhanging.

Although the major part of wallpapering, hanging straight lengths is fairly quick and straightforward. The tricky areas – corners, doorways and so on – which call for careful measuring, cutting and pattern matching are the bits that slow the job down. There's no worse eye-sore than a lop-sided pattern at a corner; but if you use the right techniques you can avoid this problem.

You have to accept in advance that the continuity of a pattern will be lost in corners and similar places; even a professional decorator can't avoid this. However, he has the ability to match the pattern as closely as possible so that the discontinuity is not noticeable, and this is what you have to emulate.

Things would, of course, be a lot simpler if all corners were perfectly square, but this is rarely the case. When you wallpaper a room for the first time you are likely to discover that all those angles that appeared to be true are anything but.

You can, however, help to overcome the problem of careful pattern matching at corners by choosing a paper with the right design (see *Ready Reference*). The most difficult of the lot to hang are those with a regular small and simple repeat motif. The loss of pattern continuity will be easy to spot if even slight errors are made. The same is often true of large, repeat designs. With either of these types, a lot more time will be involved and it could well take a couple of hours to hang a few strips around a single window reveal.

Sloping ceiling lines are another problem area and certain patterns will show it up clearly. You can understand the nuisance of a sloping ceiling by imagining a pattern with, say, regular rows of horizontal roses. Although the first length on the wall may be hung correctly to leave a neat row of roses along the ceiling line the trouble is that as subsequent lengths are hung and the pattern is matched, you will see less and less of that top row of roses as the ceiling slopes down. And, conversely, if the ceiling line slopes upwards, you will start to see a new row of roses appearing above. So, despite the fact that each length has been hung

vertically, the sloping ceiling will make the job look thoroughly unsightly.

Internal and external corners

Before you begin papering round a corner, you must hang the last full length before the corner. Your corner measurement will be done from one edge of this length. You can use a steel tape or boxwood rule to measure the gap to the corner (see *Ready Reference*) and then cut the piece required to fill it, plus a margin which is carried round onto the new wall. Since it's likely that the walls will be out of square and that the margin taken round the corner will not be exactly equal all the way down, it's obvious you would have a terrible job hanging the matching offcut strip to give a neat butt join.

For this reason you must hang the matching offcut which goes on the 'new' wall to a true vertical and then brush it over the margin you've turned onto this wall. You should aim to match the pattern at the corner as closely as possible. Since the paper overlaps, the match will not be perfect, but this is unavoidable and will not, in any case be noticeable as the overlap is tucked into or round the corner out of sight (see *Ready Reference*).

Papering round window reveals

Unless you intend to paper just one or two walls in a room you will eventually have to cope with papering round a window. Pattern matching is the problem here, but you should find cutting the paper to fit above and

below a window is not too difficult provided you work in a logical order (see box opposite). But you may have to be prepared for lots of scissor work when you cut out strips of paper for the two sides and top of the reveal to ensure the pattern matches the paper on the facing wall. (It's worth getting into the habit of marking some sort of code on the back of each piece of paper before it's cut up so you will be able to find matching pieces quickly.)

Make sure that you don't end up with a seam on the edge of the reveal, where it will be exposed to knocks and liable to lift. Before you begin work on the window wall, take a roll of wallcovering and estimate how many widths will fit between the window and the nearest corner. If it looks as though you will be left with a join within about 25mm (1in) of the window opening you should alter your starting point slightly so that, when you come to the window, the seam will have moved away from the edge of the reveal.

Where the lengths of paper are positioned on the window wall obviously depends on the position of the window, its size and the width of the wallpaper. But the ideal situation occurs when the last full length before you reach the window leaves a width of wall, plus window reveal, that measures just less than the width of the wallpaper. You can then hang the next length so its upper part goes on the wall above the window, the lower part on the wall below it and (after making two scissor cuts) turn the middle part to cover the side of the window reveal. The edge of

PAPERING ROUND A WINDOW

Top: Fill the narrow gap left on the underside of the reveal with a small offcut.
Above: The papering sequence; piece 7 fills the gap left on the reveal by piece 6.

the middle part can then be creased and trimmed so it fits neatly up against the window frame.

Go on to hang short lengths of wallpaper above the window, cutting them so their lower parts can be taken on to the underside of the top window reveal, and again trim them so they fit neatly up against the window frame. When you reach a point where the reveal on the opposite side of the window is less than the width of the wallpaper away from the last edge hung, you should stop and repeat the papering process below the window between the sill and skirting board, trimming as you go.

You can then hang the next full length in the same way as the one you hung on the first side of the window. You should, first, however, hang a plumbline over the pieces in place above the top and bottom of the window then hang the full length to the plumb-line, trimming any slight overlap on the new length if necessary. (By doing this, you will ensure that the lengths to be hung on the rest of the wall will be truly vertical.)

Often, however, the position of the last full length at the window will fall so that the paper does not cover the reveal at the side of the window, and in this case you will have to cut matching strips to fill the gap. Similarly, you

will have to cut strips to fill the gaps on the underside of the reveal at the top of the window.

Dormer windows
In attics and loft rooms there will be sloping ceilings and dormer windows with which you will have to contend. If you decide to paper rather than paint the sloping ceiling, then you treat it in the same way as you would a vertical wall; there are no unusual problems involved, other than the peculiar working angle. Remember, too, that if you choose the wrong type of paper the irregular pattern-matching could give unfortunate results.

Paper the wall alongside the window and then round the window itself, moving on to the wall below the other side of the sloping ceiling (see step-by-step photographs). Finally, you can paper the dormer cheeks.

Chimney breasts and fireplace surrounds
Special rules apply to chimney breasts. For a start, since they are a focal point in the room, any pattern must be centralised. The design of the paper will affect where you begin to hang the wallpaper. Where one length of paper contains a complete motif, you can simply measure and mark off the central point of the chimney breast and use a

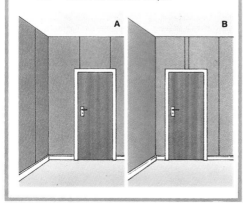

PAPERING AN INTERNAL CORNER

1 *Hang the last full length before the corner. Then measure the gap (see Ready Reference) to determine the width to be cut from the next length.*

2 *Cut from the next length a piece which will overlap 12mm (1/2in) round the corner. Then paste and fix it in position so it fills the corner gap.*

3 *Measure the width of the matching offcut strip of paper and use a plumbline to mark a guideline on the wall this distance from the corner.*

4 *Hang the offcut so its cut edge overlaps the matching edge of the first corner piece and its 'good' edge aligns with the vertical guideline.*

FLUSH WINDOWS

1 *Fix the last full length of paper before the window and pull the excess across. Cut round the sill and fix the paper beneath it.*

2 *You can then trim off the excess paper which runs alongside the window. Now press and brush the pasted paper into position.*

3 *Work along the wall underneath the window, fixing, creasing and trimming as you go. Afterwards you can fix the paper on the other side of the window.*

plumbline at this point to help you draw a vertical line down the centre. You can then begin hanging the wallpaper by aligning the first length with this line.

On the other hand, if it is the type of paper where two lengths, when aligned, form a motif, you will first have to estimate the number of widths which will fit across the chimney breast and then draw a line as a guide for hanging the first length of paper so the combined motif will, in fact, be centralised.

Your order of work should be from the centre (or near centre) outwards and you will then have to turn the paper round the corners at the sides so you form an overlap join with the paper which will be applied to the sides of the chimney breast. Follow the usual techniques for measuring and papering round external corners, remembering in particular not too take too much paper round the corner.

When it comes to fireplace surrounds, there are so many varying kinds of mantelshelfs and surrounds that only general guidance can be given. Usually the technique is to brush the paper down on to the top part of the wall and then cut it to fit along the back edge of the mantelshelf. You can then cut the lower half to fit the contours of the surround. If it's a complicated outline then you'll have to gradually work downwards, using a small pair of sharp scissors, pressing the paper into each shape, withdrawing it to snip along the crease line, then brushing it back into place.

If there is only a small distance between the edge of the mantelshelf and the corner, it's a lot easier if you hang the paper down to the shelf and then make a neat, horizontal cut line in the paper You can then hang the lower half separately and join the two halves to disguise the cut line.

PAPERING ROUND A DORMER

1 Where the dormer cheek meets the junction of the wall and ceiling, draw a line at right angles to the wall on the ceiling by the dormer cheek.

2 Draw a vertical line at right angles to the first line on the dormer cheek. You can then fix the first length of paper in place on the dormer cheek.

3 Work along towards the window, trimming as you go. Gently tear along the overlap to feather its edge so you won't get a bulky join later.

4 At the window, crease along the side of the frame by running the edge of the scissors along it. You can then carefully trim along the creased line.

5 Return to the small gap which needs to be filled at the narrow end of the dormer cheek; fix this piece in position, crease and trim.

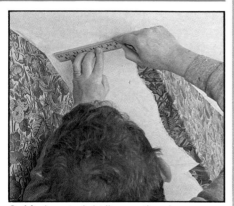

6 Mark a straight line on the sloping ceiling to serve as a guideline for fixing the first length of paper on the underside of the dormer cheek.

7 Cut a piece of paper so it reaches from the point you have marked up to the window and brush it into position ensuring that it covers the feathered edges of the overlap.

8 At the junction of the wall and ceiling you will have to cut round awkward angles. You can then go ahead and brush the paper into its final position.

9 Finally, you can brush the strip of paper which fills the gap between the wall and the underside of the dormer cheek into position to finish off the dormer area neatly.

PAPERING CEILINGS

One way to cover up a ceiling with cracks or other imperfections is to use lining paper or a textured wallcovering and then paint over it. But a good alternative is to make a special feature of the ceiling by using decorative paper.

Papering ceilings can be a rather daunting prospect, even to the experienced home decorator. In fact, once you have mastered the basic technique of paperhanging, ceilings are quite straightforward and you are likely to be presented with far fewer problems than on walls. There will be no windows, few (if any) corners and not so many obstacles with which you have to deal.

If you intend to paint the ceiling it's usually best to hang a lining paper or a textured paper like woodchip first to hide the inevitable blemishes of a plaster ceiling. Or you might decide to choose a fine decorative paper and make a feature of the ceiling with it. Most of the papers that are suitable for walls can also be used for ceilings.

But before you opt for papering, it makes sense to consider the alternative: if the sole objective is to get a textured surface which will cover up cracks and bumps, you can do it just as well with a textured paint. Using a woodchip paper would only make sense if you were skilled at papering and wanted to save money; in any case, you'll still have to paint it. However, if you want a smooth ceiling or a decorative surface of distinction then papering is for you.

The equipment you'll need
You will need the same equipment as for papering walls, with the addition of a safe working platform that spans the width of the room (see *Ready Reference*). You should check with your supplier that the paper of your choice is suitable for ceilings (some heavier types may not be) and ask him to provide a suitably strong adhesive, including fungicide if it is a washable vinyl paper. Such papers are extremely suitable for high humidity environments like bathrooms and kitchens.

Preparing the surface
The surface to which you fix the paper must be clean and sound. This means washing down existing paintwork with detergent or sugar soap and then sanding it with a fine abrasive paper or pad to provide a key for the adhesive. Distempered ceilings, often found in old houses, must be scrubbed to remove the distemper, or the paper will not stick.

If the ceiling has been papered before, you should remove the old paper completely. If you try to hang another paper over it there will be blobs and bubbles where the dampness of the new paper separates the old paper from the plaster. Any surface which is at all porous, such as bare plaster, will tend to absorb moisture from the pasted paper at too fast a rate for a successful adhesion. Such surfaces should be sized by brushing them over with a proprietary size, or a diluted version of the actual paste you're going to use. Let the size dry before proceeding.

New plasterboard, often used in modern construction, needs painting with a primer/sealer before decoration. It is also wise to fix a layer of lining paper before your main decorative paper if you are hanging heavyweight or fabric wallcoverings.

Decorating perfectionists always recommend using lining paper anyway, whatever the surface. There is no doubt it does improve the final appearance, particularly on older surfaces or with thinner papers. Lining paper comes in different thicknesses or 'weights' and you should consult your supplier about a suitable grade.

One last preparation tip: don't leave cracks and dents in ceilings for the paper to cover. Fill them and sand them smooth, particularly at joins between plasterboards, and at the wall/ceiling angle. Think of your paper as a surface that needs a good smooth base, and not as a cover-up for a hideous old mess.

Planning the job
Consult the estimator panel (see *Ready Reference*) to gauge the approximate number of rolls you will need; also think about the pattern of your intended paper. Can you cope with a complex drop pattern on a ceiling, or would you be better off with a straight match? A bold paper that looks fine on walls might be a bit overpowering above your head. Is your ceiling good enough for a plainish paper, or do you need texture to draw the eye away from the ravages of time that appear in all old lath-and-plaster ceilings?

Modern papers are designed for the strips to be butted against each other, not overlapped. This means the traditional pattern of working away from, but parallel to, the main source of natural light is not essential. You will generally find it easier working across the narrowest dimension of the room. Well-applied paper will tend not to show the joins too much anyway, particularly if the pattern draws the eye.

All ceiling papering starts from a line which is strung or marked across the ceiling 10mm (⅜in) less than the width of the paper away from the wall. The 10mm (⅜in) on the length of paper which runs next to the wall allows for the walls being out of square and its overlap is trimmed off at the wall and ceiling junction. You can chalk a line and snap it against the ceiling between two tacks to make a mark, or just pin it temporarily in place and butt the first strip of paper against it.

MARKING UP AND PASTING

1 Measure in from the width of the paper minus 10mm (³/₈in), to allow for an overlap at the wall, and mark this distance on the ceiling.

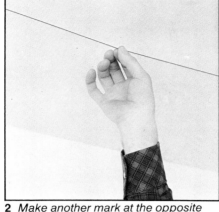

2 Make another mark at the opposite end, the same distance from the wall. Use a chalked line to link the marks, then snap the line onto the ceiling.

3 Cut or tear the lengths of paper. You should allow 100mm (4in) excess on each piece to give an overlap of 50mm (2in) for trimming at each end.

4 Apply paste to the back of the paper and fold it into concertina folds as you go. Paste enough lengths to allow adequate soaking time.

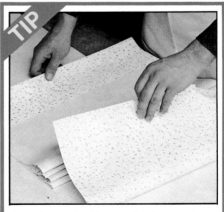

5 Take the last fold in the length to meet the first, short, fold so the edges meet without paste getting on the front of the paper.

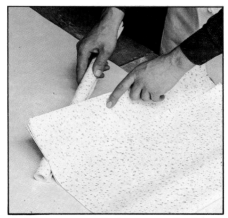

6 Slip a spare roll of paper under the folded-up length; this will serve as a support for the paper so you can carry and hold it easily.

Ready Reference

ESTIMATOR

Distance around room	Number of rolls 10.05m x 530mm (33ft x 21in)
10-12m (33-39ft)	2
12-14m (39-46ft)	3
14-18m (46-59ft)	4
18-20m (59-66ft)	5
20-22m (66-72ft)	6

TIP: WHISK YOUR PASTE
To speed up the process of mixing paste, use a kitchen whisk to beat up the mix.

A SAFE WORKING PLATFORM
Set up two stepladders and a solid plank, at a height where you can comfortably touch the ceiling with the palm of your hand.

TIP: HAVE TOOLS TO HAND
Have the necessary tools with you (in the pocket of an apron or overall) when you're on the working platform to save you scrambling up and down more than you need.

PREVENT WASTAGE
If you are pattern matching, paper in the direction which will save long bits of waste paper left over after cutting the lengths.

LINING PAPER
If you are hanging lining paper, remember that it should be hung at right angles to the paper which goes over it.

PAPERING TECHNIQUE
With the concertina-folded paper supported by the spare roll held in your left hand (if you are right-handed; vice versa if you are left-handed) pull one fold out taut and then brush it into place, working outwards from the centre to avoid trapped air bubbles. Repeat with the other folds.

TIP: TRIM ROSES NEATLY
Don't be tempted to remove the cover of a ceiling rose to trim the paper round it; inaccurate cutting may mean there are gaps when the cover is replaced. Instead:
● trim round the fitting with the cover in place leaving a slight overlap (see step-by-step photographs)
● remove the cover and press the overlap into place.

FINAL TRIMMING
When the last piece of paper has been hung you may need to spend some time on final trimming if the walls and ceiling do not meet squarely and evenly.

HANGING STRAIGHT LENGTHS

1 *Hang the first length on the 'room' side of the chalk line, not next to the wall. Brush the paper into place gently but firmly.*

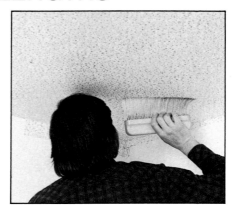

2 *Brush the ends carefully into the angles where walls and ceiling meet, and trim. Then hang the next length alongside the wall.*

3 *The lengths should be butt-jointed. Use a seam roller to ensure well-stuck edges by running it gently over the length of the seam.*

4 *Trim off the overlap at the ends and side (if necessary) of each length of paper. Use a scraper as a guide for the knife for accurate cutting.*

5 *Wipe off any excess adhesive where the overlap has been before it dries, or it will leave ugly marks on the wall surface.*

6 *You can now go ahead and hang the next length on the other side of the first piece hung. Continue until you have covered the entire ceiling.*

It makes sense to get all the lengths measured and cut out in advance, and pasted up in batches of twos or threes (depending on your speed of working) to give adequate soaking time for the type of paper you are hanging; check the manufacturer's instructions on this point. Cut all the strips, including those which will be trimmed for chimney breasts, to full room dimensions plus 100mm (4in) excess for trimming.

The concertina fold

The secret of successful ceiling papering is the correct folding technique, as you paste, so that the paper can be transferred to and laid out against the ceiling surface in a smooth manner. Each fold of the concertina should be 300mm (1ft) wide approximately, apart from the first, which can be shorter (see step-by-step photographs). It's worth practising folding with dry paper first.

Hanging the paper

Assemble the working platform securely at the correct height across the whole length of the room, beneath the area where the first strip is to be pasted. Before you get up there with a fold of wet, pasted paper, make sure you have the tools you will need to hand.

The last-to-be-pasted section of each length is first to go on the ceiling; tease off this first section and brush it into place. Continue to unfold the concertina in sections, brushing it down as you go and checking it is straight against the guideline.

Trimming and seam rolling

When you trim, you should make sure the paper butts exactly up to covings, but allow a 5-10mm (1/4-3/8in) overlap down to the surface of the walls you intend to paper later. Except with embossed papers, you should roll the butt joints between strips with a seam roller.

Light fittings or shades should always be removed, leaving just the flex hanging down. Turn the power off, to ensure safety.

If a chimney breast falls parallel to the run of the paper, you will need your scissors handy to take out an approximate piece as you work along the platform. It's worth anticipating this before you get up there; mark a rough line on the paper at the approximate position of the chimney breast. Cut out the chimney breast piece, leaving an excess of about 15mm (5/8in) for detailed trimming when the whole strip is in place.

If the strip ends at a chimney breast there are less problems. Remove any vast unwanted sections as you work and trim to fit later. External corners are dealt with by making a V-cut so that one flap of the paper can be folded down the inside alcove edge of the chimney breast (or trimmed there if you are working to a coving).

PAPERING ROUND OBSTACLES

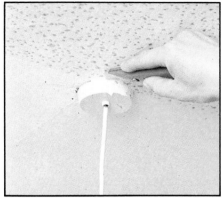

1 If there is a ceiling rose, use a knife or scissors to make a little slit in the paper so it fits round the rose; don't cut too deep.

2 Hang the next length so it butts up against the previous one; at the rose take the paper over the top of the obstacle.

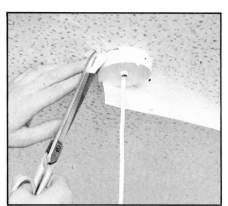

3 Again, make slits in the paper so it fits round the rose; this will allow you to brush the rest of the length of paper in place.

4 When the paper is in place, trim round the rose. Place the edge of a scraper between the knife and ceiling so there's a slight overlap.

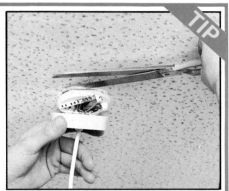

5 Turn off the power, remove the rose cover and press the overlap into place. When the cover is replaced it will conceal the cut edges completely.

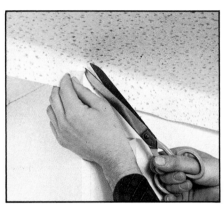

6 Where the paper meets an alcove, make a slit in the paper in line with one corner of the alcove and then in line with the other.

7 You can then brush the paper into place in the normal fashion so it fits neatly into the gap between the two corners. Trim the overlap along the wall leading to the alcove.

8 Fix the next length so it butts up against the previous one. Adhesive may ooze out when seams are rolled; so long as the paper is colourfast you can remove it with a damp sponge.

9 Measure up and cut the last narrow piece, allowing for an overlap of about 25mm (1in) at the wall and ceiling junction. Paste and brush it into place; trim to complete the job.

HANGING RELIEF WALLPAPER

If you want a change from the flat surface which ordinary wallpaper gives, you can hang a relief wallcovering with a raised, embossed pattern for a different look on walls or ceilings.

Wallcovering: Crown Anaglypta Arabesque RD132

One way of covering up a poor wall or ceiling surface is to use a relief or embossed wallcovering. It must be stressed at the outset that the wall or ceiling should be in sound structural condition, but these types of wallcoverings will provide an ideal disguise for minor defects such as hairline cracks, a rough finish or slight unevenness in the surface. Even where the surface is perfect, you may simply decide that you like the look which a raised pattern can give.

Frequently, embossed or relief wallcoverings are referred to as 'whites' because they come only with a white finish. Most of them require overpainting (you can, of course, paint them white, if you wish) so the paper is protected against dirt, moisture and reasonable wear and tear. Painting over a wallcovering normally means that it won't be an easy job to remove it later, so it's usually best to hang a relief wallcovering only if you intend leaving it in place for some time. (Although a steam stripper will make removal easier.)

There is a wide range of relief wallcoverings available which vary in design, thickness, depth of embossing, quality, strength, method of manufacture and price.

Woodchip wallpapers

One of the most commonly used of the 'whites' apart from lining paper is woodchip wallpaper. This relatively thick paper is made from soft wood-pulp with small, medium or large chips of wood added during the manufacturing process. These chips create the textured surface.

Woodchips are hung in normal fashion; you paste the back with a paste suitable for medium weight papers and butt-join lengths of paper before trimming off the overlaps. The cut lengths must be allowed to soak and become supple before hanging, but be careful that you don't oversoak them (follow the manufacturer's instructions as to the length of soaking time) or it is more likely you will tear the paper when trimming.

Low-relief embossed papers

This range of wallpapers, which includes Anaglypta, is also made from pulped wood fibre. During manufacture two sheets of paper are bonded together with a water-resistant adhesive. Before the adhesive dries, the paper is run through shaped steel rollers, one with a raised pattern and the other with corresponding indentations, to stretch the soft paper and create the embossed effect.

The back surface of the paper has hollows and you need to take extra care when hanging these types of wallcoverings to ensure that the hollows are not squashed flat against the wall. You should use a heavy-duty adhesive and, allow the paper to soak (usually for 10 minutes) and become supple before hanging. Take care that the edges are well pasted.

High-relief embossed papers

The majority of good quality high-relief 'whites' are made in a similar manner but often using cotton linters (short cotton fibres), china clay and resins rather than pulped wood fibre to produce the 'paper'. These ingredients give a more durable wallcovering and enable it to be given a greater depth of embossing. Supaglypta is the best known example of this type of paper.

Depending on the design, high-relief embossed papers can often require some depth of drop matching to maintain pattern repeats. Soaking times (use a heavy-duty adhesive) should therefore be kept as constant as possible so that each length stretches, before and during hanging, to the same degree.

Blown vinyls

Classed as 'whites' and intended to be over-painted, blown vinyls are made from a type of vinyl bonded to a paper backing. During manufacture the vinyl is heated to make it expand, then before it cools it is passed through a machine which embosses a pattern into the surface. The result is a wallcovering with a slightly soft, spongy feel. But despite this softness, blown vinyls are strong, easy to handle and create few hanging problems.

You should hang a blown vinyl wallcovering with a heavy-duty or ready-mixed paste containing a fungicide; these types of wallcovering do not require soaking. You can

PREPARING ANAGLYPTA

1 *Measure and cut the paper so there will be a 50mm (2in) overlap at the top and bottom. Mark the top so you'll hang the lengths the same way.*

2 *To ensure accurate pattern matching place the length to be cut alongside a cut length and make a slight tear to indicate where to cut.*

3 *Brush on the adhesive, filling all the hollows. If it is the correct consistency the brush will lift the paper from the table for a few seconds.*

4 *Fold the paper, taking care not to crease the folds, and leave the length to soak for 10 to 15 minutes (follow the instructions on the roll.)*

Ready Reference

LINING WALLS
It's advisable to line walls and ceilings with lining paper before you hang a relief wallcovering. Remember to:
● hang it the opposite way to which the wallcovering will run
● never overlap the edges of the lining paper; they should be butt joined or you can leave a slight gap between lengths.

TIP: DON'T ROLL SEAMS
Never use a seam roller to flatten the butt joins between lengths of a relief wallcovering or you risk flattening the embossed pattern. Use a paperhanger's brush to press the seams lightly into place.

TIP: OVERLAP JOINT
Where it is necessary to overlap lengths of a relief wallcovering at a corner, tear the edge of the first length which reaches round the corner and then run a seam roller over the feathered edge to flatten it down before fixing the adjoining length over it.

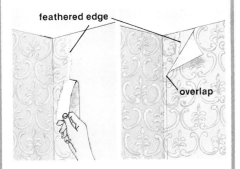

feathered edge

overlap

PAINTING RELIEF WALLCOVERINGS
Relief wallcoverings can be painted using a brush or roller. The first coat should always be an emulsion paint but you can, if you wish, follow this up with a coat of solvent-based paint. The exception is Lincrusta which should always be painted with a solvent-based paint or, if a wood effect is wanted, it can be treated with scumble, a thin oil-based covering which gives a 'grainy' effect.

TIP: FLATTEN AIR BUBBLES
The painting process will show up any air bubbles trapped behind the paper. As the paint dries the air bubble will probably flatten again but if this does not happen:
● use a razor blade to make two careful cuts diagonally across the bubble
● push more adhesive under each flap and press the paper back
● wipe off excess paste from the paper surface, allow to dry and then repaint.

then paint them like any other relief wallcovering, and they can be scrubbed clean. When you want to remove the wallcovering you peel off the vinyl layer leaving the paper lining on the wall. This can be left in place to serve as a lining paper for the next covering, or else it can be soaked and stripped off completely.

Pre-finished vinyl reliefs
Another type of relief wallcovering comes with a textured or plain vinyl surface. It is pre-finished so it does not require over-painting (though you can paint it if you wish), and it is bonded to a paper backing. These can be regularly wiped clean and are easily removed by peeling them off.

There are also vinyl relief wallcoverings with a printed decorative embossed surface designed to give the appearance of wall tiles, wood panelling or other effects.

Lincrusta types
Lincrusta is a heavy, solid, embossed wallcovering made from a combination of oxidised linseed oil and fillers bonded to a paper backing. During manufacture the putty-like surface is embossed while still soft, and is then left for 14 days to mature and dry out. It is available in two versions – one intended to be overpainted and the other already finished.

As this type of wallcovering is heavy and will easily pull away old, poorly-adhering emulsion or other paints, you should take special care in preparing the wall surfaces. They must be thoroughly clean, made good and should also be given a coat of size.

To hang Lincrusta, first cut it into drop-matched lengths, allowing an extra 50mm (2in) for later trimming at the base. The top edges of each length should be cut to fit precisely. Then trim the edges of the lengths

HANGING ANAGLYPTA

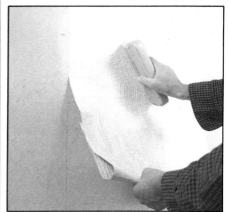

1 Mark where the first length will fall (here the edge just reaches the central point of the chimney breast) and then gently brush it in place.

2 To give you a clear guideline for trimming the relief paper, mark off the cutting line by running a pencil along the wallcovering.

3 Use scissors to trim the paper. Don't use a knife as you are more likely to tear the paper because of its softness (from soaking).

4 Fix the next length of wallcovering, butting it up against the previous length. Don't overlap; any slight gap will be filled by overpainting.

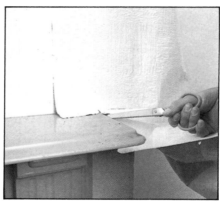

5 To fit the paper round a mantelpiece cut into the overlap at several places. Make sure that you don't cut too deep.

6 Similarly, where the paper will have to fit round an external corner, make a cut into the overlap at the top and bottom.

7 At a fire surround mark off the cutting line with a pencil, use scissors to trim the overlap, then brush the trimmed edge into place.

8 There should be at least 25mm (1in) of paper lapping round an external corner (here there's much more) which you brush into place.

9 At an internal corner brush one length into the corner. Ideally, tear the overlap (see Ready Reference), and cover it with the next length.

using a straight edge and a sharp knife. (Lincrusta is one of the few wallcoverings which require edge trimming). Offer each length up to its intended position and make any cutouts required for light switches or other obstacles.

You should then dampen the paper backing with warm water applied with a sponge to allow the material to expand fully and make hanging easier. Leave it to soak for up to 30 minutes on a flat surface with two lengths laid back to back, then wipe off any excess water.

Brush special Lincrusta glue onto the damp backing paper; work fairly quickly and aim for even coverage. Position each length immediately after it is pasted, and use a soft cloth to press the wallcovering gently but firmly into position, working from the top downwards. Trim the bottom length with a sharp knife and you can then go ahead and hang the other lengths, butting each tightly up against the next. Because of its thickness and the nature of its surface, Lincrusta does not easily bend round corners so you will have to cut and butt join it at corners as neatly as possible. As with other types of wallcoverings, you're unlikely to get perfect pattern matching at corners because the walls will probably be slightly out of true.

It is very difficult to remove Lincrusta and you are quite likely to damage the wall behind in the process if you try to remove it, so it's worth thinking carefully before you decide to hang this type of wallcovering. It is, however, extremely durable, so can be used where ordinary relief wallcoverings might be prone to damage – in stairwells, for example.

Novamura

Although not really a relief wallcovering and certainly not a 'white', there is another slightly textured wallcovering worth describing which is made from an unusual material and hung in an unusual manner.

This is Novamura, which is a foamed polyethylene wallcovering. It is extremely lightweight and supplied in standard-size rolls in a wide variety of designs. It is soft and warm to touch and possibly the easiest wallcovering to hang.

Instead of pasting lengths cut from the roll, the paste is applied directly to the wall; the roll is unfurled down the wall onto the pasted area and then trimmed. This method eliminates the need for paste tables, mixing buckets and other paperhanging paraphernalia and takes comparatively little time.

Novamura must nevertheless be treated with some care and should not be overstretched. Although it can be wiped clean it should not be scrubbed.

To remove it you simply peel it away from the wall, with no soaking or pre-treatment required.

PAINTING ANAGLYPTA

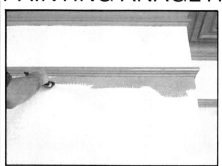

1 Use a brush to cut in at the edges; applying a silk-finish emulsion paint will emphasise the embossed effect more than a matt one.

2 The job will go more quickly if you use a roller to paint the rest of the wallcovering; paint it in bands, working down the wall.

HANGING NOVAMURA

1 Apply adhesive containing a fungicide to the wall, covering an area slightly wider than the width of the wallcovering.

2 Apply the wallcovering directly from the dry roll without cutting individual lengths. Smooth it into place with a damp sponge.

3 Crease the wallcoverings at the joins between wall and ceiling (or picture rail) and skirting, then trim with scissors or a sharp knife.

4 Hang the next piece in the same way, butting it up against the preceding piece and making sure the pattern matches as you hang it.

CHAPTER 3

USING CERAMIC TILES

**Tiled walls present one of the most attractive and hardwearing finishes available, and there is now a huge range of colours, patterns and sizes to choose from.
Ready-mixed adhesives make the fixing easy; all you have to do is plan out each area carefully before you start.**

CERAMIC TILES
for small areas

Ceramic tiles are easy-clean, hygienic and hard wearing. By starting with a small area in your home where these qualities are needed – like splashbacks or worktops – you'll not only grasp the basics but also gain confidence to tackle bigger things.

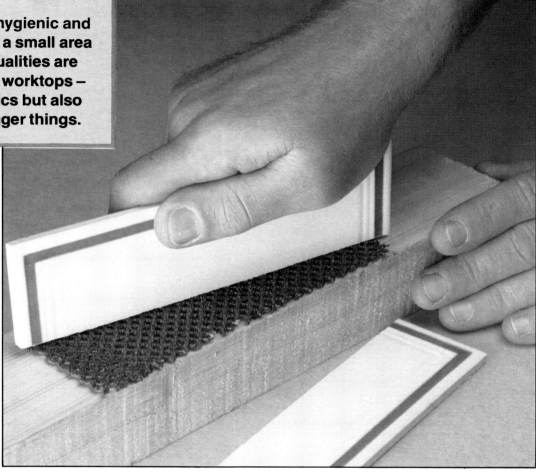

Modern ceramic tiles are thin slabs of clay, decorated on one side with coloured glazes. These are baked on to give the tile a hard, glassy surface resistant to water, heat and almost all household chemicals. The clay from which tiles are made, which is known as the biscuit, varies and you need to know the differences before you choose the tile to use. The thinnest ones with a pale coloured biscuit are good on all vertical surfaces (including doors where extra weight puts stress on the hinges).

If the biscuit is reddish/brown it has been high baked (vitrified). The thicker and darker coloured it is the more strength the tile has — floor tiles, for example, are usually big in size as well as thick in biscuit.

Work surfaces need tiles that are strong to withstand weights of heavy pots, while splashbacks and bathroom surfaces can take lighter, thinner ones.

Types of tiles
Within each range of tiles there are usually three types. *Spacer* tiles have small projections on each edge called lugs which butt up to the neighbouring tile and provide the correct space for grouting (with these it is very hard to vary the width of the grouting). *Border* tiles are squared off on all sides but are glazed on two adjacent edges — these give a neat finish to outer corners and top or side edges. *Universal or continental* tiles have no lugs and are square on all edges. All three can be used successfully in small areas, but do remember that if tiles do not have lugs you have to include grouting space in your calculations — the thinnest tiles need to be spaced by nothing more than torn-up pieces of cardboard, 6mm (1/4in) tiles are best with a matchstick width in between.

Tiles are sold by the sq metre, sq yd, boxed in 25s or 50s, or can be bought individually. Boxed tiles usually advise on adhesive and grout needed for specific areas. When buying, if there's no written information available always check that the tile is suitable.

How to plan the layout
When tiling small areas you don't have much space to manoeuvre. The idea in all tiling is to create a symmetrical effect, using whole tiles or, if any have to be cut, making them equal.

Knowing about the different sizes of tiles helps in the planning. For example, if you know the width and height or depth of the surface you intend to tile, you can divide this by the known size of tiles until you find the one that gives the right number of whole tiles. Remember that the width of grouting has to be added to the measurement with non-lugged tiles – and except with the very thinnest tiles this can be slightly widened if it saves cutting a tile.

If you're prepared to incorporate cut tiles into the planning remember:
● on the width of the tiled area, place equal cut tiles at each end
● on the height, place cut tiles at the top edge
● on the depth (eg, window-recesses) put cut tiles at back edge
● frame a fitting by placing cut tiles at each side and the top

A mix of patterned or textured with plain tiles is best done first on metricated graph paper. This will help you see where you want the pattern to fall.

Fixings should be made in the grouting lines where possible. Some tile ranges have soap dishes, towel rails etc attached to tiles so they can be incorporated in a scheme, but if these don't suit your purposes, you can drill the tiles to screw in your own fitting (see page 52).

A working plan
All tiles should be fixed level and square so it's important to establish the horizontal and vertical with a spirit level. Draw in the lines with pencil. If you plan to tile where there is no support (eg, on either side of a basin or sink) lightly pin a length of 50 x 25mm (2 x 1in) timber below the tiling line – the batten will prevent the tiles slipping.

On doors you may have to consider adding a timber surround to keep the tiles secure as they will be subjected to movement (also see section on *Adhesives* below).

Adhesives and grouting
The choice of both of these depends on where the tiles are to be fixed. In a watery situation (eg, a shower cubicle or a steamy kitchen) it is important to use a waterproof variety of both, even though you might have

Ready Reference

TILE SHAPES AND SIZES

Ceramic tiles for walls are usually square or oblong in shape. The commonest sizes are shown below. The smaller sizes are usually 4mm (⅝in) thick, while larger tiles may be 6mm (¼in) or more in thickness.

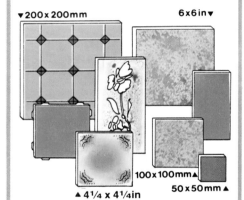

▼200x200mm 6x6in▼
100x100mm▲
50x50mm▲
▲4¼ x 4¼in

HOW MANY TILES?

Square or oblong areas
● measure lengths and width of the area
● divide each measurement by the size of tile you're using, rounding up to the next whole number if you get a fraction
● multiply the two figures to give the number of tiles needed

Awkwardly-shaped areas
● divide area into convenient squares or oblongs
● work out each one as above adding up the area totals to give the final figures

Patterns using two or more different tiles
● sketch out design on graph paper, one square for each tile (two for oblong tiles); use colours to mark where different tiles fall
● count up totals needed of each pattern, counting part tiles as whole ones

Add 10% to your final tile counts to allow for breakages

ADHESIVE/GROUT

For each square metre of tiling allow:
● 1.5kg (about 1 litre) of adhesive
● 150g of grout

TIP: AVOID NARROW STRIPS

Less than about 25mm/1in wide is very difficult to cut. When planning, if you see narrow strips are going to occur you can:
● replan the rows to use one less whole tile with two wider cut pieces at either end
● or increase the grouting space slightly between every tile in the row

HOW TO HANG TILES

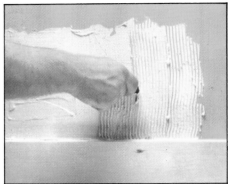

1 Spread ceramic tile adhesive to cover 1 sq metre, then 'comb' with notched spreader. To support tiles where no other support exists, pin a horizontal timber batten to the wall.

2 When positioning tiles it is important to twist them slightly to bed them. Don't slide them as this forces adhesive between joints.

3 Form even grouting spaces between tiles without lugs with pieces of matchstick. Or you can use torn-up cardboard from the tile packaging or similar if you want only a narrow grouting space.

4 Remove matchsticks or card after all tiles are hung, and grout 12-24 hours later. Press grout into the spaces using a small sponge or squeegee, making sure no voids are left in either vertical or horizontal spaces.

5 After 10 minutes, wipe off excess grouting with soft cloth. Use fine dowelling (sand the end to round it) to even up and smooth the lines. Fill any voids that appear with fresh grout to prevent water penetration.

6 When grouting is dry, polish the tiles with a soft cloth so the area is smooth. All the surface needs now is an occasional wipe-down although non-waterproof grout may tend to discolour as time goes by.

to wait for 4-5 days before exposing the tile surface to use.

All ceramic tile adhesives are like thin putty and can be bought ready mixed in tubs or in powder form to be made up with water. They are what is known as thin-bed adhesives in that they are designed to be applied in a thin layer on a flat even surface. The spread is controlled by a notched comb (usually provided by the manufacturer but cheap to buy where you bought the tiles) to make furrows of a specified depth. When the tiles are pressed on with a slight twist, the adhesive evenly grips the back of the biscuit.

Special latex-based adhesives (usually, two-part products which have to be mixed before using) have much more flexibility and are good for tiles where there is any movement (eg, on doors).

Spread the adhesive on an area no more than 1 sq metre (1 sq yd) at a time, or it will lose its gripping power before you have time to place the tiles. If you remove a tile, before refixing comb the adhesive again.

Grout gives the final finish to the tiled area, filling the spaces between the tiles and preventing moisture getting behind them and affecting the adhesive. Grouting can be done 12-24 hours after the last tile has been pressed into place. Grout can be standard or waterproof (with added acrylic), and both are like a cellulose filler when made up.

If you only make up one lot of grouting, you can colour it with special grouting tints – but remember that it's hard to make other batches match the colour. Waterproof grouting cannot always take these tints.

Press grout between the tiles with a sponge or squeegee and wipe off excess with a damp sponge. Even up the grouting by drawing a pencil-like piece of wood (eg dowelling) along each row first vertically, then horizontally. Do this within 10 minutes of grouting so it is not completely dry.

Leave the tiles for 24 hours before polishing with a clean dry cloth. Wash clean only if a slight bloom remains.

Tiles should never be fixed with tight joints for any movement of the wall or fittings will cause the tiles to crack. Similarly where tiles meet baths, basins, sinks etc, flexibility is needed – and grout that dries rigid cannot provide it. These gaps must be filled with a silicone rubber sealant

Techniques with tiles

To cut tiles, lightly score the glaze with a tile cutter to break the surface. Place the tile glazed side up with the scored line over matchsticks and firmly but gently press the tile down on each side. If using a pencil press on one side, hold the other. Smooth the cut edge with a file. Very small adjustments are best done by filing the edge of the whole tile.

CUTTING TILES

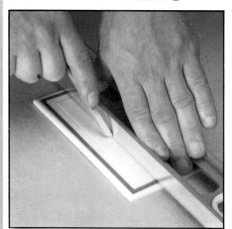

1 *Before a tile will break, the glaze must be scored — on the edges as well as surface. Use a carbide-tipped cutter against a straight-edge.*

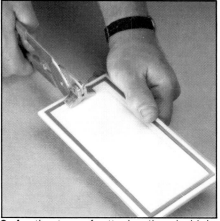

2 *Another type of cutter has 'jaws' which clasp the tile during breaking. (It also has a small 'wheel' for scoring through the glaze on the tile).*

3 *No special tools are needed with other tile-breaking methods. For medium thick tiles use a pencil, for thin tiles use matchsticks.*

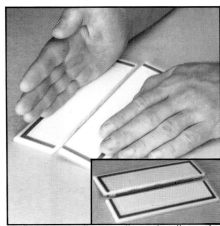

4 *Place pencil centrally under tile and score line, hold one side and press firmly on other. With thin tiles, press lightly both sides.*

To remove a narrow strip of tile, score the line heavily by drawing the tile cutter across the tile more firmly several times in the same place. Then use pincers to 'nibble' the waste away in small pieces and smooth the edge. Glaze on broken tiles is as sharp as glass, so be careful not to cut yourself.

Templates for awkwardly shaped tiles are not difficult to make. Cut the shape in card, place on a tile and score a line freehand with the tile cutter. Any straight score marks can be deepened afterwards, using a straight edge for support. Then nibble away the waste with pincers. If there's a large amount to be cut away, score the waste part to divide it into sections, then nibble away. A good tip is to do this on a soft or padded surface so the tile doesn't break in the wrong place.

Suitable surfaces

The ideal surface for tiling is one that's perfectly flat, dry and firm. Small irregularities will be covered up, but any major hollows, bumps or flaking, need to be made good.

Plastered walls and asbestos cement sheets: perfect for tiling, but wait a month after any new plastering to allow the wall to dry out completely. Unless surface has been previously painted, apply a coat of plaster primer to prevent the liquid in the tile adhesive from being absorbed too quickly.

Plasterboard: again, ideal for tiling as long as it's firmly fixed and adjacent boards cannot shift. (If they did the joins would probably crack). To prepare the surface, remove all dust, wipe down with white spirit

Ready Reference

TOOLS FOR TILING

Tile cutter: essential for scoring glaze of tiles before breaking them. Score only once (the second time you may waver from the line and cause an uneven break).
Pincers: these are used for nibbling away small portions of tile, after scoring a line with the cutter. Ordinary pincers are fine for most jobs, but special tile nibblers are available.
Special cutter: combines a cutting edge (usually a small cutting wheel) with jaws which snap the tile along the scored line.
Tile file: an abrasive mesh, used as a file to 'shave' off small amounts.

TIP: TO DRILL A TILE

● make a cross of masking tape and mark the point where you want the hole
● drill after adhesive and grouting have set using lowest speed or a hand drill with masonry bit — too much speed at the start will craze the tile
● once through the glaze, drill in the normal way

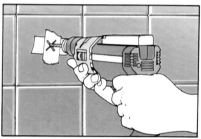

● cut tile into two along line corresponding with centre point of pipe; offer up each half to the pipe
● mark freehand semi-circles on tile to match edge of pipe; score line with tile cutter and nibble away waste with pincers

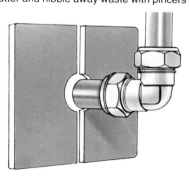

SHAPING TILES

5 Edges of broken tiles need to be smoothed off — use a special tile file mounted on wood, a wood file or rub against rough concrete.

6 To cut an awkward shape, make a card template. Place it on the tile and score glaze on the surface and edges with the tile cutter.

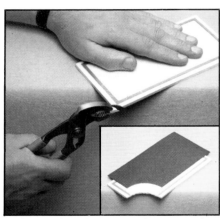

7 On a soft surface, use pincers to take tiny nibbles out of the tile. If you're over enthusiastic you'll break off more than you intended.

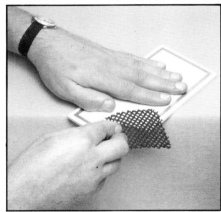

8 Once the waste has been slowly but surely nibbled away, smooth up the edge. Files are also useful when a whole tile needs a slight trimming.

to remove grease, then treat with primer.
Paint: old emulsion-paint needs to be cleaned thoroughly with sugar soap or detergent to remove all traces of dust and grease. Gloss paint needs to be cleaned thoroughly; remove any flaking paint then roughen up whole surface with a coarse abrasive to provide a good key for the adhesive.
Wallpaper: DO NOT tile directly onto wallpaper, as this can be pulled away from the wall by the adhesive. Strip it off completely.
Wood and Chipboard: perfect for tiling as long as it is flat and adjacent boards cannot shift. Treat with an ordinary wood primer.
Laminates: joins and small, minor blemishes in the surface can be covered up so long as the entire sheet is soundly fixed and absolutely flat. Its smooth face must be roughened with course abrasive to provide a key for the tile adhesive.
Old ceramic tiles: the thin biscuit ceramic tiles are excellent for tiling over as they add little to the wall's thickness and won't protrude beyond existing fittings. Loose and cracked tiles will have to be removed. Scrape out the grouting surrounding the tile using an old, thin screwdriver or something similar, then, beginning in the centre and working outwards, remove the tile using a club hammer and cold chisel.

Small sections or mis-shapen pieces (as around a new fixture) can be built up level with neighbouring tiles with cellulose filler.

The area should then be sealed with plaster primer or emulsion paint to finish the surface.

CERAMIC TILING WALL TO WALL

Ceramic tiles are an ideal decorating material for they make a room look good for years and require virtually no maintenance. But covering several walls with tiles is a large-scale job which needs a methodical and careful approach if you are to achieve the best results.

The all-in-one look that wall-to-wall tiling can give has to be planned carefully to avoid expensive and time consuming mistakes. How to do this may depend on whether you want to include special patterns in the design, but following certain rules will give a desirable symmetry to the look.

One of the hardest tasks will probably be choosing the tiles for there's a vast array of shapes, sizes and colours available. Having picked out the ones you want though, don't buy until you've done the planning – for the plans of each wall should tell you whether the pattern will work in the room or would be lost in the cutting or amid the fittings.

Plans on paper also give you an instant method of working out how many tiles to buy (counting each cut one as a whole, and adding 2-5% for unintended breakage) including the number which will need to be border (two glazed edges) or mitred (on square or rectangular universal tiles) for the top row of half-tiled walls or external corners. Buy all the tiles at once, but do check each carton to make sure there's no variation in the colour (this can occur during the firing of different batches).

Planning on paper

The best possible way to start planning for a large expanse of tiling is not on the wall, but on paper. Graph paper is ideal, particularly if you intend including a mix of plain and patterned tiles, or a large motif that needs building up. Of course, advance planning is also essential if you're tiling round major features like windows, doors, mirrors, shower cubicles and so on.

You need separate pieces of graph paper for each wall you intend tiling. Allow the large (1cm) squares on the paper to represent your tiles — one for a square tile of any size, two for a rectangular tile; this will give you a scale to work to. Now mark up sheets of greaseproof paper with your actual wall sizes using the scale dictated by the tile size on the graph paper. Measure and outline on the see-through paper the exact position and in-scale dimensions of all fixtures and fittings (see the planning pictures on page 54).

At this stage, the objective is to decide how to achieve the best symmetrical layout for your tiles — the 'ideal' is to have either whole or equal-size cut tiles on each side of a fixture.

First you have to mark in the central guide lines. For instance, on *walls with a window* draw a line from the sill centre to the floor, and from the centre of the top of the window to the ceiling. If there are *two windows* also draw in the central line from floor to ceiling between them. Mark the centre point above a *door* to the ceiling and also indicate the horizontal line at the top of the door. In the same way draw in a central line from the top of a *basin or vanity unit* to the ceiling.

For all these lines use a coloured pen for you have to be aware of them when deciding where whole tiles should be positioned. But they're only the starting point — other potential problems have to be looked at too.

Place the see-through paper over the tile sizes on the graph paper so you can see how the tiles will fall in relation to the guide lines. Now take into account the following important points:

● The first row above the lowest level — either the floor, the skirting board or a wall-to-wall fitting — should be whole tiles. If necessary, change this to prevent a thin strip being cut at the ceiling.

● Check where tiles come in relation to fittings. If very thin strips (less than 38mm/ 1½in) or narrow 'L' shapes would need to be cut, move the top sheet slightly up, down, left or right till the tiles are of a cuttable size — areas to watch are around windows, doors and where one wall meets another.

Placing patterns

When you are satisfied that you have a symmetrical and workable arrangement you can tape the top sheet in the right position on the graph paper, then start to plan where you're going to position your patterned tiles. Use pencil this time in case you change your mind and want to make adjustments. These are the points to watch:

● Don't place single motif patterns at internal corners where they would have to be cut — you won't find it easy to match up the remaining piece on the adjacent wall.

Jem Grischotti   Tiles: Rustica Roberta pattern   Flooring: GAF terra cotta cushion vinyl Coburg

Ready Reference

TILING SEQUENCES

You can use the 'step' method (see page 55), or build 'pyramids'. Here are the sequences for different bonds.

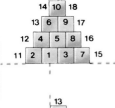

Running bond staggers the tiles. Place the first one centrally on your vertical line.

Jack-on-Jack has the joints lined up. Work either side of your vertical line.

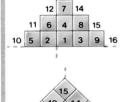

Diamond bond puts plain or outlined tiles at an angle. Place the first centrally on the vertical, fill in 'triangles' last.

● If the pattern builds up vertically and horizontally over four or more tiles, 'centre' the pattern on the wall so that cuts are equal at both ends. If pattern loss can't be avoided with designs of this type at least it can be kept to internal corners.

● Whole tiles should be used on both faces of external corners.

Now butt each of the wall plans up to the other to make sure that the patterns relate both vertically and horizontally.

Planning on the wall

When there are no complicated tiling patterns involved and walls are free of interruptions such as windows, it's often easier to do the planning directly on the wall itself. Here, the simple objective is to place the tiles symmetrically between the corners. And to do this, all you need is a tiling gauge which you can make.

A tiling gauge is like a long ruler, except that it's marked off in tile widths. Use a long, straight piece of timber ideally about 25mm square (1in square) and remember to include the grouting gap between tiles as you rule off the gauge. If you're using rectangular tiles, mark the widths on one side, the lengths on the other.

Holding the gauge against the walls —

first vertically, then horizontally — tells you instantly where the whole tiles will fit in and where cut tiles will be needed. But first you must find the centre of each wall. Measure the width — doing this at three places will also tell you if the corners are vertical (hang a plumb line or use a spirit level to make absolutely sure) — and halve it to find the centre point. Use the tiling gauge to mark this vertical centre line with a pencil, then hold the gauge against it. Move it up or down until you have at least a whole tile's width above the floor or skirting board — this can be adjusted slightly if it avoids a thin piece of tile at ceiling height — then mark off the tile widths on the vertical line itself.

Now hold the tiling gauge horizontally, and move it to left or right of the vertical line if thin pieces of tile would have to be cut near windows or fittings, or to make cut tiles at both ends of the wall equal. Following this adjustment, mark the wall and draw in a new vertical line if necessary. The wall can now be marked horizontally with tile widths. Keeping to the same horizontal, mark up adjacent walls in the same way.

At corners, whether internal or external, don't assume they're either square, vertical or even. An internal corner is the worst place to start your tiling for this very reason, but it

doesn't matter if you position cut tiles there. On external corners use the tiling gauge to work inwards in whole tile widths.

You can also use the tiling gauge to check that your graph plan is accurate, and make any necessary adjustments.

Putting up battens

Once you have determined that your plan is correct, fix a length of perfectly straight 50mm x 25mm (2in x 1in) battening across the full width of the wall — use a spirit level to ensure that the batten is horizontal. Use masonry nails to fix it in place but do not drive them fully home as they will have to be removed later. If using screws the wall should be plugged. The batten provides the base for your tiling and it's important that its position is correct.

If more than one wall is being tiled, continue to fix battens around the room at the same height, using the spirit level to check the horizontal. The last one you fix should tie up perfectly with the first. If there are gaps, at the door for example, check that the tile level either side is the same, by using a straight-edge and spirit level to bridge the gap.

Once the horizontal battens are fixed, fix a vertical batten to give yourself the starting point for the first tile. Use a spirit level or plumb line to make sure it's positioned accurately.

Fixing tiles

Begin tiling from the horizontal base upwards, checking as you work that the tiles are going up accurately both vertically and horizontally. Work on an area of approximately 1 sq metre (1 sq yd) at a time, spreading the adhesive and fixing all the whole tiles using card or matchsticks as spacers as necessary. Make sure no excess adhesive is left on the surface of the tiles.

Next, deal with any tiles that need to be cut. You may find the gap into which they fit is too narrow to operate the adhesive spreader properly. In this case spread the adhesive onto the back of the tiles.

When all the tiling above the base batten has been completed wait for 8-12 hours, before removing the battens, and completing the tiling. Take care when removing the base batten that the tiles above are not disturbed — the adhesive is unlikely to be fully set.

Dealing with corners

Your original planning should have indicated how many border or mitred tiles you will need for tiling external corners or for the top line of tiles on a half-tiled wall. You will find external corners, those which project into the room, in virtually all tiling situations — around boxed-in pipework, or around a window or door reveal, or in an L-shaped room.

Where you are using universal tiles at an

PLANNING TILE LAYOUT ON PAPER

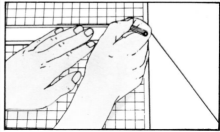

1 *On graph paper with large (eg, 1cm) squares, let each square represent one whole square tile. Strengthen the grid lines with coloured pen if necessary.*

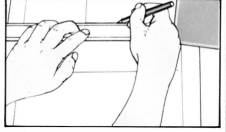

2 *On tracing paper, draw the outline of each wall to be tiled, and mark in doors and windows. Use the scale 1cm = the actual tile size (eg, 150mm).*

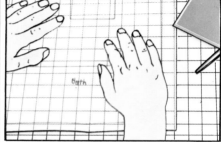

3 *Place greaseproof over graph paper and move it around till you get the most manageable size cut tiles, especially near fixtures, ceiling and floor.*

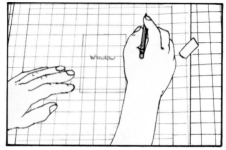

4 *Tape the top sheet in place, then mark the pattern in with pencil. Do each wall the same so that the alignment of the horizontal is correct.*

Jem Grischotti

external corner, start at the corner with a whole tile — it should project by the depth of the mitre so that the mitre on the other face neatly butts up against it with a fine space for grouting in between.

With window reveals the correct method is to tile up the wall to sill level, cutting tiles if necessary. Fit whole tiles either side of the reveal, then again cut tiles to fill the space between those whole ones and the window frame. Attach whole border or mitred tiles to the sill so they butt up against the wall tiles. If using square-edged tiles the ones on the sill should cover the edges of those on the wall so the grouting line is not on the sill surface. If the sill is narrower than a whole tile, cut the excess from the back — not the front. If the sill is deeper than a whole tile, put cut tiles near the window with the cut edge against the frame. Continually check the accurate lining up of tiles with a spirit level.

Some vertical external corners are not as precisely straight and vertical as they should be and this can lead to problems of tile alignment. The use of a thick-bed adhesive will help to straighten out some irregularities where a corner goes inwards (a thin-bed helps where the wall leans outwards). Buying a 'flexible' adhesive will give you both qualities. As a general rule it is

PLANNING ON THE WALL

2 Use a plumb line to check that the wall is vertical.

1 (inset) Mark the tiling gauge in tile widths (and lengths if they are rectangular).

3 Draw verticals down the wall, marking off the exact tile widths to give an accurate guide.

4 Check each horizontal with a spirit level, then mark tile positions from floor to ceiling.

5 Place horizontal batten at least a tile's width above floor or a fitting using masonry nails or screws.

6 Fix vertical batten and begin to tile where the battens meet. Spread adhesive to cover 1 sq metre (1 sq yd).

Ready Reference

TACKLING TILING PROBLEMS
Whenever a fitting, a door or window interrupts the clean run of a wall, it becomes the focal point of the wall. So you have to plan for symmetry *round* the features. Here are some guidelines:

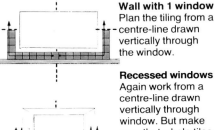

Wall with 1 window
Plan the tiling from a centre-line drawn vertically through the window.

Recessed windows
Again work from a centre-line drawn vertically through window. But make sure that whole tiles are placed at the front of the sill and the sides of the reveals. Place cut tiles closest to the window frame.

Wall with two windows
Unless the space between the two windows is exactly equal to a number of whole tiles, plan your tiling to start from a centre-line drawn between the two.

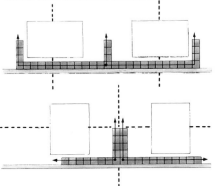

Wall with door
If the door is placed fairly centrally in the wall, plan your tiling from a centre-line drawn vertically through the door. If, however, the door is very close to a side wall, the large expanse of wall is a more prominent focal point. So plan the tiling to start one tile's width from the frame. If the frame is not exactly vertical, you'll be able to cut tiles to fit in the remaining space.

MAKE YOUR OWN TILE BREAKER

1 Use a timber offcut wider than the tile as the base. Use 3mm (¹/₈in) ply for the top and sides.

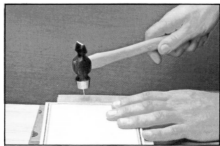

2 Stack ply strips on both sides till the same height as the tile, then pin. Nail on the top piece.

3 The breaking part needs to be as wide and deep as the tile, with the opening on the top a half tile long.

4 Score the glaze on the top and edges with a carbide-tipped cutter. Put the tile into the main part.

5 Slip on the breaking part so the score line is between the two. Hold one side while you press the other.

6 The tile breaks cleanly. This aid costs nothing and will save you time when tiling a large expanse.

TILING CORNERS

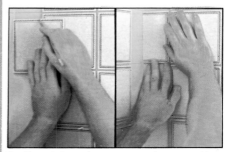

1 At an internal corner, mark amount to be cut at top and bottom. Break the tile, then fit in position.

2 File the remainder until it fits the adjacent area with enough space left for a fine line of grout.

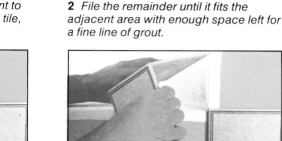

3 On a window sill, use a whole tile at the front and make sure that it overlaps the one on the wall-face underneath.

4 Mitred edges of universal tiles and glazed edges of border tiles give a better finish to external corners.

better to concentrate on lining up your border or mitred tiles perfectly vertically with only minute 'steps' between tiles, then bedding spacer or ordinary tiles behind to correspond with the line. Don't forget that if you do have to create a very slight stepped effect, you can reduce the uneven effect between the corner tiles and others by pressing in extra grouting later.

Internal corners seldom cause serious problems as cut tiles can be shaped to suit fluctuations from the truly vertical. Don't assume when cutting tiles for a corner that all will be the same size — the chances are that they will vary considerably and should be measured and cut individually. Another point: don't butt tiles up against each other so they touch — leave space for the grouting which will give the necessary flexibility should there be any wall movement.

Tiling around electrical fittings

When tiling around electrical fittings it is better to disconnect the electricity and remove the wall plate completely so that you can tile right up to the edge of the wall box. This is much neater and easier than trying to cut tiles to fit around the perimeter of the plate. Cut tiles as described in the illustration on pages 51 and 52 and fit them in the normal way with the plate being replaced on top, completely covering the cut edges of the tiles. This same principle applies to anything easily removable. The fewer objects you have to tile around the better, so before starting any tiling get to work with a screwdriver.

You have the greatest control over the end result if at the planning stage you work out where you want to place fittings such as towel rails and soap dishes, shelves and the like. Some tile ranges offer them attached so it's only a matter of fitting them in as you put the tiles up.

Tiling non-rigid surfaces

On surfaces which are not totally rigid or which are subject to movement, vibration or the odd shock, tiles should not be attached using adhesive which dries hard as most standard and waterproof types do. Instead use adhesives which retain some flexibility. These may be cement-based types with a latex rubber content, or acrylic adhesives. You may have to surround a non-rigid surface with wooden lipping to protect the tiles.

TILING AROUND FIXTURES

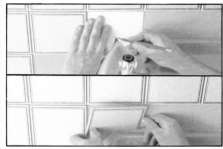

1 At awkward corners use card to make a tile-size template. Place it on the tile and score the shape, then gently nibble out the waste with pincers — the smaller the bits the better.

2 Where basins, baths, kitchen sinks or laundry tubs meet tiles, seal the join with silicone caulking to keep out water. Caulking comes in various colours to match fixtures.

3 After the adhesive has had time to set, the tiles are grouted both to protect them and to enhance their shape and colour.
Accessories can be bought already attached to tiles, can be screw mounted after drilling the tile, or if lightweight can be stuck on to tiles with adhesive pads.

CHECK FREQUENTLY

● the vertical (with a plumb line)
● the horizontal (with spirit level)
● that tiles don't project beyond each other

TIP: MAKING TEMPLATES

Cut the card tile-size then make diagonal snips into the edge to be shaped. These pieces will be forced out of the way and an accurate cutting line can be drawn.

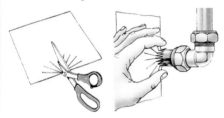

ADHESIVE AND GROUT

You need 1 litre of adhesive and 0.25kg of grout per sq metre (a little less for 1 sq yd), but for large areas buy in bulk: adhesive comes in 2½, 5 and 10 litre buckets; grout in 1.5 and 3.5kg packs.

WHEN GROUTING

● don't press mixture in with your fingers (it can abrade and irritate your skin)
● do wear light flexible gloves
● don't leave excess on tiles till dry
● do grout or caulk between tiles and window or door frames
● don't forget to grout edges of universal tiles if run finishes halfway up the wall
● use an old toothbrush to get grout into awkward places

TIP: GROUTING WALLS

On a large expanse, it's less tiring to use a rubber float to push grout between tiles – work upwards, then across; remove excess diagonally.

TILING SHOWERS

● use water resistant or waterproof adhesive and grout
● tile at least 1 row above shower head
● on ceiling use large drawing or upholstery pins to hold tiles till adhesive dries
● do floor and ceiling before walls
● don't expose tiles to water for 1 week

MOSAIC TILING

You don't have to be a skilled craftsman to decorate a surface with modern ceramic mosaic tiles. They come in a variety of designs and their small size makes it easy to tile round curves and obstacles.

Decorating a surface with mosaics – small pieces of material such as stone, glass, tile or shell – is an art form with a long history. The main drawback with the traditional method was that you needed an artist to design the mosaic and, usually, a highly skilled installer to fit them – all of which was expensive. Today, however, there are mosaics available as ceramic tiles that you can lay yourself.

Modern ceramic mosaic tiles come in a wide variety of shapes, sizes and patterns and can be used both indoors and out. In the kitchen they are ideal as wall surfaces or as a practical and attractive worktop which will be easy to clean and extremely hardwearing. An alternative to a completely tiled worktop is to have an inset area of mosaic tiles close to the hob on which you can put hot pans (see *Ready Reference*). In the bathroom, mosaics can be used as a splashback to the basin and bath, to tile the floor and walls or as an attractive finish to the inside of a shower cubicle.

Elsewhere in the house, mosaic tiles can be used for interesting effects. You don't have to stick to wall or floor surfaces either; mosaics will also make an unusual coffee table top, or could be set into a wooden frame to create a pot stand or even a cheeseboard. The small size of the tiles makes them easy to apply to curved surfaces: the smallest ones can even be used to cover unsightly columns or large pipes.

Types of mosaics
Most mosaic tiles are supplied on backing sheets. This means that the sheet itself can be cut to fit the tiles round doors, windows, light switches and fittings. In effect, it keeps the cutting of tiles themselves to a minimum.

The tiles are available glazed or unglazed, and come in various shapes, from 22mm (¾in) square, to round, hexagonal or Provencale (see *Ready Reference*). The number of tiles on a sheet varies from 12 to about 80 depending on the size and shape of each tile. Some sheets come with a paper facing over the front of the tiles, and this has to be removed after the adhesive has set so

that the grouting can be completed. The disadvantage in using such sheets is that you cannot see the overall effect of the tiles right away. To overcome this problem, most mosaic tiles are now produced with either a nylon or perforated paper backing. The added advantage with this type is that you can, if you wish, make minor adjustments to the placing of each tile during laying, by cutting through the backing mesh with a sharp knife and sliding the tile to its ideal position.

Buying mosaics
Ceramic mosaic tiles may be available from local do-it-yourself shops, but specialist ceramic tile shops will usually have a far greater selection. The staff in a specialist shop may also be able to advise you on the right mosaic tiles for the job you have in mind – they're not all suitable for kitchen work surfaces, for example, because of the lead content of the glaze.

Adhesives and grout
Adhesives and grout for mosaic tiles are the same as are used to fix other ceramic tiles. You can either buy separate products, or go for a combined adhesive and grout that will do both jobs. If the mosaic tiles are to be fixed in an area likely to get wet, as in a

shower, bathroom or kitchen, use a waterproof type. For outdoor use (eg, tiling a porch floor) pick a frostproof adhesive. Remember you can add colour pigments to grout to obtain a coloured, rather than the usual, white, finish. This technique can be most effective, especially if it's used on a work surface where a darker coloured mosaic is used.

MARKING UP THE

1 *Measure across the wall to find the central point to help you determine where to fix the first whole sheet of tiles at the corner of the room.*

FIXING TILES ON A WALL

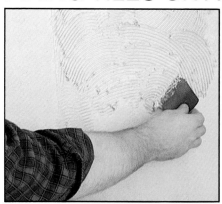

1 *Spread adhesive on the wall to take the first sheet of tiles. Don't use too much adhesive at a time or it will set too soon and be wasted.*

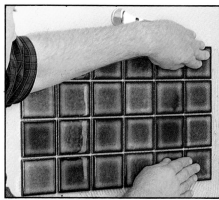

2 *Press the first whole sheet of tiles firmly into place, checking it is in the right position. Continue fixing whole sheets of tiles and then off-cut strips.*

3 *When the whole sheets and off-cut strips are in place, you can mark off tiles which need cutting to fill the gaps at the end of the wall.*

4 *Fix the cut tiles in place, leaving a grouting gap between them and the whole tiles. Clean off excess adhesive with a damp sponge as you work.*

TILE POSITION

2 *Measure up from the floor where you want to fix tiles. Aim to have a whole sheet of tiles fixed immediately above the lowest point of the floor line.*

3 *Draw a line across the wall to show where the top line of the tiles will come to. You can use this as a guide for getting the tile sheets straight.*

Ready Reference

SHEET SIZES FOR MOSAICS
● Small, square mosaics usually come in sheets measuring about 300mm (12in) square, though larger sheets measuring 600 x 300mm (24 x 12in) are available.
● Shaped tiles are available on sheets measuring 470 x 300mm (18½ x 12in) or 547 x 350mm (21 x 14in).

TILE SHAPES
Most mosaics are square or rectangular, but other shapes are also available – round, hexagonal and Provencale are the commonest.

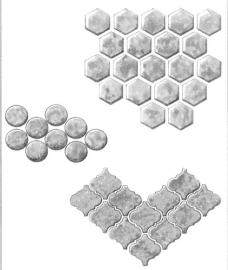

CHOOSE THE RIGHT TYPE
Check that the tiles you intend using are suitable:
● for exterior use (eg, on a patio) mosaics must be frostproof or vitrified
● for floors, select flooring quality mosaics
● for kitchen work surfaces, check that the glaze on the tiles does not contain lead.

THE TILING GAUGE
Use a 2m (approx 6ft) length of 50 x 25mm (2 x 1in) softwood and mark the width of a number of mosaic sheet sizes along it, allowing the same gap between sheets as between individual tiles. In small rooms use a shorter batten.

CUTTING TILES

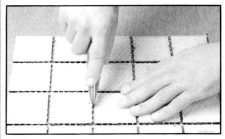

1 *To cut off strips of tiles from a sheet, simply trim through the mesh or perforated paper backing with a sharp knife to get the right number of rows.*

2 *To cut a single tile, score a cutting line with a tungsten-carbide-tipped tile cutter. Break the tile along the line using a tile cutter with angled jaws.*

3 *To cut shaped tiles mark off a cutting line using a template as a guide, then score along the cutting line using a tungsten-carbide-tipped cutting tool.*

4 *Nibble away at the waste area with a pair of tile nips taking out only small pieces at a time. Smooth any rough edges with a carborundum stone.*

TILING ROUND A WC

1 *Lay a whole sheet of tiles so the outer row fits round the corner of the WC base. Tear off individual tiles which will need to be replaced by cut tiles.*

TIP

2 *With the remainder of the tiles in the sheet fixed in place, mark off a cardboard template for cutting tiles. Once cut to shape, fix the tiles in place.*

3 *Lay tiles over the rest of the floor area. Make sure you work in small areas at a time so the adhesive doesn't harden before you're ready.*

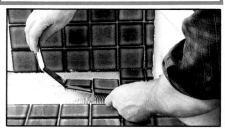

4 *Fix strips of tiles to the floor in the same way as fixing a whole sheet; allow for a grouting gap. Mark off the tiles for cutting at the edges.*

Preparing the surface

The surface on which you are tiling should be clean, flat, dry and firm. You should allow a newly plastered surface to dry out for at least a month before tiling it; make sure old plaster is sound by removing all loose particles with a brush. Dusty or porous plaster can be treated with a stabilising primer to prevent the liquid from the adhesive being absorbed too quickly.

Mosaics can be applied on top of paint as long as the paint film is sound. If the paint is flaking, you should scrape it off as thoroughly as possible. Don't use a chemical stripper, and avoid using a solvent-based adhesive for fixing the tiles (most are water based, but check first).

Old ceramic tiles provide a suitable surface if they are perfectly flat. Any chipped or broken tiles should be removed and the gap filled with mortar or adhesive, and any loose tiles should be firmly restuck. You should also remove dirt and grease from the surface of the tiles.

Don't attempt to lay mosaic tiles on concrete unless it is absolutely sound and dry. (If it's not perfectly flat, the small size of the mosaic tiles will be able to accommodate any unevenness, but it'll still show.) If you want to tile over wooden floorboards, cover the floor first with sheets of plywood or chipboard (special water-resistant, resin-bonded sheets are available for very 'wet' areas like bathrooms). This will prevent any slight movement of the floorboards causing the tiles or the grouting to crack.

Where to start on floors

The best way of planning your tiling and deciding where to start is to treat a sheet of tiles as one tile. In effect this means you can use a tiling gauge to find the correct starting point in the same way as for laying ordinary ceramic floor tiles (see Chapter 5 pages 118-123). Where a

GROUTING TILES

1 *Use a sponge to spread the grout over the tiles, taking care to press it down firmly into the gaps so they will be properly sealed off.*

whole sheet won't fit, you simply cut whole tiles off the sheet – and leave the cutting of individual tiles until last. Check with a square that you have a right-angled starting point, and adjust your starting point if the cut pieces are too thin for convenience.

In a small room where there is a prominent feature such as a WC, it may be more sensible to begin tiling outwards from the feature and work towards the walls. In cases like this you should measure up and find the central starting point. Adjust its position if it means you will have to cut very thin pieces of tile by including one less mosaic tile in each complete row.

Mosaics on wall surfaces

On a wall you can use a tiling gauge to mark off where complete sheets of tiles will fall, and so establish your starting point in the same way as for fixing larger ceramic wall tiles (see Ceramics tiling, pages 53-57). Use a plumbline and a spirit level to establish a true vertical and horizontal. Aim to position the tiles so there will be a whole mosaic sheet width (with a grouting gap at the bottom) immediately above the floor line or skirting board.

Find the centre point of the wall or the centre of a window, and measuring from this point work out where the last whole sheet of tiles in each row will be; then mark off your starting point by finding where one of these will fall at a suitable level – usually just above the skirting board. Again, adjust your starting point if you will have to cut pieces of tile which are too thin. On a reasonable size wall you can fix a horizontal and vertical batten which meet at the starting point to serve as guides for fixing the sheets. On a small area this is not essential.

Fixing mosaics

It's easier to work in small areas when fixing the tiles, one sheet at a time, otherwise there's a risk of the adhesive going off before you've finished making the final adjustments. Spread the adhesive over an area no greater than 1 sq m (about 11 sq ft) and fix the first sheet of tiles in place. You can then lay the other whole sheets, remembering to leave the same gap between each sheet as there is between the individual mosaics. On a floor you can gently tamp the sheets of mosaic down with a wooden batten to make sure they are level and securely fixed. When all the whole sheets are in place, the next step is to cut the strips of mosaic to fill the gaps at the perimeter of the wall or floor. Then, if necessary, mark off any individual pieces of mosaic to be cut, and fix these in place.

Mosaics are ideal for tiling round curved fixtures, such as a WC. You simply butt a sheet of mosaics against the base of the WC and push it up so some of the tiles will fit round the corner. You can then tear off individual tiles to fit round the front part of the WC base. Usually you will still have to fill some gaps with cut, shaped tiles. For this you will need to make a cardboard template of the required shape and mark this off on the individual tiles to be cut. With very small gaps, a bit of extra grouting won't look out of place or upset the clean lines of the tiles.

Grouting mosaics

You should allow the adhesive to set before applying the grout and follow the manufacturer's instructions carefully. As when you are applying adhesive, work over only about 1 sq m (11 sq ft) at a time. Allow the grout to dry for about 24 hours before walking on the floor. However, if the mosaics have a paper facing, you can apply the grout to the back of the sheet making sure all the gaps between the tiles are well filled. The tiles should then be laid quickly on the adhesive and when dry the paper facing has to be removed (see Ready Reference). Then the grouting can be finished neatly as shown below.

2 Use a smooth rounded stick, such as a length of dowel, to smooth off the joins in the grouting so there won't be any ugly bumps or gaps.

3 Remove excess adhesive with a damp cloth or sponge before the grout dries. When the grout has set, you can complete final polishing with a dry cloth.

TILING WORKTOPS

You can update your kitchen by tiling one or more work surfaces in it. There's a range of specialist tiles available which makes what would be the awkward bits – going round corners and sealing the edges – a comparatively straightforward task.

M any kitchen worktops, or vanitory units in bathrooms and bedrooms, become scuffed or discoloured with time, while the base units remain in good condition. If you are faced with this situation and don't want the expense or upheaval of a complete change, it is possible to revitalise the units with new worktops, without spending too much time or money in the process. For example, you could create a country-style look for the kitchen with tiled worktops on heavy wooden or traditional coloured kitchen furniture. You could use ordinary ceramic wall tiles, but purpose-made worktop tiles are a far better option as they will withstand the heat and knocks from heavy saucepans. You can also buy special lipping tiles which finish the front edge of the worktop, and back-stands which seal the top to the wall. Internal and external angle pieces are available to solve the awkward problem of going round corners.

Tiles can be used on any existing worktop including ones of plastic laminate, melamine-coated chipboard or worktops which are already tiled. If you are installing new units and plan to have ceramic tiles on the work-tops, you can put them onto a firm timber, chipboard or plywood base. But it must be solid enough to prevent bowing or movement with the weight of the tiles, otherwise they could eventually crack.

Tools and equipment
Apart from the tiles, adhesive and grout you will need a notched adhesive spreader, a ·tungsten carbide-tipped tile cutter, a spirit level, pincers or tile nips, a pencil and straight-edge, coarse glasspaper or a carborundum stone, a sponge and a spirit level. You'll also require a lath of wood the length of the work top; a straight piece of wood about 30x30mm (1¼x1¼in) will be suitable. With tiles without spacer lugs to keep them apart you'll need spacer cards or matchsticks.

Planning and preparation
Before you begin tiling you should plan out the work. Open and check the boxes of tiles, the edging, corner pieces and mitres. Mix the contents from the boxes so you get a random effect if there's any colour variation. Sort out any patterned tiles if you plan to make a design on the worktop. If you are tackling a fairly straightforward job, lay out the tiles on the area to be covered, starting at the front of the work-top. If the tiles need to be cut to fit, the cut ones should be placed close to the wall and the whole tiles at the front of the worktop. Your preparatory layout will give you an idea of how wide the cut tiles should be. Remember to allow for the worktop trim at the front edge, and plan for the corner pieces and internal mitres (see *Ready Reference*).

If you are in doubt, or the job is likely to be complicated (for example where you'll need to allow for cutting round a sink or basin), you can plan the tile layout on a piece of card or stiff paper, cut as a template to fit the work surface. Square up and mark the tile positions on this and number the tiles to indicate their position on the plan. Do this planning on paper if you are incorporating a design.

Once you are happy with the plan, make sure the surface is firm, smooth, clean and dry.

Cutting tiles
Most tiling jobs involve cutting several of the tiles; some require just a simple straight cut, but others may need shaping which will involve 'nibbling' away some of the surplus tile so that it fits accurately. Mark the glazed side of the tile where it is to be cut and score with a tile cutter. Place a matchstick under the scored line. Press the edges of the tile firmly down and it should snap cleanly along the line you've scored. If you have to cut a tile to fit round an area or object, you should score the tile in the same way and then nibble away at the excess with pincers or tile nips. There are also tile-cutting hacksaw blades available and you may find one of these a useful aid to this job. Any rough edges can be sanded.

Tiling the worktop
Prepare the surface as required. You should then mark a base line on which to put the first row of tiles. For this, place the straight trim in position on the worktop along the short vertical edge. Mark with a pencil. Repeat two or three times along the length of the worktop. Draw straight lines connecting the marks to give you the base line. You can then fit a lath up to the base line and nail it lightly in position. Fix the tiles as described in the step-by-step photographs; you may have to cut away the corners of the existing worktop to get a good fit. When the adhesive has set you can grout the tiles.

TILING WORKTOPS

1 Place a straight trim tile on the edge of the worktop. Mark its position, move it along and mark again. Then draw a straight line connecting the marks.

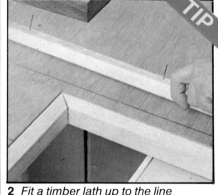

2 Fit a timber lath up to the line you've drawn and temporarily pin it in place. It will serve as a guide for getting the first row of tiles straight.

3 Apply the adhesive with a notched spreader and lay the whole tiles using pieces of card or matchsticks as spacers. You can then lay the cut tiles.

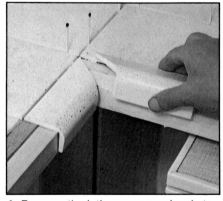

4 Remove the lath so you can begin to lay the trim at the edges. At an internal corner you use tiles which have been specially mitred to form a neat angle.

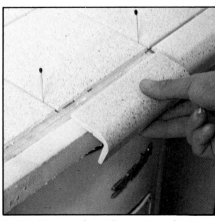

5 Working out from the corner pieces, lay the stright tile trim, taking care that each piece aligns with the appropriate row of whole tiles.

6 At the outer edge, fix a corner trim. When the worktop has been tiled, remove the spacers, allow the adhesive to set (remove any excess first) and then grout.

Ready Reference

SUITABLE TILES
Make sure you buy tiles which are of a suitable thickness and quality for a worktop. Some tiles are too porous and could stain easily, while others are too thin to stand up to the heat and other punishment they are likely to get during food preparation, cooking and serving. You will need the special ranges which include the edging or 'trim' tiles, with the necessary corners, mitres and angles.

TILE LAYOUT
It is important, when laying out and planning, to ensure that the cut tiles are situated near to the wall and that tiling starts at the front of the worktop with a full tile. The diagram below shows the correct way to lay out the tiling and trim. When laying out, take into account the position of the tiles relative to the internal mitres and corner pieces.

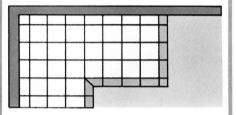

WHEN TO CUT TILES
You can cut the tiles to the required size and shape after you've laid them out and before you fix them. Alternatively, you might prefer to cut the tiles which go at the back of the worktop as you are tiling. This second method may be more practical, particularly in a kitchen where the wall is not perfectly straight and the tiles therefore have to be cut to a slight angle.

TIP: START STRAIGHT
It's essential that you begin tiling to a straight line; it you don't the layout will end up askew. After you've established your base line you can loosely nail a timber lath up to it. This will give you something to work against and will keep the tiles in line.

GROUTING WORKTOPS
You will need to buy special grout for worktops; this will not stain or discolour and is unaffected by the acids found in some foods. To get good results:
● wait at least 12 hours after tiling
● compact the grout to finish flush with the tile surface
● remove the excess with a clean damp sponge
● run a rounded stick along the joins
● polish the whole surface with a clean, dry cloth.

CHAPTER 4

EXTERIOR DECORATING

**Painting the outside of your house can seem more of a chore than a pleasure, simply because of the size of the job.
By breaking it down into separate, manageable areas and using time-saving tools and techniques, you can keep the weather at bay and complete the task more quickly than ever before.**

EXTERIOR PAINTING 1: the basics

The main reason for decorating the outside of your house is to protect it from the elements. But paint can also transform the appearance of your house and increase its value, so it's a job worth doing well.

The outside of your house is under continuous attack from rain, frost, heat and light from the sun, dirt and pollution. Properly applied paint or varnish is the best way of protecting the fabric of the house, and it should last for about five or six years before it needs renewing. If the outside hasn't been touched for several years it's probably looking rather shabby by now and you should start to think about repainting.

Modern paints come in a very wide range of colours and are very easy to apply. A little time spent preparing and painting your house now can transform a drab old building into a desirable residence; and increase the value of the house with very little outlay.

The main parts of the house that have to be painted are the woodwork, metalwork, and possibly the walls. Plastic gutters and pipes do not need to be painted. It's up to you whether you paint the walls or not. Brick, pebbledash, stone and rendering can all be left in their natural state, but if the walls are in need of repair or are porous, stained and dirty, a good coat of paint will both protect the surface and brighten up the house.

The first thing to do is to take a long, critical look at your house to assess what needs to be done. Search for any defects that may affect the final paintwork. A common fault on older houses is leaking gutters. These can leave unsightly stains on the wall or cause woodwork to rot. They can be easily sealed or even completely replaced with new gutters. Other common faults are flaking and peeling paint, rotten window sills and cracked rendering. The illustrations on the next page show many different defects that need repairing. It's unlikely you'll find all of these faults on one house, but you'll probably find a few. It is very important that you remedy every fault you find before you begin to paint or the paint won't be able to do its job and your house will only deteriorate further. This preparation will usually be the most time consuming part of the decoration and will often be quite hard work. But it has to be done if you want your new paintwork to last. Details on how to prepare each different type of surface – wood, metal, brick, render etc – will appear in a later article.

When to paint

Outside painting should only be done in dry weather and after at least two days without rain, fog or frost. The ideal time is late summer when the wood has had a good time to dry out and the weather is usually quite settled. Even a small amount of moisture trapped under a new paint film will vaporise, causing blisters and peeling. For the same reason you should wait an hour after sunrise to let the dew dry out, and stop work an hour before sunset. On the other hand, don't paint under the full glare of a hot sun as this will dry out the surface too quickly, leaving relatively soft paint underneath which may cause wrinkling as it dries in turn. The ideal practice is to follow the sun, and only paint when it has dried one part of the house and passed on to another. Unfortunately this advice is often difficult to follow in practice as some walls may never see the sun, so you'll have to look for the best compromise.

What to paint first

There is a logical sequence of painting which holds for nearly all houses. In general it's best to start at the top and do larger areas before smaller ones. So if you're going to paint the whole of your house try to follow this order: do the fascia boards and barge boards first, followed by the gutters. The rendering (if any) comes next, then the windows and doors and finally the downpipes. The reason for doing it in this order is that splashes of paint dropped onto a wall beneath a fascia or gutter, even if wiped off immediately, will leave a mark; but subsequent painting of the wall will cover them up. Also, since windows and doors are smaller in area than the rendering, it will be easier to 'cut in' (that is, leave a finer edge) when painting them, so giving a much neater finish.

You will need to follow this sequence three times in all, first to do the preparation, then to apply primers or under coats, and finally to paint on the top coat. If this sounds like far too much work to do all at once there's no reason why you shouldn't split it up and do just a part each year. You could, for instance, do the walls this year, the woodwork next year and the gutters and downpipes the year after. It may even be better to do it this way, spread over several years, as you'll be more aware of the condition of the paintwork and will be able to touch up bits and make small repairs as you go along, when the first signs of wear show. (But remember that this will restrict you to using the same colour as you have at present. It's going to look odd if you change the colour only gradually.)

COMMON SURFACE DEFECTS

Before painting your house, give it a thorough going over to find out where any faults and defects may lie. You're certainly not likely to find all the faults shown here, but the drawings do point out the problem areas. All faults must be put right before you start to paint, otherwise you are likely to achieve a poor result and will waste much time and money in the effort.

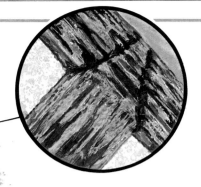

Decorative woodwork like this, as well as fascias and barge boards, are very exposed. Scrape off loose paint and fill holes.

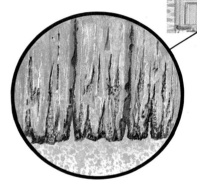

Over the years, rendering can crack and come loose. Clean and fill all holes and sterilise mould and algae growth.

The bottom edge of a garage door may start to rot and break up. You'll have to replace it with new pieces or a whole new rail.

Small holes in asbestos or iron roofs can be repaired, but extensive damage may mean replacing parts of the roof.

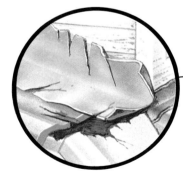

Weatherboards are sometimes painted only on the surface and if rain gets in they will warp and rot, and paint will flake off.

Old flashing can crack and tiles can come loose, letting damp inside. Renew flashing and replace tiles.

Any cracks and blisters in paint will let in water, and metal will start to rust. All rust must be removed and the metal primed.

TESTING A PAINTED SURFACE

1 Try this easy way of testing your paint surface to see if it's suitable for repainting. First, score a double cross in the paint with a sharp knife.

2 Stick a piece of adhesive tape over the length of the cross cuts and press it down firmly. Then pull the tape away from the surface slowly.

3 If the tape is clean, the paint surface is sound and safe for painting. If flakes of paint are pulled off you must strip off the old paint first.

A blocked gutter can overflow, joints can leak and iron gutters can rust – causing damp patches and stains on the wall.

The white deposit (efflorescence) is caused by damp; it should be brushed off and the source of damp treated.

Old, dry putty can fall out and must be replaced; knots should be stripped and treated; rotten wood must be cut out and holes filled.

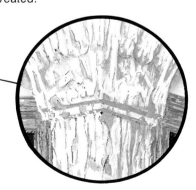

Flaking paint on render should be scraped off and the render brushed down. Fill holes and, if the surface is powdery, apply a stabiliser.

WORKING SAFELY AT HEIGHT

Ladders are an easy and convenient way of reaching heights, but since most domestic accidents involve ladders, it's worth taking time to secure them safely.

Always lean the ladder at a safe angle so that for every 4m of height, the base is 1m from the wall. Always tie it securely at the top or bottom to stop it slipping, and overlap an extension ladder by at least three rungs.

You'll need a roof ladder if you want to paint or repair the chimney or the dividing wall between two roofs. If your house has overhanging eaves, use a ladder stay to hold the ladder away from the wall.

Right: if you have a wide clear area round your house a tower platform is the safest way of getting up high. Make sure it stands perfectly level.

Left: often the gap between two houses is too narrow to put up a ladder at the correct angle. The only answer is to use a special narrow tower.

Special brackets fit on a pair of ladders to provide a long working platform which is useful for reaching the area over a bay window. A third ladder is needed to gain access to the platform.

Tower platforms can be assembled in a cantilevered structure to bridge an outbuilding or a bay window. Protect the roof with sacking and blocks of wood, or use sandbags if the roof is very steep.

Working in safety

To paint the outside of your house in comfort and safety you need the right tools and equipment. There's nothing worse than balancing dangerously on a makeshift working platform with a paint pot in one hand, trying to reach into an awkward corner with the other. But as long as you follow a few simple rules you should be able to work easily and safely. Always work from a step-ladder or an extension ladder and make sure it stands on a firm and level surface. If the ground is uneven, push wedges under a board until the board is level then stand the ladder on this. You'll have to put down a board on soft ground too. If you're working on grass there's a danger of the board slipping, so drive in two stakes on either side of the ladder and rope the ladder to these. On a slippery surface put down some canvas or sacking, and put a board on soft ground. Don't use plastic sheeting as a dust sheet, because the ladder could slip on it.

If you're working high up it's best to tie the ladder to something solid at the top. Don't tie it to the gutter or downpipe as these are not designed to take the extra weight and wouldn't support a ladder if it started to slip. The best way is to fix big screw eyes into sound woodwork such as a window sill, fascia or barge boards and tie the ladder to these. Or, if convenient, you can tie the ladder to the centre mullion of an open window. If there's no sound woodwork, it's advisable to drill and plug the wall to take the screw eyes. Fix them at intervals of about 2m (6ft) and leave them in place when you've finished so they're ready the next time you have to decorate.

Be sure to position the ladder square against the wall so it won't wobble, and lean it at the correct safe angle of 4 to 1, that is, for every 4m of height the bottom should be 1m out from the wall.

When you're working on a ladder don't lean out too far as it's all too easy to loose your balance. Never work from the very top of a step ladder as you'll have nothing to hold on to. A paint kettle, to hold your paint, is an essential piece of equipment as you can hook it on to a rung of the ladder, leaving both hands free.

A safer alternative to a ladder or step-ladder is a tower platform which you can hire from most hire shops. The tower comes as a set of interlocking sections which you build up to the required height; you then lay boards across to provide the platform. A handrail fits around the top and there is plenty of room for tools and paint. The towers can be extended over bay windows or round chimneys so you can reach all parts of the house in safety. If you have a wide, flat area around your house, choose a tower with locking castors so you can move it along more easily. Always lock the castors before using the tower, and always climb up on the inside, NEVER on the outside.

THE TOOLS YOU'LL NEED

It saves a lot of time and trouble to have the right tools to hand before you start any job. The tools shown here are the ones you'll need to prepare and paint the outside of your house – the walls, metalwork and the woodwork. Some large items (not shown here) which you'll also need are a dust sheet, a large bucket and a ladder or tower platform.

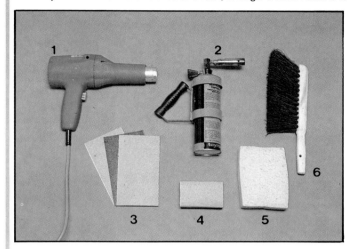

1 Hot air electric stripper for stripping unsound paintwork.
2 Gas blow lamp may be preferred as it saves trailing wires about.
3 A selection of fine, medium and coarse grades of sandpaper for woodwork, and emery paper for metal.
4 Sanding block to hold sandpaper.
5 Sponge for washing down woodwork.
6 Stiff brush for removing dust from masonry.

1 Small trowel for repointing brickwork and repairing holes.
2 Combination shavehook for scraping paint from mouldings.
3 Scraper for flat areas of woodwork.
4 Filling knife for filling holes and cracks.
5 Narrow filling knife for tricky areas round window frames.
6 Putty knife for re-puttying windows.
7 Wire brush for removing rust and paint from metal.

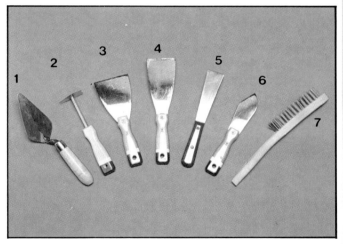

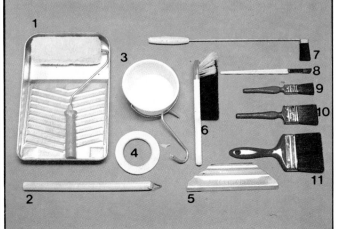

1,2 Long pile roller with extension handle and tray for large areas of masonry.
3 Paint kettle and hook to hold the paint when working on a ladder.
4,5 Masking tape and shield protect areas you want unpainted.
6 Banister brush for painting rough textured surfaces.
7,8,9,10 A selection of brushes for wood and metalwork.
11 Wide brush for smooth surfaces.

EXTERIOR PAINTING preparation

Whether you like it or not, preparing the outside of your house before painting it is a job that has to be done. If you provide a sound surface the paint will last much longer.

If your house is in good order and has been decorated regularly, then the paintwork may need no more than a quick wash down and a light sanding before it's ready for re-painting. But if your house is in a rather worse state than this, take some time now to make a really good job of the preparation and you'll have a much easier time in the future. The preparation may seem rather time-consuming, but don't be tempted to miss out any of the steps. Properly applied, paint will protect your house for several years, but it won't stick to an unsound surface.

The most convenient order of working is to start at the top of the house and work down, and to do all the preparation before you start to paint so that dust and grit won't fall on wet paint. When working at a height, make sure the ladder or platform is firm and secure.

Gutters and downpipes

Gutters manage to trap a surprising quantity of dirt and old leaves, so clear this out first. It's a good idea to check that the gutter is at a regular slope towards the nearest downpipe. You can easily check this by pouring a bucket of water into one end and seeing if it all drains away. If puddles form, you'll need to unscrew some of the gutter brackets and adjust the level of the gutter until the water flows away freely. Check all the joints for leaks and if you do find any, seal them with a mastic compound applied with a gun.

Plastic gutters need little maintenance, and they don't need painting. But if you want to change their colour, simply clean them thoroughly and wipe them over with a rag dipped in white spirit or turps to remove any grease spots before starting to paint. There's no need for a primer or undercoat, but you may need two top coats for even coverge.

Metal gutters and pipes need more attention as all rust has to be removed. Scrape off flaking paint first, then use a wire brush and emery paper to remove the rust. A wire brush attachment on an electric drill would make the cleaning easier (but wear a mask and goggles while using one). You can buy an anti-rust chemical from paint shops which is useful for badly rusted metalwork. It works by turning iron oxide (rust) into phosphate of

iron which is inert and can be painted over. In any case, prime all bare metal immediately with either a red lead primer or a zinc chromate metal primer. Metal primers contain a rust-inhibitor which protects the metal against further corrosion, so don't miss them out. If the gutters and pipes are in good condition with no sign of rust, simply wash them down and sand the surface lightly to key it ready for repainting.

Fascias and barge boards

Fascias and barge boards run along the top of a wall just below the roof. Fascias support the guttering below pitched roofs and edge flat ones, while barge boards are fitted beneath the roof tiles on gable ends. Because they are so high up, don't worry too much about their appearance; the main consideration is protection as they are in such an exposed position. Clean out well behind the gutters as damp leaves or even bird's nests can be lodged there. Then, using a wide scraper, remove all loose flaking paint, sand down the whole board surface and prime the bare patches. Fill holes and cracks with an exterior-grade filler or water-proof stopping and smooth it level while still damp using a filler knife. You can prime the filler when it's dry.

Walls

The main surface materials and finishes used on the outside of your house are brick, stone, wood and render.

Walls of brick and stone, especially when

weathered, have a beauty all of their own and don't really need painting. But the surface can become cracked and dirty and a coat of paint will cover up repairs that don't match the original surface, and protect the wall from further damage. Examine the pointing and, if it has deteriorated, rake out the damaged parts and re-point with fresh mortar. Use a mixture of about 1 part cement to 4 parts of fine sand, or buy a bag of ready-mixed mortar. Use a small trowel and try to match the original pointing in the surrounding brickwork. Don't worry about hairline cracks as these will easily be covered by the paint. The white crystalline deposit which sometimes appears on brickwork is known as efflorescence. It is caused by water-soluble salts in the brick being brought to the surface, and should be brushed off with a dry brush. Don't try to wash it off as this will only make it worse.

The main types of render are plain, roughcast and pebbledash. Plain render can be applied to give a smooth, finish or a textured 'Tyrolean' finish, for example. Roughcast consists of pebbles mixed with mortar before application, and with pebbledash the pebbles are thrown on while the mortar is still wet. Pebbledash deteriorates more quickly than the other types of render as, over the years, differences in rates of expansion between each pebble and the surrounding mortar may result in small surface cracks causing the pebbles to become loose and fall out. Paint will bind in the pebbles and protect small cracks.

PREPARING THE WALLS

1 *Before painting an exterior wall, brush it down well to remove any loose material. Start at the top and use a fairly stiff brush.*

2 *Kill mould and algae with a solution of 1 part bleach to 4 parts water. Leave for two days, then wash down and brush off.*

3 *Rusty metal and leaky gutters can easily cause stains, so cure the leaks and clean and prime all metal first. Sterilise the stain and brush down.*

4 *Holes in the wall are often created when old downpipe brackets are removed. Brush them out well and damp the surface with a little water.*

5 *Fill the hole with a sand and cement mixture using a small trowel. Small bags of ready-mixed mortar are ideal for jobs of this size.*

6 *If the wall is powdery or highly porous, or if a cement-based paint has been used previously, seal the surface with a stabilising primer.*

Ready Reference

CHOOSE THE RIGHT PRIMER
Different materials require different primers; be sure to choose the right type.

Wood

softwood &	wood primer or
hardwood	acrylic primer
resinous wood	aluminium wood primer

Metal

iron and steel	calcium plumbate primer, zinc chromate primer or red lead primer
galvanised iron	
(new)	calcium plumbate primer
(old)	calcium plumbate or zinc chromate primer
aluminium	zinc chromate primer
brass, copper and lead	none necessary: allow new lead to weather

Masonry etc

brick, stone, concrete & render	stabilising primer alkali-resisting primer, acrylic primer

Other materials

asbestos	stabilising primer, alkali-resisting primer or acrylic primer
bitumen-coated wood	aluminium wood primer
bitumen-coated metal	aluminium spirit-based sealer

PROPERTIES AND COVERAGE
Where there is a choice of suitable primers, it's often helpful to know something more about each type. For instance, many primers are toxic and you should choose a non-toxic one if you're painting anything in a child's room.

● Acrylic primer – white or pastel shades, water-based, quick drying, non-toxic, 13-18m² (140-190sq ft) per litre.

● Alkali-resisting primer – needs two coats on very porous surfaces, non-toxic, 3-10m² (30-110sq ft) per litre.

● Aluminium wood primer – dull metallic grey, self-knotting, non-toxic, 16m² (170sq ft) per litre.

● Calcium plumbate primer – off-white, rust inhibiting, toxic, 8-12m² (90-130sq ft) per litre.

● Lead-free wood primer – white or pink, non-toxic, 10-12m² (110-130sq ft) per litre.

● Red lead primer – bright red, rust inhibiting, only for exterior use, toxic, 12-17m² (130-180sq ft) per litre.

● Lead-based wood primer – white or pink, only for exterior use, toxic, 12-14m² (130-150sq ft) per litre.

● Zinc chromate primer – yellow, rust inhibiting, non-toxic, 11m² (120sq ft) per litre.

PREPARING THE WOODWORK

1 Start preparing the woodwork by scraping off all the loose flaking paint. Large areas of unsound paint are better if stripped completely.

2 Sand and prime all the bare wood, taking care to work the primer well into cracks and any exposed end grain, then leave the surface to dry.

3 Where joints have opened up, scrape off the paint and rake out the gap with a knife or shavehook. Clean out all the loose debris.

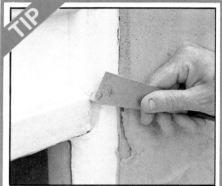

4 Small cracks can be filled with putty, but use exterior-grade filler or waterproof stopping for larger cracks and holes.

5 Gaps often appear between the window frame and the wall. Fill these with a mastic compound to provide a continuous water-tight seal.

6 Make sure the drip groove underneath the window sill is clear of paint, then thoroughly sand down the whole of the window frame.

REPLACING OLD PUTTY

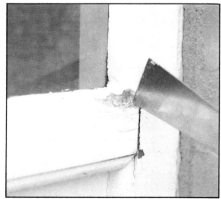

1 Old, damaged putty must be raked out. Scrape old paint from the glass, and clean the glass with methylated spirit to remove any grease spots.

2 Work the putty in your hands until it has an even consistency. If it's too oily, roll it on newspaper first. Press it firmly into the gap.

3 Smooth the new putty level with the old using a putty knife, then run a soft brush over it to make a water-tight seal with the glass.

TREATING KNOTS

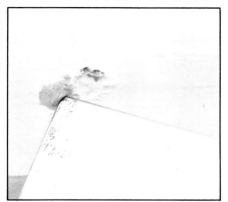

1 *Active knots like this ooze out a sticky resin which quickly breaks through the paint surface, leaving a sticky and unsightly mess.*

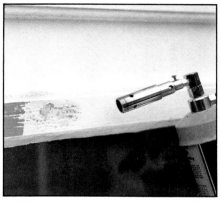

2 *The paint must first be stripped off to expose the knot. Use any method of stripping, and scrape the paint off with a shavehook or scraper.*

3 *Use a blow-torch to heat the knot until the resin bubbles out. Scrape off the resin and repeat until no more of it appears.*

4 *Sand the knot with fine glasspaper, then wipe over the area with knotting applied with a soft cloth. Prime the wood when it has dried.*

When repairing any of these surfaces, try and achieve the same finish as the original, or as near as you can, so that when it's repainted the repair won't be too noticeable. Stop up cracks with mortar, using a mix of 1 part cement to 5 parts sand. Chip away very wide cracks until you reach a firm edge, then undercut this to provide a good key for the new mortar. Dampen the surface, then stop up with a trowel. Use a float if the surface is plain, or texture the surface to match the surrounding area. Where the rendering is pebble-dash, throw on pebbles with a small trowel while the mortar is still wet, then press them into the mortar lightly with a flat piece of wood.

Mould and stains

If there's any sign of mould or algae on the wall, treat this next. Mix up a solution of 1 part household bleach to 4 parts water and paint this on the affected area. Be generous with the solution and cover the area well. Leave for 48 hours for the bleach to kill off all the growth, then wash off thoroughly and brush down with a stiff brush.

Rusty gutters, pipes and metal fittings can all cause stains if rusty water drips down the wall. So cure any leaks first and clean and prime all metal to ensure there's no trace of rust. Mould and algae thrive on damp walls; even if you can't actually see any growth on a damp patch, there may be some spores lurking there, so you should make absolutely sure that you sterilise all stains with the bleach solution just to make sure.

Dusty or chalky walls

All walls, whether dusty or not, should be brushed down thoroughly to remove any loose material. But if, after brushing, the wall is still dusty or chalky, if a cement-based paint was used previously to decorate it, or if the wall is porous, you'll have to brush on a stabilising solution. This will bind together loose particles to allow the paint to stick, and it will seal a porous surface and stop paint from being sucked in too much. The stabiliser also helps to waterproof the wall and you can paint it on as an extra layer of protection whether it's really necessary or not. Most stabilisers are colourless, but off-white stabiliser/primers are available and this would be a good choice if you were planning to paint your house in a light colour, as it could save one coat of the finishing colour. These off-white stabilisers, however, are not recommended for use on surfaces painted with a cement-based paint.

Stabilisers must be painted on a dry wall and should be left to dry for 24 hours before painting on the top coat. Don't paint if rain is expected. Clean your brush in white spirit or turps as soon as you stop work.

Timber cladding

If the cladding or weatherboarding is bare and you want to leave the natural wood surface showing, it should be treated with a water-repellent wood preservative to give protection against damp penetration and decay. The preservative is available clear or pigmented with various colours.

If the wood has been varnished, scrape off the old varnish and sand down well, following the grain of the wood. Fill cracks and holes with plastic wood or a tinted stopper to match the colour of the wood.

If you wish to paint the surface you'll have to wait a year or so for the water-repellent agents in the preservative to disperse before priming with an aluminium wood primer.

Woodwork

If the paintwork on the windows is in good condition all you need do is give them a wash and a light sanding. If the paint is cracked and flaking, a little more preparation is needed. To check if the paint surface needs stripping, lay on a piece of sticky tape and see if it lifts off any paint. Occasional chipped or blistered portions can be scraped off and cut back to a firm edge. As long as the edge is feathered smooth with glasspaper, it shouldn't show too much. If previous coatings are too thick for this treatment, build up the surface with outdoor grade hard stopping until it is just proud of the surrounding paint, then sand level when it's dry. Don't allow the stopping to extend too far over the edge of the damage or it'll be difficult to sand it smooth.

There comes a time, however, when the condition of the old coating has become so bad that complete stripping is advisable.

A blow-torch or an electric hot air stripper are the quickest tools to use. Start at the bottom softening the paint, and follow up immediately with a scraper. Hold the scraper at an angle so the hot paint doesn't fall on your hand, and don't hold it above the flame or it may become too hot to hold. Try not to concentrate the flame too long on one part or you're likely to scorch the wood,

PREPARING METAL

1 *Metal pipes and gutters are often in a very bad state of repair and need a lot of preparation. Scrape off all the old flaking paint first.*

2 *Brush well with a wire brush to remove all traces of rust. Badly rusted pipes should be treated with an anti-rust chemical.*

3 *Hold a board or a piece of card behind the pipe to keep paint off the wall, and paint on a metal primer, covering every bit of bare metal.*

4 *A small paint pad on a long handle is a useful tool for painting behind pipes, especially when they are very close to the wall.*

New doors and windows

New wooden windows and doors may already have a coat of pink primer applied at the factory, but it's best not to rely on this for complete protection. Knots, for instance, will rarely have been properly treated, and the primer film will have been damaged here and there in transit. So sand down the whole surface, treat any knots with knotting compound and apply another coat of wood primer overall. It may be advisable to paint doors while they're lying flat; certainly it's vital to paint the top and bottom edges before you hang them in place. It's very important to paint the bottom as rain and snow can easily penetrate unpainted wood causing it to swell and rot. Paint also protects the wood against attack from woodworm.

Metal and plastic windows

Metal doors and windows should be treated in the same way as metal pipes and gutters. So sand them down and make sure all rust is removed before priming. Aluminium frames can be left unpainted, but if you do want to paint them you must first remove any surface oxidation which shows as a fine white deposit. Use a scraper or wire brush, but go very gently and try not to scratch the surface. Prime with a zinc chromate primer. Plastic window frames should not be painted.

Galvanised iron and asbestos

You're likely to find galvanised iron used as corrugated iron roofing, gutters and down-pipes. The zinc coating on galvanised iron is to some extent 'sacrificial', so that if a small patch becomes damaged, the surrounding zinc will, in time, spread over to cover the damage. But this weakens the coating and an application of paint will prolong its life. If the galvanising is new and bright, simply clean it with a rag dipped in white spirit or turps to remove any grease, and apply a calcium plumbate primer. If it's old and grey-looking, first remove any existing paint by rubbing lightly with a wire brush, trying not to scratch the surface. Then clean with white spirit or turps and apply zinc chromate primer.

Asbestos is often used for guttering, fascia boards, as walls on out-houses and as corrugated sheeting for roofs. Asbestos is a very dangerous material and for this reason great care should be taken when dealing with it. It'll probably need cleaning before painting and the only safe way is to wet it thoroughly first and scrub it down with a scrubbing brush. Be sure to wear rubber gloves and a face mask. Leave it to dry, then prime it with a stabilizing primer, an alkali-resisting primer, or simply a coat of thinned-down emulsion paint. Asbestos is very porous, so always paint both sides of any asbestos sheet to prevent damp penetrating from the back.

though this rarely matters on exterior woodwork which will be over-painted again. Always be extremely careful when using a blow-torch, and keep a bucket of water or sand nearby in case something does catch fire. A chemical paint stripper is the best method to use near glass in case the glass cracks under the heat of a blow-torch.

Knots, putty and holes

Check the woodwork for any live knots which are oozing out resin. If you find any, strip off the paint over them and then play a blow-torch or electric hot air stripper over them to burn out the resin. Sand lightly and treat with knotting, then prime when dry.

You should also check the putty fillet round each pane of glass, and if any has disintegrated, rake it out with an old knife. Then sand and prime the wood and bed in new putty using a putty knife. Use linseed oil putty on wood and metal glazing or all purpose putty on metal-framed windows. Smooth the putty with a damp cloth and leave it for about a week before painting.

Rake out any cracks in the wood and cut back wood which is starting to rot. If a large amount of wood is rotten – usually along the bottom edge of a sash window – a larger repair is needed. This could involve replacing a section or all of the window. Prime the bare wood, working the primer well into cracks and end grain as this is where the weather gets in. Small cracks can be filled with putty, but larger ones should be filled with exterior grade hard stopping or filler. Sand level when dry and spot-prime. Gaps between the window frame and wall should be filled with a flexible, waterproof, mastic compound applied with a special gun.

Finally, sand down the whole of the woodwork to make it ready for repainting.

EXTERIOR PAINTING
completing the job

The first two parts of this article described how to prepare the outside of your house to make it ready for repainting. This last part shows you the best way to paint the walls, pipes, windows and doors to give a professional look to your home.

If you have completed all the cleaning, repairs and preparation on the outside of your house, and if the weather has been dry for the past couple of days and looks settled for a while, you are now ready to start painting. Tackle the painting in more or less the same order as the preparation, starting at the top and working downwards.

Gutters, fascias and barge boards

If you have plastic gutters and want to paint them, simply apply a thin coat of gloss paint to the outside surface. This is the only case outside where paint is used purely for decoration rather than protection. Iron gutters can be painted on the inside with a bituminous paint as this will provide a waterproof coating and protect the iron. Paint the outside of gutters and downpipes with the usual gloss paint system. You'll need a small paint pad or crevice brush to get into the narrow gaps at the back of gutters and pipes. Protect the fascia with a piece of board held behind the guttering. Don't miss out these awkward bits as this is where the rust will start up again. You can use bitumen paint on the inside of asbestos gutters too, but it's best to use

TEXTURED WALLS

1 Use a 'banister' brush or 'dust pan' brush for painting rough-textured finishes such as pebbledash or a randomly-textured finish.

2 Paint brickwork with a well-loaded old brush. Small cracks are bridged by the paint, but larger cracks have to be filled first with exterior filler.

3 Alternatively, use a roller on brick to give a thicker coat of paint and a slightly textured finish. Special rollers give even deeper textures.

emulsion paint rather than solvent-based gloss ones on the outside. Asbestos is porous and needs to be able to 'breathe'. Gloss paint would trap moisture within the asbestos, and this would eventually cause the paint to blister.

Fascias and barge boards are so exposed that it's best to give them an extra coat of gloss. You'll need your crevice brush or paint pad again to paint behind the gutters.

Walls

There is a wide range of paints available for exterior walls, and full information is usually available from suppliers. As for tools, a 100mm (4in) brush is the easiest size to handle; anything larger would put too much strain on the wrist. An alternative is a long-pile roller which has the advantage of being much quicker to use – about three times quicker than a brush. An extra long-pile roller is needed for roughcast or pebbledash; choose one with a pile 32mm (1¼in) deep, or use a banister brush instead. Use a cheap disposable brush or roller for cement paints as they are almost impossible to clean afterwards.

A large plastic bucket or paint kettle is essential when working up a ladder. Stir the paint thoroughly first, then pour some into the bucket until it's about one third full. If you're using a roller, use a special roller tray with a large paint reservoir, or else stand a short plank in the bucket (see step-by-step photographs, page 77) to allow you to load the roller evenly.

Hook the bucket or tray onto a rung of the ladder with an S-hook to leave both hands free. Lay a dust sheet below to catch any drips and you're ready to start.

Application

Start at the top of the wall and paint a strip across the house. Work from right to left if you're right-handed, and left to right if you're left-handed. Be sure to secure the ladder to prevent it slipping and allow a three-rung overlap at the top.

Use a brush to cut in under the eaves or fascia boards and to paint round obstacles, then fill in the larger areas with a brush or roller. Paint an area only as large as you can comfortably manage and don't lean out too far, your hips should remain between the ladder's stiles at all times.

If you have an awkward area which is too far away to reach, push a broom handle into the hollow handle of the roller, or buy a special extension handle. Protect pipes by wrapping them in newspaper, and mask any other items you don't want to paint. Leave an uneven edge at the bottom of each patch so the join won't be too noticeable, then move the ladder to the left (or right) and paint another strip alongside the first. The principle is always to keep working to the longest wet

edge so the joins won't show. When you've done the top series of strips, lower the ladder and paint another series across the middle. Lower the ladder again or work from the ground to do another series along the bottom. Working across the house like this means you have to alter the ladder height the least number of times.

Woodwork

You can choose either a non-drip gloss or a runny gloss for the exterior woodwork. The non-drip jelly paints combine the properties of undercoat and finishing coat so a separate undercoat is not required. But this single coat won't be as long-lasting as the undercoat-plus-runny-gloss system and you'll have to apply two or three coats to build up a thick enough paint film to give adequate outside protection. Inside, however, one coat of non-drip paint would be quite sufficient.

The sequence of painting all jointed woodwork – windows, doors and frames – is determined by the method of construction. In nearly all cases the rails (horizontal bars) are tenoned into mortises cut into the stiles (uprights). Therefore, you should paint the rails and cross bars first, then deal with the stiles. By painting in this way, any overlaps of paint from the rails and bars are covered up and leave a neater finish. An even edge on the glass is best achieved freehand, but if you doubt the steadiness of your touch, use a paint guard or masking tape. Bring the paint onto the glass for up to 3mm (⅛in) to protect the edge of the putty. If you are using masking tape, remove it shortly after painting round each pane; the paint may be peeled off if it is left to harden completely before the tape is removed.

When a visitor calls at your house, he'll stand face to face with your front door and have nothing to do but examine it while he awaits your answer. So it's here you should put in your best work. Remove all the door furniture such as knobs, knockers, locks, keyhole covers and letterbox. Prepare the woodwork carefully and wipe it down with a tackrag (a soft cloth impregnated with a sticky varnish) to collect any remaining dust. Tackrags are obtainable from any good paint shop. Use a perfectly clean brush, preferably one that has been used before so that no loose bristles will come adrift. Wedge the door ajar and cover the floor with a dust cloth or old newspapers. Use paint which doesn't need straining, and pour about 50mm (2in) into a small container or paint kettle.

All coats of paint should follow the grain of the wood. Don't attempt to cross-hatch – that is, apply a primer in one direction, undercoat at right angles and finishing coat in the direction of the primer. If you do, you'll get a criss-cross effect when the paint dries which produces a poor finish.

HOW MUCH MASONRY PAINT?

The spreading power of masonry paints varies according to the porosity and texture of the surface. Roughcast, for instance could take twice as much paint as smooth render. These spreading rates are usually given on the side of the paint tin but in general the coverage is:
● smooth surfaces – 6 to 10m² (65 to 110sq ft) per litre
● lightly textured surfaces – 4 to 6m² (44 to 65sq ft) per litre
● pebbledash, roughcast and Tyrolean – 3 to 4m² (33 to 44sq ft) per litre.

CALCULATING THE AREA

To estimate the area of a house wall, simply measure out its length and multiply by the eaves height. Only allow for window area if this is over one fifth of total wall area.

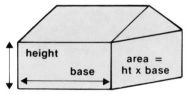

● if you don't know the height, measure the length of the lowest whole section of a downpipe and multiply this by the number of sections making up the complete pipe drop
● for triangular areas, measure the base of the triangle, multiply by the height and divide the answer by two.

$$area = \frac{ht \times base}{2}$$

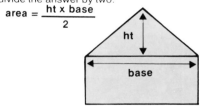

TIP: CLEANING BRICKWORK

Paint splashes from previous careless work can be removed with a chemical paint remover. The paste type is best as it won't run down the wall. This will only strip off the surface paint, however, and some will have soaked into the brick. You may be able to remove this with a wire brush, but if not, apply a poultice of whiting and ammonia kept in position with a piece of polythene taped down at the edges. This will leave a light patch which can be disguised by rubbing with a piece of old, dirty, broken brick. By the time the brick dust has been washed out by rain, natural weathering will have evened out the tone.

PAINTING WALLS

1 A roller is much quicker to use than a brush, but make sure you have a large enough bucket to dip the roller in. Fill this about ⅓ full.

2 Cut a short plank of wood to the same width as the roller and put it in the bucket so you can load the roller evenly by pressing against it.

3 When painting the house wall, start at the top right hand corner (if you are right-handed) and use a brush to cut in round the edges.

4 Using the roller, cover a strip on your right-hand side. Don't lean over too far and only make the strip as long as you can easily manage.

5 Move the ladder to the left and paint another strip by the first, without overlapping too much. Touch in round obstacles with a brush.

6 Using the brush again, carefully paint round the window. Try to leave a neat edge with the woodwork and wipe off any splashes with a damp cloth.

7 Continue painting a strip at a time from right to left, then lower the ladder and paint a further series of strips until the wall is covered.

8 Protect pipes by wrapping old newspaper round them and securing it with adhesive tape. Use a brush to paint the wall behind the pipes.

9 Be very careful when painting the bottom edge of the wall, and don't load the brush too thickly or paint will run onto the path.

Ready Reference

HOW MUCH GLOSS PAINT?

The coverage of a litre of gloss paint depends on several factors, including the smoothness of the surface and whether it is interrupted by edges and mouldings. Also, a lot depends on the painter's technique. However, as a general guide, for one litre of paint:
● runny gloss covers 17m² (180sq ft)
● non-drip gloss covers 13m² (140sq ft).

CALCULATING AREAS

It would be very difficult to calculate the area of every bit of wood and metal you wanted to paint. But you need to make a rough estimate so you'll know how much paint to buy. The following examples are intended as a rough guide and they should give you an idea of how much paint you'll need, assuming you're using **runny gloss** and you give everything **two coats of paint.** If you're using non-drip gloss you'll have to buy about 25% more paint:
● a panelled front door will take ⅓ litre (½ pint)
● a flush door will take about ⅕ litre (⅓ pint)

panelled door   **flush door**

3 doors/litre   **5 doors/litre**

● a sash window, about 2x1m (6ft 6in x 3ft 3in) with an ornate frame will take about ⅙ litre (¼ pint)
● a modern picture window of the same size with a plain frame will take only ⅛ litre (⅕ pint)

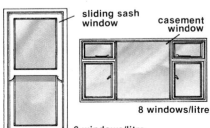

sliding sash window   **casement window**

8 windows/litre

6 windows/litre

● to find the area of a downpipe, simply measure round the pipe and multiply by the height, then add a little for clips and brackets. For two coats of paint, one litre will cover 18m (60ft) of 150mm (6in) diameter pipe and 27m (90ft) of 100mm (4in) pipe.

PAINTING WINDOWS

1 *Start to apply undercoat at the top of the window. Prop the window open, tape up the stay and paint the frame rebates first.*

2 *Paint the rebates on open casements next. If you get paint on the inside surface, wipe it off immediately with a cloth dipped in white spirit or turps.*

3 *Close the window slightly and paint the area along the hinged edge. You may need to use a narrow brush (called a fitch) to reach this part.*

4 *A neat paint line on the glass is best achieved free-hand, but if you find this too difficult, use a paint shield or apply masking tape.*

5 *The general order of painting is to do the cross bars (rails) first, followed by the uprights (stiles) and then the window sill.*

6 *When the undercoat is dry, sand it down with a fine grade glasspaper, then apply the top coat in the same order as the undercoat.*

PAINTING SEQUENCES

Windows and panelled doors are tricky areas to paint properly but you shouldn't have any trouble if you follow the correct sequence of painting shown here.

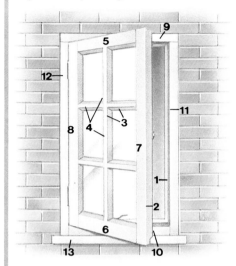

Start with the rebate on the frame (1), then paint the outside edge of the window (2). Do the putty (3) next, followed by the glazing bars (4) and the rails and stiles (5 to 8). Paint the frame (9 to 13) last.

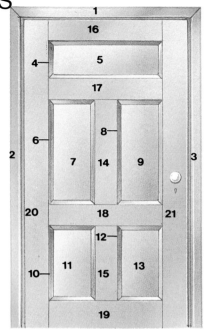

Wedge the door ajar and paint the frame (1 to 3), the hinged edge of the frame and door. Do mouldings and panels next (4 to 13) followed by the muntins (14,15), the rails (16 to 19) and finally the stiles (20, 21).

Deal with the door frame first (the top, then the sides) so that any splashes can be wiped off an unpainted surface immediately. Then do the door itself, following the sequence of painting shown on this page. Don't put too thick a coat on the inner edge of the door frame because although gloss paint dries fairly quickly, it won't oxidise (ie, thoroughly harden) for about a week. So in that period, when you close the door, paint may 'set-off' from the frame onto the door, producing a vertical streak an inch or so from the door's edge. A good idea to prevent this is to insert a thin strip of polythene sheeting round the door's edge after the paint has become touch dry, and leave it until the paint has thoroughly hardened.

If you want to apply two finishing coats, wait at least 12 hours but not more than a week between coats. There's no need to sand down between coats because the solvent used in modern gloss paints is strong enough to dissolve the surface of the previous coat and so to ensure a firm bond between the two layers.

Weatherboards

Weatherboards and timber cladding can be left in their natural state as long as you treat them with a wood preservative, and you can use wood stains to enhance or change their colour. If you prefer a glossy finish, use a suitable external varnish such as an oil-resin varnish (marine varnish), rather than a one-pack polyurethane varnish which can prove brittle and difficult to over-coat in future. If you wish to paint the wood you'll have to apply one coat of wood primer, followed by an undercoat and two finishing coats of gloss.

Galvanised iron and asbestos

Because it is waterproof, bituminous paint is best for galvanised or asbestos roofs. In addition to the customary black it can be obtained in shades of red, green or brown to simulate or match tiles. These colours are more expensive than black and may have to be ordered specially from a builders' merchant. Bitumen soon loses its gloss and its surface tends to craze under a hot sun. But that doesn't matter as roofs are not usually visible.

Paint the walls of asbestos outhouses with outdoor-grade emulsion in a colour to match the rest of the house. Thin the first coat to allow for the porosity of the asbestos and follow this with a normal second coat. Apply emulsion on the interior surface as well to minimise moisture absorption. Galvanised iron on vertical surfaces should be painted with gloss paint.

When painting corrugated surfaces, give the high parts a preliminary touch-up with paint, leave it to dry and then paint the whole lot. If you apply paint all over in one go it will tend to flow from high to low parts, giving an uneven coating.

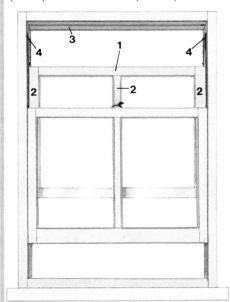

Sliding sash windows need to be painted in two stages. Pull down the top sash and paint the top rail of the inside sash (1) and the sides as far as you can go (2). Do the runners at the top of the frame (3) and a short way down the outer runner(4). Almost close the windows, then paint the bottom runners (5,6), and the remainder

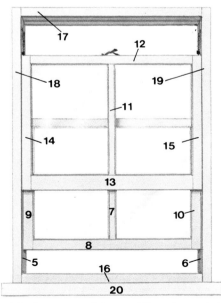

of the bottom sash to meet the other paint (7 to 10). Paint the whole of the top sash including the bottom edge (11 to 15) and finally the window frame (16 to 20). This view shows the interior of the window: for the exterior the sequence is identical except of course, that you start with the top sash.

SPRAYING EXTERIOR WALLS

Painting the exterior walls of your home with a brush or roller can be a fairly time-consuming job. But with a properly-used spray gun you can soon finish the job.

Painting the exterior walls of your house with a brush is hard and tedious work; even if you switch to a roller, things will not be a lot simpler. To avoid this drudgery, you can use an alternative method: you can spray the paint onto the walls. It's quicker, easier and, because it tends to give a more even coverage, should give more durable results, particularly on rough surfaces where brushes and rollers tend to leave tiny gaps through which moisture can penetrate to undermine the paint film.

If the only experience you have had of spray painting is retouching scratches on a car with an aerosol, then spraying houses may seem very novel. But it isn't a new idea. Specialist contractors have been doing it for years, though their advertising has tended to concentrate on the fact that they use special, very durable paints. In fact you'll find that you don't need special paint; so long as it's of a type suitable for exterior use.

Types of spray gun
Although you don't need special paint, you do need costly special equipment: you need a spray gun. Fortunately, these are widely available at a modest rental from good local tool hire shops. The important thing is that you choose the right kind of spraying equipment for the paint you wish to use. Choosing the gun can, in fact, be rather complicated – there are so many different kinds available – so you could tell the hire shop what you want to spray and leave the decision to them.

The simplest type of spraying equipment you are likely to be offered is called an airless spray unit. It is a straightforward pump which takes paint from a container (any container will do) and then squirts it out through a spray nozzle. It is very efficient in terms of labour and use of materials and very fast. It is capable of delivering up to 2.25 litres (4 pints) of paint per minute (a practised operator would normally cover about 240sq m/262sq yd in an hour). This type of gun does, however, have a few drawbacks. To begin with the paint must be thinned before it can be sprayed, which may mean applying an extra coat in order to achieve the required coverage and colour density. Also, with the pump at ground level, problems may arise when you are working on buildings higher than about two storeys. The machine may not be powerful enough to pump the paint that distance. In addition, this type of unit will not handle paints containing fillers.

An alternative is a machine that works a bit like an old-fashioned scent spray: the air flow is provided by a compressor which may or may not be rented out as a separate item (if you do have to hire the compressor separately, make sure it is sufficiently powerful for the application you have in mind). Reaching heights with a machine of this type should not be a problem. The only limitation is the length of the hose between the compressor and the spray gun, but many hire shops supply 10m (30ft) hoses. A point here: not all compressor-operated units are the same and you should check that you are using a suitable type. At the bottom end of the scale, you'll find small portable units primarily designed for spraying cars and the like. So long as you use a paint that does not contain fillers, these can be used to spray walls, but since the integral paint container normally has a capacity of less than a litre (1½ pints), you will spend a lot of time running up and down to refill. Larger 'industrial' versions using more powerful compressors are available and these are faster and have feed cups of around 1 litre (1½ pints). They too will only handle ordinary resin- and water-based paints.

If you want to spray on a reinforced paint there are a number of options, with different suppliers calling them by different names. Those able to cope with most ordinary filled exterior paints may have a shoulder-carried, or back-pack style, paint container. Those capable of spraying anything from reinforced paint to very heavy, plaster consistency materials tend to be fed from a gravity feed hopper on top of the spray gun, or from a separate pressurised tank – see step-by-step photographs.

Whatever you decide on, do double-check that the gun is suitable for the material you wish to spray; even if the basic equipment is right for the job a different nozzle may be required. Also make sure you get adequate instructions on using and cleaning the equipment before you take it home. If you damage it or return it dirty, you may lose some or all of your deposit. Again, bear in mind that some compressors are electric and some petrol-driven, but the smaller units are almost always electrically operated (check that you get a 240V model, not a 110V one).

Choosing access equipment
Since the main virtue of spray painting walls is speed, it's only sensible to choose a means of reaching the heights that allows you to get up, down and along with the minimum of fuss. This means that a scaffold tower, even one on castors, although excellent when you are preparing the surface, is not a particularly

PREPARING THE WALLS

1 *Most exterior wall paints will fill hairline cracks when sprayed on. Rake out and fill larger cracks and holes with mortar or exterior-grade filler.*

2 *The paint will not adhere properly to a dusty, crumbly surface. Go over areas like these with a stiff brush to remove dirt and any loose material.*

3 *Where old paint has begun to crack and flake off, use a scraper to remove it from affected areas of the wall. Prime bare areas with paint before spraying.*

4 *Look out for green spots, which are a sign of mould growth. To prevent any further outbreaks, brush on a solution of bleach or apply a proprietary fungicide.*

good choice for spraying unless you have a suitable flat, hard 'road' running right round the area you wish to paint. A step ladder (or possibly two, spanned by a scaffold board) for the lower levels, and a lightweight, aluminium extension ladder for the rest is generally a better bet.

Having said that, you should not, of course, allow speed to take precedence over safety. It's probably true that as there is no physical contact with the wall, you are less likely to push yourself off balance than you would be if using a brush or roller and that as spraying is quick and easy you are less likely to over-stretch in order to reach that extra little bit before climbing down and moving the ladder along. But don't take any chances. Always make sure that the ladder is set at the correct angle on a firm, level footing and that it is roped in place at the top. If necessary, spend an hour or two fixing stout hooks at

intervals into the top of the wall to make roping off easier. You'll find they come in handy wherever you need to scale a ladder.

Preparing the site

You should thoroughly prepare the surface so it is clean, dry and sound. In particular, fill any cracks which are wider than about a millimetre with mortar, and check that all rendering is securely adhering to the surface underneath. Also, you should treat dusty surfaces with stabilising primer and kill off any mould or algae using a proprietary fungicide or algicide.

Masking off will normally be your next step (see *Ready Reference*). This can take time and you may feel it rather cancels out the benefits of spraying. This is true to some extent, but wielding a heavy brush can hardly be compared with snipping away at a length of sticky tape. However, it is possible to do

MASKING OFF

1 *Masking off takes some time, but it's essential that you do it properly. Cover drainpipes with newspapers, working from the bottom up.*

2 *For larger areas such as windows it's easier to use larger sheets (paper is cheaper than polythene). Tape all edges and joins carefully for the best results.*

3 *To prevent the spray from falling over surrounding areas, it's a good idea to protect the ground at the bottom of the wall with dust sheets.*

SETTING UP THE EQUIPMENT

1 *Make sure you've got all the equipment you need. Then assemble the components; here, start with the gun and paint hose.*

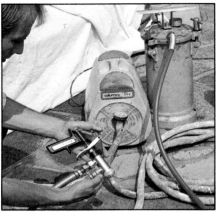

2 *Link the other end of the paint hose to the pressurised paint tank. Then connect the air hose to the turbine and the gun. Tighten all connections fully.*

3 *Fill up the paint tank to the level recommended by the hire company. If thinning is necessary, do it now and then stir the paint thoroughly.*

4 *Fit the lid of the tank back on. When you are sure it's correctly placed, screw it down so the tank is properly sealed and can be pressurised.*

5 *Next, pressurise the container by pumping with the integral pump. Don't exceed the recommended pressure level shown on the gauge.*

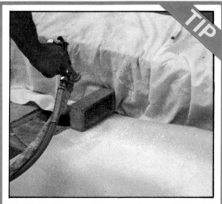

6 *Test the gun by spraying paint onto an old board, and adjust the nozzle on the front of the gun as necessary to give a uniform spray pattern.*

82

SPRAYING THE WALLS

1 *If you are right-handed, begin at the top right-hand corner (or the top left if you are left-handed). Spray towards a natural break such as a downpipe.*

2 *As soon as you've completed one band of paint you can begin work on the next. Here, the two windows neatly define the next area to be tackled.*

3 *Keep the gun at right angles to the wall surface when you are spraying. Spray over the edges of the masked-off areas; the paper will protect them.*

4 *Before you reach the end of the wall, make sure that you have covered up any adjacent areas which you don't want to be splotched with paint.*

5 *Remove the masking tape before the paint dries. Otherwise it would be more difficult to remove and you also risk peeling off the paint.*

6 *If your masking-off has been effective there should only be small areas left for you to fill in by hand. A small brush is best for cutting-in work.*

away with masking; though you will still need to protect the ground. All you do is stop spraying when you get too close to whatever it is you don't want painted; normally within 300-600mm (1-2ft). These 'safety zones' can then be painted in using a brush or roller. Do be warned though: a sudden puff of wind or a momentary loss of concentration could have disastrous consequences. If you intend using this technique you should be prepared to have to paint the woodwork and metalwork soon after and to keep some white spirit (turps) or water (according to the type of paint) handy to wipe off any spray that strays onto the window panes.

Spraying technique

The basic technique for spraying walls is to aim to cover the surface with a series of barely overlapping stripes. You should keep the gun moving a constant distance from the surface at a constant speed: slow enough to ensure good coverage and fast enough to avoid the runs that result from applying too much paint. If you don't get a perfect result at the first attempt you can put things right by applying another coat.

Keep on working as blockages may occur if you stop spraying. When you have to stop clean the equipment thoroughly.

Order of work

As when you are brushing on paint, you should follow the sun round the house so your new paintwork won't be exposed to the full blistering heat of the sun until the next day.

It's certainly worth dividing the area into manageable sections using features such as drainpipes and window bays to provide sensible boundaries. This not only gives natural cues for rest breaks but also helps boost morale. Having completed a section, you'll feel you're really getting somewhere.

Similarly, for the sake of comfort and efficiency, tackle each section working down and across, starting at the top right if you are right-handed, top left otherwise. Overstretching is dangerous so climb down and move the ladder.

You'll have to take the weather into account. Don't work in the rain, or if rain is likely within the next few hours, and don't start work if the surface is wet with rain or dew; give it time to dry out. The heat of the sun can damage new paint and will exacerbate the problem of paint drying in the gun so avoid working when the weather is really scorching.

And don't forget the wind. The stiller the day the easier it will be to spray accurately and the less paint you will waste. With a reasonably powerful modern gun, you should be alright working in anything up to a gentle summer breeze, possibly a bit more. But if you have trouble when you first start work, take a rest and try again later.

CHAPTER 5

FLOORCOVERINGS

Changing your floorcoverings can be an expensive job, and
certainly means considerable upheaval while the old flooring
is lifted and the new one laid.
Using the right techniques ensures a perfect fit and long life,
whether you're laying materials off the roll or in tile form.

STRIPPING TIMBER FLOORS

Sanding wooden floorboards is dusty, time-consuming work, but it's not difficult. You'll find the effort well worthwhile when the boards are transformed into an attractive floor surface.

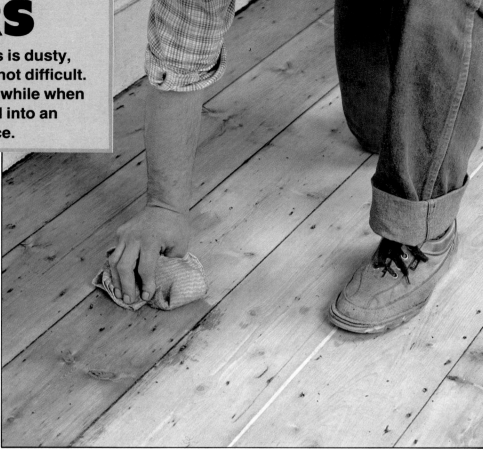

Using floorcoverings can be expensive, particularly if you have to deal with passages, stairs or landings as well as main rooms. As an alternative you could decide to leave a wooden floor uncovered after treatment to make it an attractive surface in its own right. Since timber is one of the most versatile flooring materials there is, it will fit in with most styles of decor, whether modern or traditional. It's extremely hardwearing and easy to look after. And, just as important, it has a warmth you don't get with most modern floorings of comparable durability.

You can, if you wish, lay a new timber floor, if the old one is rotten or in a bad state of repair, finishing it with stains or varnish to bring out the natural beauty of the wood. But the chances are you won't need to go to this expense. You may well have a wooden floor already which you've covered up. The old floorboards may not look much when you first expose them but if you sand them smooth to take off the uneven top layers engrained with dirt you'll be surprised how beautiful they can become, especially after they've been coated with varnish to make the grain pattern clear.

Checking out the floor
Of course, ordinary floorboards are not intended to be displayed, so you cannot guarantee good results. A particularly unattractive, inferior grade of timber may have been used. Or the boards may have been badly laid or badly looked after. The only way to find out is to lift any floorcovering and see for yourself. You can make a preliminary survey simply by lifting a corner of the floorcovering; but to be absolutely sure the whole floor should be exposed.

When you lift the existing floorcovering, take care to remove any fixing nails and the remains of flooring adhesive. Many flooring adhesives are soluble in white spirit (turps) or petrol. But obviously, if you're using petrol you must ensure the room is adequately ventilated. Don't smoke while you're doing the work.

The look of the timber grain is important, but here much depends on personal taste. Some people like wooden floors to have

even, restrained grain patterns; others feel that, unless the pattern is striking and irregular, the floor doesn't look like real wood. It's up to you, but do allow for the fact that any grain pattern will become slightly more pronounced once the boards have been sanded and sealed.

You should also see if the floorboards have been stained, and if so, whether or not the staining covers the entire floor: it was once popular to stain the edges and cover the central unstained portion with a carpet or linoleum square. If the staining has been carried out over the whole of the floor area there shouldn't be any problem with sanding and sealing later. Thoroughly sand a trial area by hand to get an idea of the finished result. If you don't like the way the floor looks, you can try restaining it experimentally; alternatively try to lighten or remove the existing wood stain with a proprietary wood bleach. Border staining can be more of a problem because of the need to match the border with the unstained part of the floor. Again, experimenting with stains and bleaches is the only answer; make sure you sand the test area first. If, when later you come to tackle the job in earnest, you give the floor its main sanding

after staining, there is a risk that the old and new stains will respond in rather different ways.

Preparing the surface
When you've got a good idea of what the final result will look like, you can turn your attention to the physical state of the floor. Are there lots of large gaps, wider than 2 or 3mm (up to ⅛in) between boards? If there are, the finished floor may well turn out to be excessively draughty so you will have to fill the gaps before sanding. To maintain the floor's 'natural' look involves tailoring a fillet of timber for each gap and you may well decide, as a result, that a wooden floor simply isn't worth the effort. Watch out, too, for signs of excessive localised wear resulting in dips and ridges that no amount of sanding will remove. And, finally, check for signs of woodworm. This must be treated, but, remember, woodworm treatment will not restore the appearance of the affected wood.

If, at this stage, things don't look too promising, there are three remedies to consider which may provide you with the solution you require.

The first is a cure for gaps. All you do is lift every single board and re-lay them closer together: not difficult but very hard work. Next there is the remedy for boards disfigured by wear or woodworm, and you can also use it to overcome the problems associated with stained boards. Again, all you do is lift and re-lay the boards, but this time, you re-lay them with what used to be the underside uppermost. This is also very hard work, and there is a possibility that the underside of the boards may look no better; a good builder should have laid the boards with the worse side face down when the house was built.

Because of the amount of work involved with both of these solutions it's best to consider them as a last resort. You could instead adopt the third remedy: give up the idea of sanding the existing boards and cover them with new ones. Such 'non-structural' boards are available in a variety of hardwoods and softwoods, so the results can be very rewarding indeed in that you will end up with a very attractively coloured and grained floor surface. However, this type of floor is likely to prove very expensive and rather tricky to lay. The actual techniques involved will be covered in a later article.

If, on the other hand, you check the boards and discover that they are suitable for sanding, you should fill any gaps and make sure there are no protruding nails or screws. These should be driven well below the surface otherwise there could be dire consequences when you are sanding (see *Ready Reference*). Giving screws an extra half a turn should do the trick; otherwise unscrew them, drill out a deeper countersink and replace them. For nails which cause you a problem you will need a nail punch (if you don't have one you can use an old blunt nail instead) to drive the offending nails home so they can't cause any further nuisance.

Sanding the floor

Sanding floorboards is in essence, no different to sanding any piece of natural timber. You must work your way through coarse, medium and then fine grades of abrasive until you achieve the desired finish. It's simply that you are working on a larger scale than usual.

However, this question of scale does create a few complications. First, there will be a great deal of dust flying about, and a lot of noise, so you must protect yourself with the appropriate safety equipment (see *Ready Reference*). You must also take steps to stop the dust being trodden all round your home. Second, the job will be far too large for sanding by hand and, in any case, the average DIY power sander wouldn't be up to the task. What you need are two special floor sanders, and these you will have to hire. (See below for tips on hiring).

The first sander looks a bit like a lawn mower, but is in fact a giant belt sander and its role is to tackle the bulk of the floor. It has a revolving rubber-covered drum set on a wheeled frame which can be tilted backwards to lift the drum from the floor. You wrap a sheet of abrasive round the drum to provide the sanding surface. There is a bag attached to the sander into which a fan blows the wood dust and particles produced by the sanding process. The second sander is a sort of heavy duty orbital sander, and it is used to tackle the parts the main sander cannot reach. It works on the same principle as the large sander (you attach an abrasive sheet to a rubber pad) but, being small and lighter, it's easier to manoeuvre.

You won't be able to rely entirely on these labour-saving devices, though. After machine sanding there will be small unsanded patches left, usually at the edges of the floor and these will have to be sanded by hand or scraped with a shave hook or some other form of scraper.

The need to hire equipment raises a further complication: careful planning is needed to keep the cost to a minimum. As always, the best way to start is by shopping around the hire shops in your area to find the best price. In particular, look for firms that give discounts for extended periods of hire (for example, one where the weekly rate is cheaper than say, four or five days at the day rate) and find out how much flexibility there is in allowing you to switch rates should you decide to keep the sanders for a day or two longer than originally anticipated. This is important because, although it's only sensible to keep the period of hire to a minimum by doing all the preparation (punching nail heads below the surface and so on) before you pick up the equipment, and returning it as soon as you've finished, floor sanding is physically very demanding, and may well take longer than you think.

Check up, too, on the cost of the abrasives. If there is a marked difference in price between two shops, it may be due to the fact that, while one offers ordinary glasspaper, the other offers a more modern synthetic paper which will last longer and clog less readily, and so works out cheaper than it appears. You will also encounter differences in the way abrasives are provided. For example, some shops will give a refund for any abrasive you don't use. A point to remember here is that as it's difficult to estimate exactly how much abrasive you will need it's wise to take an amount which appears surplus to requirements. If you take this precaution you will avoid the annoying situation where you have to down tools and buy extra abrasive.

PREPARING THE FLOOR

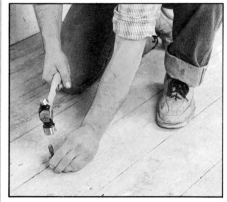

1 *Go over the entire floor, punching all nail heads well below the surface. If screws have been used, check they're adequately countersunk.*

2 *Cut thin fillets of wood to fill gaps between the boards; hammer them in, protecting the edges of the fillets with a block of softwood.*

3 *Plane the fillets flush with the surrounding surface, taking off a little at a time to prevent chipping and splintering.*

ORDER OF WORK

After you have checked that the floor is in a suitable condition for sanding, with gaps filled and no protruding nails or screws, you should adopt the procedure indicated below when using the large and small sanding machines. The arrows indicate in which direction the sander should be moved.

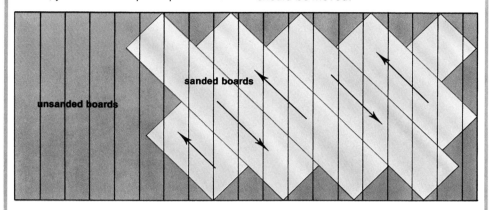

1 *Use the large sander in a diagonal direction across the boards in order to flatten them out and remove thoroughly the top dirt-engrained layer.*

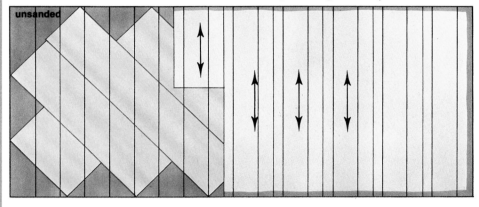

2 *Work in strips along the boards. Work down a strip, then with the machine on, move back along the strip. Switch off when you reach your starting point.*

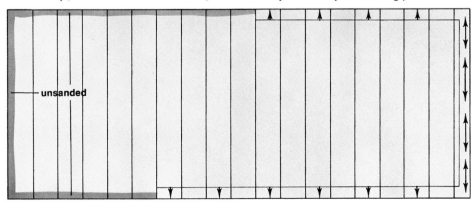

3 *When the floor has been sanded as in (2), with first coarse, then medium and fine abrasives, you can use the small sander on the perimeter of the floor.*

Ready Reference

PUNCH NAILS DOWN
Make sure there are no protruding nails or screws in the floor surface before you begin sanding, because:
● if screws or nails are less than 2-3mm (1/12-1/8in) below the surface of the boards there's a good chance they will tear the abrasive sheets
● a protruding nail will cause an explosion of flying bits of abrasive which can be dangerous; it may also damage the sander.

KEEP DOORS AND WINDOWS CLOSED
To prevent dust from permeating other areas of the house, keep doors closed. Close the windows, too, to allow the dust to settle so it can be vacuumed up.

SAFETY EQUIPMENT
Sanding is extremely dusty, very noisy work, so you should wear the appropriate equipment to protect yourself. A mask, to prevent you from breathing in dust, is a must; you should also consider ear muffs to protect your ears from the din, and goggles so dust and flying bits of grit don't get in your eyes.

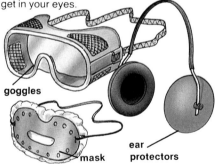

goggles

mask

ear protectors

ELECTRICAL SAFETY
To prevent nasty accidents, you should make sure the electrical cord is out of the path of the sander. One way to do this is to drape the cord over your shoulders as you are working.

FLATTEN WARPED BOARDS
Use the weight of the sander to flatten the edges of any warped boards in the first stage of sanding by running the sander diagonally across the boards.

SAND WITH THE GRAIN
When you are sanding in strips down the length of the room in the second stage of sanding, work in the same direction as the grain of the timber or you will cut deep, difficult-to-remove scratches in the surface.

SANDING AND SEALING THE BOARDS

1 Fit a large floor sander with a coarse grade of abrasive; the paper is locked into a slot in the revolving drum of the machine.

2 You can now start sanding the floor by running the sander diagonally across the floorboards to remove the rough and dirty surface layer.

3 Continue sanding the floor in this way until the bulk of the floor area has been treated; the sander will flatten out any warped boards.

4 Sand a strip down the length of the room. Work in the same direction as the boards and allow the sander to pull you along.

5 Sand this strip again, dragging the sander backwards. Repeat for the rest of the floor. Afterwards, sand using medium then fine grades of paper.

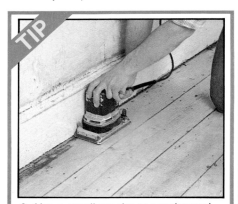

TIP

6 Use a small sander to sand round the perimeter using progressively finer grades of paper. Work in the direction of the grain.

7 You can use a shave hook to scrape stubborn areas at the edges. Other areas that the machines have missed will have to be sanded by hand.

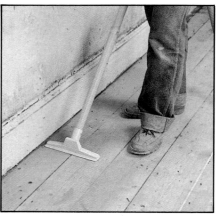

8 Allow the dust to settle, then vacuum the floor clean, paying particular attention to the gaps between the floor and skirting.

9 To reduce the amount of sealant needed, apply polyurethane varnish, diluted with white spirit on a clean cloth to prime the boards.

Finally, you should make sure that the shop from which you hire the equipment will give you adequate tuition on how to use and clean the sanders. If you damage them through misuse, or return them dirty, you will have to pay more.

Finishing the floor

Having dealt with the sanding, the final thing you have to consider is how to finish the floor: that is, add to its decorative quality and protect the boards from scratches and other types of wear.

If you feel that the boards are too dark to leave as they are after sanding you can apply bleach to lighten them. Use a proprietary wood bleach and follow the manufacturer's instructions for applying it. The fumes from the bleach can be at the least unpleasant and at worst dangerous, so make sure you keep the windows open and wear a protective face mask.

You may want to change the colour of the boards, as well as lighten them. You could use coloured polyurethane varnish for this, but as the surface of the floor becomes subject to wear, so the colour may become thin in some places, highlighting the wear more strongly than you would wish. So it's better to use wood stains which colour the timber itself and then seal with clear polyurethane varnish. Again apply the stain according to the manufacturer's instructions as to the number of coats needed. Work in the direction of the grain when you are applying the stain. (Stains, which come in a variety of colours, allow you to go in for different attractive decorative effects.)

Polyurethane varnish is by far the best choice for sealing the floor, simply because it is so hardwearing and easy to look after. You should choose a brand that is available in large cans rather than in the small tins you are probably familiar with. You'll need a lot to give the floor the two or three coats it requires, and buying such a large amount in small cans can work out very expensive. It's up to you whether you choose a polyurethane giving a high gloss, a satin look or a matt finish; it all depends on the style of the room as a whole. However, it's worth bearing in mind that a very high gloss will show marks more readily and may make the floor rather slippery.

Care and maintenance

To look its best, a wooden floor should be kept free of dust; regular vacuuming will attend to this. If you like a shiny look you can polish it with a proprietary floor polish. Dirty marks can be removed with a damp cloth or mop; more stubborn marks may require treatment with a proprietary cleaner. Where the finish or floorboard has been slightly damaged, such as by a cigarette burn, you will have to sand down the affected area until the signs of damage are removed and then apply polyurethane to reseal it. If there is more extensive damage you will have to remove the affected floorboards, replace them (or use them with the undamaged side face up), sand to provide a smooth surface and reseal.

Take care when you are moving bits of furniture about that they don't scratch the surface (see *Ready Reference*). There's not much point in spending the time and energy it takes to get an attractive varnished wooden floor surface only to spoil it in a few careless minutes.

10 *Follow the priming with at least two, preferably three, coats of polyurethane varnish applied with a brush, working with the grain.*

11 *Allow each coat to dry, then rub lightly down with medium glasspaper to provide a key for the next. Use a damp cloth to remove dust.*

LAYING FOAM-BACKED CARPET

Having wall-to-wall carpet is most people's idea of floorcovering luxury. You can even lay it yourself if you choose the right type of carpet.

carpet from Allied Carpets

Carpet is warm and luxurious underfoot, a good insulator, which is particularly important in flats and upstairs rooms, and still something of a status symbol when fitted in every room – particularly in the bathroom. Modern methods of weaving carpets, and the development of new synthetic fibres, have made some forms of carpeting relatively inexpensive, but it is silly to buy carpet just because it is the conventional thing to have; or for its luxurious image and status.

Consider whether it is a practical proposition for your home. Carpets in bathrooms where there are young children splashing about, (or where the lavatory is situated in the same room) may not be a wise choice. Carpets in kitchens (even the special 'utility' area type) are not always practical at the cooking/washing up end of the room, (although the eating end can be carpeted to co-ordinate with a more easycare surface at the 'business' end of the room). In family rooms, childrens' bedrooms and playrooms, halls and dining rooms, a washable surface may be the answer, softened with large cotton rugs (these can be cleaned in a washing machine), a carpet square or rush matting. But for the sitting room, master bedroom, stairs and corridors, there is really no substitute for carpet.

Choosing carpets

So how do you decide exactly which type of carpet to buy? Of course, you will start by looking for a colour or pattern you like, but a trip to a local carpet specialist or department store can often result in complete confusion once you have seen the range. As a general guide, you should choose the best quality (and consequently the most expensive) you can afford for heavy 'traffic' areas such as hallways, stairs, landings and main living rooms. You can then select the lighter weights and cheaper grades for the rooms which get less wear, like bedrooms, bathrooms and so on.

The carpet industry has produced a labelling system which divides the carpets into categories. In each case the label gives details of how the carpet is made, what fibres have been used and how durable it is likely to be.

This is quite a useful guide, but you should also ask for advice from the salesman. Here are some of the terms it helps to know.

Carpet weaves

The traditional types of carpet are known as Axminster and Wilton, terms which refer to the way they are woven.

An **Axminster** carpet is usually patterned and has an extensive choice of colours within the design. The backing is jute or hessian, sometimes strengthened by polypropylene. Different fibres and blends of fibres are used, but an Axminster is frequently woven in an 80 per cent wool and 20 per cent nylon mixture, and also from acrylic fibres, which resemble wool in appearance and feel.

Axminsters come in many different widths, up to 5m (16½ft) wide. They also come with bound and finished edges, known as carpet 'squares', although they are not necessarily square in shape. This type of carpet can be turned round within a room to even out the wear.

A **Wilton** carpet is usually plain or two-tone, although there are some patterned Wiltons made with a restricted number of colours. The carpet is generally close-textures with a velvet, looped, twist-and-loop, or a mixed cut-and-loop pile (called sculptured or carved). Any yarn not used on the face of the carpet is woven into the backing, to add to the thickness, and the backing is usually jute or hessian.

Different fibres and blends of fibres can be used in the construction, but Wiltons are usually made with 100 per cent wool pile, the 80/20 blend (as Axminster) or from an acrylic fibre.

Wilton carpet is woven in widths from 700mm (27in) to 2m (6ft 6in), which are then seamed together when the carpet is to be fully fitted; 3.75m (12ft) widths are also available in some ranges and can be bound to form a carpet 'square'.

Tufted carpets are a more modern type which has been developed during the last 25 years. Tufted carpets come in many different fibre mixtures including wool and wool blends. Widths vary from 1m (3ft) to 5m (16½ft). The tufts are 'needled' into a ready-woven backing and anchored by adhesive; when the main backing is hessian, this can be given a coat of latex to secure the tufts. Foam backing can then be stuck to the main backing; a high-quality foam-backed tufted carpet does not need an underlay.

Bonded carpets are made face-to-face, with the carpet pile held between two specially-treated woven backings. The carpet is then 'sliced' down the middle at the finishing stage, and becomes two carpets. The pile can be cut to different lengths to give a carpet with a texture ranging from a shaggy pile to a velvety velour. Fibres can be wool, wool blends or several different synthetics, and the carpet is usually plain. Widths are as for Axminster carpets.

Needlefelt or needleloom carpet is not really woven. A fibrous material is needled into a strong backing to create a looped ribbed pile or one which looks like dense felt. The fibres used are normally synthetic and the carpet has a rather harsh texture. The backing can be resin-coated hessian or foam, and the surface can be printed or plain. Various widths are available.

Broadloom or body?
These are terms used to describe the width of carpet. **Broadloom** carpets are 1.8m (6ft) or more wide, and are the practical choice for fitted carpets in all but the smallest rooms. **Body** carpets are usually 700 to 900mm (27 to 35in) wide, and are intended for use on stairs and in corridors, although they can be seamed together to cover larger areas.

Carpet fibres
All the carpets previously mentioned can be made in several different types of fibre or different blends, which creates still more confusion.

Acrylic fibres are the synthetic fibres most similar to wool. They have long-lasting qualities, and good resistance to flattening, but are not quite so springy as wool. They tend to soil more easily than a natural fibre, but they can be treated to resist staining and to be anti-static. Acrylic fibres come under many brand names, such as Courtelle and Acrilan.

Nylon is a hardwearing fibre, which has a characteristic shiny look. It soils easily, and can look flat and sad if it is the only fibre used in the carpet construction, but when added to other fibres it increases the durability con-

siderably. Nylon is frequently used in an 80/20 mix with wool.

Polyester is a soft fibre, used to create fluffy light-duty carpets. It is not very hard-wearing and does become flattened easily, but it can be blended with other fibres.

Polypropylene is a fairly tough fibre, which is often used to create 'cord' effect carpet. It does not absorb liquid, so it is often used for carpet tiles and carpets for kitchen and utility rooms.

Viscose rayon is not used very much these days, and has poor wearing and soiling qualities, but it can be used as part of a blend of fibres quite successfully.

Wool is the traditional carpet fibre, and no real substitute for it has yet been found. Wool is warm, hard-wearing, resilient and does not soil easily; from the safety point of view it also resists the spread of flame. It is used alone, or blended with other fibres. The most widely-used blend, 80 per cent wool and 20 per cent nylon, gives the best performance.

Other carpet types
Apart from the diferent methods of carpet making, and the various blends of fibres, you will find there are many other words in the carpet salesman's vocabulary, which loosely cover what might be called carpet styles, or types.

Cord carpets, for example, come in several styles. Originally the only type was a haircord, which was made from natural animal fibres, and was very hardwearing. This is now very expensive and is not frequently used, but there are some blends of animal hair with synthetic fibres available, and some much cheaper cords which are not particularly hard-

PREPARING THE FLOOR

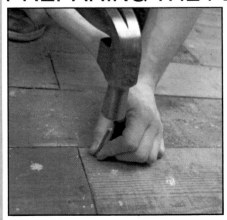

1 *Lift old floorcoverings completely, and remove all traces of underlay. Nail down any loose boards securely with 38mm (1½in) nails.*

2 *Use a nail punch and hammer to ensure that all the nail heads are flush with, or driven below, the surface of the boards.*

Ready Reference

THE TOOLS YOU'LL NEED
For cutting and laying foam-backed carpet you will need:
- a handyman's knife plus spare blades
- an old broad-bladed knife or scissors
- a staple gun (useful for fixing lining to floorboards)
- a steel tape measure.

EQUIPMENT AND FITTINGS
To anchor the perimeter of foam-backed carpet in place, use either
- double-sided carpet tape, or
- carpet tacks every 100mm (4in) – best on long-pile carpets that conceal the tack heads.

At door thresholds, use proprietary edging strips to finish off the carpeted area. Different types are available for linking two carpets (A) or one carpet and one smooth floorcovering(B).

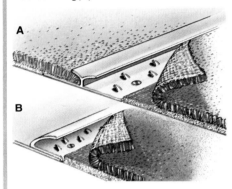

LINING OR UNDERLAY?
Always cover floors with paper or nylon linings before laying foam-backed carpets. Staple the lining to timber floors, tape it to solid ones. With foam-backed carpets, underlay is not needed.

ORDER OF WORKING
First unroll the carpet in the room where it will be laid, and position it roughly, with an even overlap at the skirting boards all round. Check that the excess will fit into
- alcoves beside chimney breasts
- other recesses, such as bay windows
- door openings
Then make the first trim along the longest uninterrupted wall (1) and tackle the other walls in sequence (2 to 4).

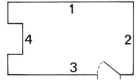

wearing. Other types of cord carpet include the Berbers, which have a looped pile and look homespun. Originally these were made from un-dyed, coarsely-woven wool, by Berber tribesmen. Now they are made in many different fibres, including blends of wool and synthetic fibres. These are often called Berber-style.

Hardtwist is a curly, crush-resistant pile, which is sometimes called twist pile. This is frequently found in high-quality Wiltons, in wool or wool blends, but may also be found in all-synthetic carpets.

Shag pile carpets have a long pile, which can be plain or kinked and with a richly textured shaggy surface. The pile needs raking if it is very long, to maintain its appearance, and it is not a practical carpet to choose for areas which get a lot of wear, on stairs, or in halls for example.

Shadow pile is another fairly new development in carpet style. The pile is dyed so it has contrasting colour or tone, usually darker at the base, lightening towards the tip. The pile is usually shiny (synthetic fibres) and when the carpet is walked on the dark tones show as 'shadows'.

Sculptured pile is usually made by combining a looped and cut pile to form a self-coloured pattern, although sometimes different colours can be used. Fibres can be natural, synthetic or a mixture of both.

Printed carpets are another fairly recent development. The carpet is woven and then a design is printed on the surface via computer-controlled dye injection systems. They often resemble Axminsters in colour and design, but on closer examination you can see the pattern does not go right through to the backing. The fibres used in this range are usually synthetic, and the pile is frequently very close and sometimes looped or corded.

Planning and estimating

As with any other floorcovering, start your planning by taking accurate measurements of the room at ground level with a steel tape or yardstick. If possible, work out a scale plan on squared paper, marking in the recesses, corners, angles, projections and so on. Take this with you when you shop for carpet, so the salesman can work out exactly how much you need. It is usual to multiply the room measurements to get square yards or square metres, and you will find most carpeting is sold by the square yard or metre, although some types are still sold by the linear yard or metre.

With the more expensive types of carpet with hessian backing, it is wise to call in an expert to lay the carpet for you, unless you have had a great deal of experience laying other types of carpet and floorcovering. Otherwise you risk marring an expensive carpet if you make a cut in the wrong place; what's

LAYING THE LINING

1 Unroll the lining down the length of the room. Smooth out the strip and staple down both sides 50mm (2in) in from the edge.

2 Using a sharp handyman's knife, cut off a strip of the lining 38mm (1½in) wide between the line of staples and the skirting board.

3 To fit the lining into an alcove, lay the strip up against the face of the chimney breast and make a cut with your knife in line with its corner.

4 Staple down the cut end of the length as before, after ensuring that it is perfectly flat. Then cut off the border strip next to the skirting board.

5 Continue covering the rest of the floor with the lining, overlapping each succeeding strip with the previous one by about 25mm (1in).

6 Stick double-sided self-adhesive tape down all round the edge of the room where you have cut off the strip of lining. Do not remove the release paper.

POSITIONING THE CARPET

1 Unroll the carpet parallel with the longest wall, and position it so that there is an overlap at the skirting board all round the room.

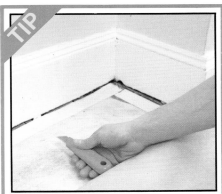

3 At fireplaces gauge the depth of the alcoves using your cutting knife as a guide. Add 75mm (3in) to allow for the final trimming.

5 Cut across the end of the tongue of carpet that fits into the alcove, taking care not to cut into the pile underneath the tongue.

2 Roughly trim off the excess carpet with a sharp handyman's knife to leave a 75mm (3in) overlap all round; cut through the foam backing behind.

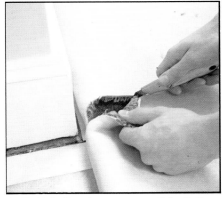

4 Cut into the alcove as you did with the lining. Make the first cut parallel with the side of the chimney breast and allow the tongue to fall into place.

6 At the corner of the chimney breast, make a diagonal cut on the underside of the carpet, and trim across the face of the chimney breast.

Ready Reference

CUTTING IN AT DOORWAYS

At doorways carpet should extend to a point under the centre of the door. To get an accurate fit round architraves and door stops, start making release cuts in the overlap at one side of the door opening, until the tongue falls neatly into the door opening. Then trim it to fit neatly under the threshold strip (see *Ready Reference*, page 91).

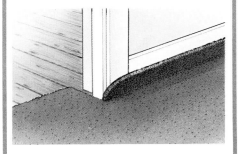

COPING WITH BAY WINDOWS

It's often easier to cope with odd-shaped bay windows by trimming the two flanking walls first. Then
● pull the carpet down the room until its edge is across the 'mouth' of the bay

● measure the depth of the bay, and cut a strip of wood to match this measurement
● use it to trace off the profile on the carpet, marking the line with chalk

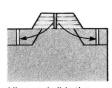

● trim along the marked line and slide the carpet back into place against the wall containing the bay.

FITTING ROUND PIPEWORK

Where pipes to radiators come up through the floor, you will have to cut the carpet to fit neatly round them. To do this
● make an incision in the edge of the carpet, parallel with one edge of the pipe
● measure the distance between wall and pipe, and cut out a small circle in the carpet at this distance from the edge
● fit the carpet round the pipe.

FITTING ANGLES

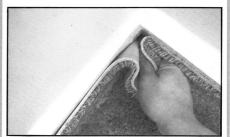

1 *To fit the carpet tightly into an angle, press your thumb firmly down into the corner as shown.*

2 *Pull up the corner, keeping your thumb in place, and make an incision just beyond the end of your thumb.*

3 *Cut cleanly across the corner in line with the incision, and press the carpet back in position.*

TAPING SEAMS

1 *Carefully trim the edges of the two pieces to be joined, and check that they butt neatly together.*

2 *Cut a piece of carpet tape to the length of the join, peel off the release paper and bed one carpet edge on it.*

3 *Position the other piece of carpet over the tape, and press it down firmly right along the join.*

FINAL TRIMMING

1 *Press the carpet tightly into the base of the skirting board with the back of an old knife or a pair of scissors.*

2 *Turn back the carpet and cut off the excess, using the score mark made by the knife back as a guide.*

3 *Peel off the release paper from the border tape and press the carpet firmly into place.*

more, it will wear out prematurely unless it is tensioned correctly during installation. This involves fitting special toothed gripper strips all round the perimeter of the room, and hooking the carpet on to the teeth once it has been pulled taut across the room.

The foam-backed types are, however, easier to lay yourself, because tensioning is not necessary.

If you are having the carpet professionally laid, ask for a written estimate and check carefully to see whether the price includes underlay or not, and if not, how much extra this will be. With an expensive carpet it may be wise to get several quotes from different firms. Some firms quote a price for carpet 'laid', but again check to see whether underlay is included in the price.

There are several different types of underlay – at different prices. The cheapest is the conventional brown felt, but there are also rubber and synthetic foams, including one on a coarse hessian backing. Foam-backed carpets definitely do not need underlay.

Laying carpet

It is usual to plan and lay carpet so the seams (if any) come in the least obvious place and where the 'traffic' is lightest. When the carpet has to be seamed, both pieces must be laid so the pile is going in the same direction, otherwise the colour would appear slightly different on each side of the seam. The floor should be clean, level and free from dust and debris. Punch down any nail heads that are proud of the floor surface, and nail down any loose boards. If the boards are very uneven, cover them with sheets of hardboard pinned down at 230mm (9in) intervals to disguise the ridges. Otherwise simply lay stout brown paper or nylon lining to prevent dust from blowing up between floorboards.

Never lay a new carpet down on top of an existing one; the worn areas will quickly transfer themselves to the new carpet. It is not wise to use old underfelt either.

Do not lay a carpet with a latex backing, or a latex underlay, in rooms which have underfloor central heating, as you could find it gives off an unpleasant smell.

LAYING HESSIAN-BACKED CARPET

There's no denying that laying hessian-backed carpet requires a fair degree of skill. But with care and some practice you can learn how to use a knee kicker to stretch this type of carpet into place and so provide a longlasting floorcovering.

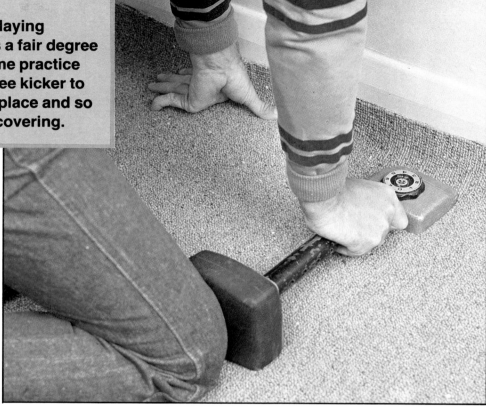

M ost really heavy quality carpets will not have a foam backing and therefore need to be laid with a separate underlay. A traditional method of securing such carpet is to 'turn and tack' it; the carpet is folded under at the perimeter of the room and non-rusting tacks are then driven through the fold to hold it to the floor. The underlay is cut to size so it meets the folded-under edge of the carpet. The problem with this method is that the tacks will be visible and will leave indentations in the carpet; also, you are likely to end up with scalloped edges and the carpet will be difficult to remove.

Consequently, most carpets which do not have a foam backing are laid using a system without tacks: the carpet is stretched over wooden or metal strips containing two staggered rows of angled pins which hook into the back of the carpet. This method provides an invisible fixing and it's quite simple to lift the carpet off the pins if you want to take it up later. But it's a much more complex method of fitting and fixing carpet than sticking down a foam-backed carpet (see pages 90-94).

Your chief problem is likely to be the stretching process: if you stretch the carpet too much it will tear; if you stretch it too little there will be lumps, which apart from being unsightly, will wear through quickly because of their exposed position.

A good professional fitter will be able to get the tension right according to the feel of the carpet. So at the outset it's worth considering the benefits of calling in an expert. Your chief guideline here will probably be cost and value for money. Fitting charges are, in fact, similar whether you are laying an inexpensive or a costly floorcovering. So, obviously, the costs of professional fitting relative to an expensive carpet make more sense than with a cheap one.

Bearing all this in mind you may decide you want to go ahead and fit your own carpet. There are many examples of successful DIY carpet fitting and yours may well be one of them. To ensure a good result it is worth practising fitting techniques on an old carpet you're going to discard before you begin on your new one. And it's certainly worth

tackling a simple rectangular room, with no awkward alcoves or bays, first of all, so the job will not be too complicated.

Tools and equipment
After you have measured up you can order the amount of carpet and underlay you'll need. Take a scale plan of the room along to your supplier so he can work out how much you need and check with him on the type of underlay which will suit the carpet you have chosen. A good quality underlay improves the feel of the carpet underfoot and, by serving as a buffer between the carpet and floor, helps to ensure even wear. It will also compensate for small defects if the floor is level but not perfectly smooth. For extra protection against dirt and dust rising up through the floorboards on a wooden floor you can lay paper or nylon lining underneath, so you will need to buy this as well.

You will also have to buy adequate carpet gripper. Gripper strips (commonly called smooth edge) can be nailed or glued to the floor. Strips intended for nailing come complete with pins for fixing to timber floors or masonry nails for fixing to solid floors. You will, obviously, have to buy adhesive of a suitable type (check with your supplier) if you are going to glue the strips in place.

In addition, you will require hessian tape

and adhesive for joining lengths of carpet and, if you are going to fix the underlay, staples (and a staple gun), tacks, adhesive or self-adhesive tape.

You will probably already have most of the tools required for this type of work: knife, shears, tin snips for cutting the gripper, hammer, bolster chisel and steel tape or wooden measure. You will also need a knee kicker to hook the carpet onto the gripper. This is relatively expensive, so it makes sense to hire one if, as is likely, you don't intend to go in for regular carpet fitting.

Preparing the floor surface
The floor surface must be level, smooth and dry. Wood floors can be sanded or covered with hardboard or an underlay; if the only problem is protruding nails you should punch the nails down or countersink the screws. Damp may also be a problem which needs tackling at a more basic level. If the floor is concrete, or has a composite surface, unevenness can be treated with a self-levelling screed (see pages 122-123 for more details of how to do this).

The first stages
If you have decided to fix a paper lining, you will have to spot-glue, staple or tack it to the floor. You can then fix the gripper in place;

FIXING GRIPPER STRIPS

1 *Cut the strips to length and nail them down so there's a gap of just less than the carpet thickness between them and the wall.*

2 *Cut short lengths and lay them with small gaps between them to follow a curve. Use a minimum of two nails to fix each piece in position.*

LAYING THE UNDERLAY

1 *Roll out the underlay and then position it so one end just comes up to the edge of the gripper strips fixed along one wall.*

2 *Cut the underlay so the end of the first length reaches the edge of the gripper strips along the opposite wall. Cut and lay other lengths.*

4 *Neatly trim what's left of the overlap so it fits exactly up to the edges of the gripper strips in the same way as for straight lengths.*

3 *At a curve or an angle, leave an overlap, and cut it at intervals so it fits around the obstacle. Then roughly trim off the excess.*

Ready Reference

TIP: AVOID BURIED PIPES

Solid floors often have pipes running close to the floor surface, so if there is a radiator in the room it's better to stick down the gripper along the length of the wall to which the radiator is attached rather than risk nailing it.

GULLY WIDTH

The space between the edge of the gripper and the wall is known as the gully. Its width should be slightly less than the uncompressed thickness of the carpet.

FIXING THE FIRST EDGE

To hold the carpet firmly down during stretching you will have to use what's known as the 'starting edge technique'. This is used to hook the carpet along the first two walls to be fitted; the carpet is hooked along the other two walls by stretching. Select a starting corner (one where you will have a reasonably uninterrupted run of walls is best) and follow this procedure:

● ease the edge of the carpet up the wall about 10mm (⅜in)
● rub your fingertips along the carpet over the gripper with a steady downward pressure so the back row of pins start penetrating the warp (A)
● use a hammer to press the carpet down between the gripper and the wall (B)
● don't try to turn the compressed carpet into the gully at this stage or you will release the pressure on the pins.

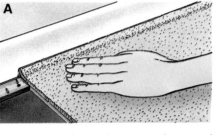

LAYING THE CARPET

1 *Place the carpet roughly over the underlay, then adjust its position more exactly. Arrange it so the edges 'climb up' the walls all round.*

2 *Trim off most of the surplus so there's an overlap of about 50mm (2in) at the wall and floor join; this makes the carpet easier to handle.*

3 *Adjust the teeth of the knee kicker so they grip the carpet backing, hold the head down firmly, then 'kick' the pad with your knee.*

4 *When making the next 'kick' use a bolster to hold down the carpet where you made the previous one so it doesn't spring back off the pins.*

5 *When all the carpet has been stretched and fixed in place, trim off the excess so there's about 10mm (3/8in) lapping up against the walls.*

6 *Use a bolster or thin piece of wood to press the overlap neatly into the gully between the gripper strips and the walls ensuring a snug fit.*

lengths of gripper can be placed end-to-end on straight walls. Recesses, bays and projections can be tackled by cutting the gripper into small pieces which you position to follow the contour of the wall. You can tack or stick the gripper down as you go along or when it is all in position. Tacking will also anchor the paper-felt lining. Where it is being stuck and a lining has been used, be careful to stick the gripper to the floor and not just to the lining, which should in fact be cut away within about 50mm (2in) of the wall all round the room.

With all the gripper satisfactorily in place, you can put down the underlay. It does not have to be fixed to the floor; lengths can simply be placed so they butt join without being secured. If you handle the carpet carefully, it should not disturb the underlay when you pull it over. If you feel happier securing the underlay, you can spot-stick it to the subfloor or anchor it to board floors with tacks or a stapling gun and tape successive lengths together where they abut.

If you have stuck the gripper down and it has been in place for the time recommended in the manufacturer's instructions, it's worth going round and trying to pull it off to make sure the adhesive has set really hard.

Laying the carpet

Unroll the carpet and place it roughly in position with the excess 'climbing up' the walls. Make sure the pattern (if any) is square and that the pile is leaning away from the light to prevent uneven shading in daylight. Position it so any seams will not be in areas of hard wear, such as doorways. You can roughly trim the overlap so the carpet is less cumbersome to handle when you are fitting it. Make sure you have left nothing under the carpet which shouldn't be there. You can then walk all over it and leave it to settle so that it flattens out.

As with foam-backed carpet, when you are trimming the carpet, and specially when you are cutting down into the overlap so it will fit round a corner or curve, make sure you do not cut too deeply or you will ruin the final effect. This and getting the tension right are likely to be your two major problems. Go round the room hooking and stretching in the required direction (see *Ready Reference*). Once you have hooked the carpet, stand back and take a look at it. It may not look straight and you might feel that it would be worth taking it off and starting again. Remember that one of the benefits of the tackless gripper method is that it's easy to hook and unhook a carpet so that you can get the adjustment right.

Where the carpet meets another type of floorcovering in a doorway, you can secure it with a threshold strip. You simply nail this down and then press the carpet onto the pins in the strip.

TRIMMING EDGES

1 *Where the corner forms a curve, cut down into the overlap so the carpet will fit round the curve; take care not to cut too deep.*

2 *At an external angled corner turn the carpet back and cut diagonally at the corner for a short distance and then straight towards you.*

3 *Trim off the bulk of the overlap, let the carpet flap back against the walls and then trim the overlap again for a perfect final fit.*

JOINING LENGTHS

1 *Lay the lengths of carpet so they butt against each other, then cut a length of hessian tape and place it so it fits beneath the two edges.*

2 *Use a small carpet offcut to spread adhesive along the tape. Take care that you don't get adhesive on the front of the carpet.*

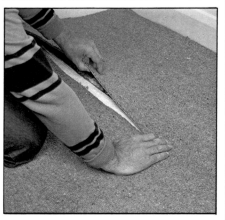

3 *You can then flap the edges back into position so they are held in place by the adhesive, and press the carpet down firmly along the seam.*

Ready Reference

STRETCHING CORRECTLY

To fit the carpet properly you should carry out the stretching and hooking in the following order:

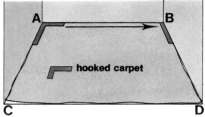

● start at corner A and hook the carpet about 300mm (12in) along walls AB and AC. Stretch from A to B and hook on about 300mm (12in) of carpet along wall BD

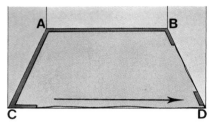

● hook the carpet along the full length of wall AB, then repeat in direction A to C. Stretch the carpet from C to D and hook it on. Stretch across the width of the carpet from wall AB as you hook onto wall CD

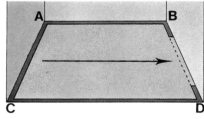

● stretch across the full length of the carpet from wall AC as you hook on the wall BD.

ADJUSTING THE KNEE KICKER

There are two sets of pins of different widths in the head of the knee kicker. The thinner pins are adjustable, so the amount they project from the head can be increased or decreased. You adjust them to suit the type of carpet, so:
● if you are laying a shag pile carpet, the thinner pins should project enough to grip the carpet backing; if they are too short they will snare the pile; if too long, they will become embedded in the underlay and will pull it out of place
● for smooth pile carpets you will need to use the thicker pins only.

LAYING CARPET ON STAIRS

Carpet provides an attractive covering for stairs, and will cut down considerably on noise levels in the home. Fitting a stair carpet is relatively straightforward providing you use the right techniques.

If you intend to fit a stair carpet you will first have to make sure that the carpet you have in mind is a suitable type. Since stairways are subjected to a lot of use, the carpet must be durable and hardwearing. The label on the carpet may help you make your choice; for example, carpets suitable for light wear only may be labelled as 'not recommended for stairs'. On the other hand, some ranges will be labelled as being specifically suited for use on stairs and others as being suitable for the whole house, including stairs. If the staircase is very heavily used and you require the carpet to last a long time, you will have to go for one of the toughest quality.

Foam-backed carpets are generally unsuitable for stairs; the cheaper light-weight ones tend not to be sufficiently durable and the heavier ones can be too inflexible to fit properly. You should also avoid carpets with a long pile which could impede movement and make the edges of the treads more difficult to locate. Again, some carpet patterns may obscure the outline of the treads or make people feel dizzy. Carpets with these kinds of patterns can be a safety risk, especially where elderly people will be using the stairs.

After you have chosen the carpet you must decide either to call in a professional to lay it or to go ahead and lay it yourself. The complexity of the job is a factor to take into account here; for example, if you want to cover a spiral staircase with a carpet fitted 'edge to edge', that is across the complete width of the stairs, it would normally be advisable to have a professional installation. A straight flight is likely to cause less problems, particularly if you intend to have a carpet runner which simply runs down the centre of the stairs and doesn't cover the complete width.

Measuring up

You will then have to work out how much carpet you'll need. The amount will be affected by the way you intend fitting the carpet; that is, edge-to-edge or as a carpet runner. If you have decided on an edge-to-edge fitting and the staircase is a regular width all the way up, you may find that this measurement coincides with one of the regular widths in which carpet is supplied. If the staircase is narrower than a regular width, you can buy the regular width, trim the carpet to size and seal the cut edge. Where the staircase is a width which is going to waste a great deal of carpet in trimming you might decide to buy broadloom carpet and cut it into strips to match the stair width.

To calculate the length of stair carpet required you should add the height of all the risers to the depth of all the treads and then add on an additional 38mm (1½in) for each step to allow for the space taken by the underlay. Where there are curved nosings at the edges of the treads you will also have to allow for these – add 50mm (2in) for each nosing. Where you are using a carpet runner you can add on an extra 500mm (20in) to the length so you can reposition the carpet later to even out wear (see *Ready Reference*).

On a curved staircase measuring up is more complicated. You will have to calculate the bends separately, taking the largest dimensions of the winder treads which go round the corners.

As well as the quantity of carpet, you will also have to work out how much underlay to order. The underlay is cut in strips, with a separate piece used for each step. Order an amount of underlay which will ensure that each strip is big enough to cover the treads and lap round the nosing so it can be secured to the riser beneath. Check with your supplier about a suitable type of underlay to use with the carpet you have chosen (remember that the better the quality the more wear and sound insulation it will give).

The preparation

As when you are fitting carpet on a floor, the stair surface must be in a suitable state; both treads and risers should be flat, smooth and dry. Check that they are in sound condition; this may involve nailing down loose treads or removing and replacing faulty treads or risers with new timber.

Unless you happen to have bought one of the few types of foam-backed carpet which are suitable for stairways you will have to fit an underlay before you go ahead and lay the carpet. And before you do this, if you are using the tackless gripper system, you will have to nail the gripper strips to the treads and risers. Fix the grippers to the back of each tread and the bottom of each riser so the pins face into the angle. The gap between the grippers on tread and riser should be

FIXING THE GRIPPER AND UNDERLAY

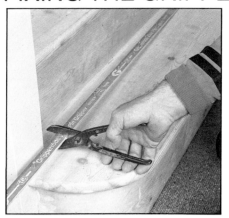

1 *Use tinsnips to cut the gripper to size; its width should match that of the tread, measured where the tread meets the riser.*

2 *Fix the gripper strips to the treads by driving in the nails with a hammer; check that the gripper's teeth are not flattened as you do this.*

3 *Fix the gripper to the risers; there should be a gap of 15 to 18mm (⁵⁄₈ to ³⁄₄in) between the gripper strips on the tread and riser.*

4 *On a landing, nail the gripper strips in place so the gully between the strip and wall is just less than the carpet thickness.*

5 *Place a strip of underlay in position on the landing and then trim it so it reaches the edges of the gripper strips.*

6 *Trim the underlay on the landing so it just reaches down to the edge of the gripper strip fixed to the first riser beneath the landing.*

7 *Use a staple gun to fix the underlay securely in place on the landing and then to fix it above the gripper strip on the riser beneath.*

8 *Work down the stairs, continuing to cut strips of underlay to size and fixing them in place between the gripper strips.*

9 *Where there is a bullnose tread at the bottom of the stairs you will have to cut the underlay so it fits the shape of the curved tread.*

equal to about twice the thickness of the carpet, to allow the carpet to be tucked down between the grippers. If you are using special right-angled stair grippers, you don't have to worry about a gap. Where you are fixing a carpet runner you should cut the gripper strips 38mm (1½in) shorter than the width of the carpet so the method of fixing won't be obvious when the carpet is finally fixed in place.

You will have to cut the underlay into strips so there is a separate piece for each step. If you are fitting a carpet runner the width of the underlay should be about 38mm (1½in) less than the width of the carpet so it won't be visible under the carpet edges. Where you are using gripper strips, each piece of underlay should just reach the edges of the gripper strips on the tread above it and the riser below it. If you are using tacks to fix the carpet, each piece of underlay can be slightly longer, but you must allow enough room (ie, stair uncovered by underlay) to drive in the tacks which secure the carpet. The underlay can be tacked down, or, to make the job go more quickly, you can use a staple gun to staple it in place. If you are using a carpet runner, you should make sure the underlay is centrally placed (measure and mark off its position before you attempt to secure it). At the same time as you mark off the position of the underlay you can mark the position of the carpet runner so it too will eventually be centrally placed. Care taken at this stage will save you spoiling the look of the stairs later.

Where you are fitting edge-to-edge carpet, treat a landing as you would a floor; that is, cover it with underlay, except that the underlay should lap down over the edge of the landing onto the first riser beneath it. Where you will be fixing the carpet with gripper strips this overlap should reach to just above the gripper strip which you have fixed in place on the top riser.

Laying the carpet
Of the various methods you can use to secure the carpet in place, stair rods provide the simplest one and the tackless gripper system the most difficult (but it also gives the most 'professional' look). Don't forget that if you are using a foam-backed carpet, you can use stair rods instead of special right-angled grippers to hold it in place. You may already have stair rods holding an old stair carpet which you want to replace: these can be removed and used again. Or you may choose to buy new ones; they come in a range of types, including simple streamlined ones and more ornate versions, so you should be able to choose a variety which gives you the look you want for your staircase. Remember that it is simple to move a carpet if you have used stair rods to secure it and that they are the easiest of the various fixing methods to

take up and re-fix. So do bear this in mind.

With the next method, tacking, you should start at the top tread. First, centre the carpet if it is a runner and allow an extra 13mm (½in) for turning under where the carpet meets the top riser. This riser will be covered by the carpet which laps down from the landing. Turn the allowance under and tack the carpet down in one corner, then stretch it so it fits smoothly across the tread and tack it down at intervals of about 100mm (4in) across the riser. Then continue down the stairs, tacking it at the edges in the angles formed by the treads and risers. Make sure it's firmly stretched over the nosings as you go. To complete the job, drive in more tacks at 100mm (4in) intervals across the risers at the angles between treads and risers and, where you have made an allowance for moving the carpet at the bottom, tack up the sides of the folded-under carpet on the bottom step.

For an invisible fixing you will have to use the tackless gripper system. You can use a bolster to stretch and fit the carpet over the gripper strips (see step-by-step photographs) and in this case you should again begin work from the top downwards. But, if you prefer, you can instead use a knee-kicker to get the tension you want, in which case you will be working from the bottom step upwards. With the roll of carpet resting further up, push the carpet into the gully on the first (bottom) step so it is tightly held. Then roll the carpet further up the stairs and, using the knee-kicker on the second tread to pull the carpet tight, push the carpet into the gully between this tread and the second riser. Continue in this way, pulling the carpet tight (but not too tight) as you go, until you reach the top of the stairs.

Left-over carpet at the top and bottom can be tucked into the top and bottom risers and tacked firmly down. Sometimes it is tucked under another carpet at the top and bottom of the stairs; sometimes it continues to meet another carpet, and at other times it is finished with a binder bar. It all depends on the existing arrangements at the top and bottom of the staircase.

On stairs with winders where you are fitting edge-to-edge carpet, you will have to cut separate pieces for each step (see *Ready Reference*). To help you get the shape right it's worth making a paper template of each winder and using this as a guide when you are cutting the carpet.

Where you have cut the carpet to width from a wider measure you will have to seal it at the edges before you lay it. Otherwise the backing will fray, tufts will work loose from the edges and the appearance of the carpet will be spoiled. To seal the edges, run strips of latex adhesive along the underside and allow it to dry before you go ahead and fit the carpet.

Ready Reference

TIP: CENTRE THE CARPET
Before you lay a carpet runner which does not completely cover the width of the treads, mark out the positions of the carpet edges to help you get the borders equal.

FIXING METHODS
There are three ways of fixing stair carpet. They are:

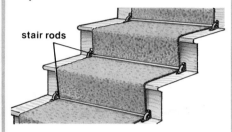

● using stair rods which are anchored with side clips; this is the simplest method and the rods form part of the stair decoration.

● tacking the carpet down with special carpet tacks

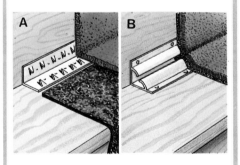

● using tackless gripper strips or right-angled metal stair grippers (A) (a pinless type is available for foam-backed carpet (B)).

TIP: CHECK PILE DIRECTION
Always make sure the pile of the carpet is facing *down* the stairs to prevent uneven shading and to ensure longer wear. If you move a carpet runner, never be tempted to reverse the pile direction.

FITTING THE CARPET

1 Cut the carpet so it fits the landing and overlaps onto the riser beneath. Stretch and fix it in place using a knee-kicker.

2 With the carpet hooked in place on the gripper at one side of the landing, use a bolster to push the overlap down into the gully.

3 On the other side of the landing, where the carpet and the balustrade meet, cut into the overlap so you can fit the carpet round the corner.

4 Fix the rest of the carpet on the landing and then use a bolster to press the carpet down onto the gripper strip on the riser beneath.

TIP

5 With the carpet loosely secured, go over it again with the bolster, this time tapping it with a hammer to fix the carpet firmly in position.

6 Trim off the overlap with a sharp knife to expose the gripper strip fixed to the tread below the riser where the carpet is secured.

7 Again use a bolster to push the carpet down onto the gripper on the tread; go over it again, tapping the bolster with a hammer.

8 Unroll the length of carpet down the stairs and press the folds securely in place onto the gripper strips with your bolster.

9 Finish a straight flight by trimming the carpet off at floor level; with a bullnose tread, cut it off below the last-but-one riser.

CARPETING A BULLNOSE TREAD

1 *If you have a bullnose tread at the foot of the flight, lay a piece of carpet across it and cut it 50mm (2in) bigger than the curve all round.*

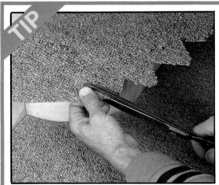

3 *Then cut up to the edge of your thumb with shears to get the correct depth of the zig-zag cut. Cut in this way right round the curve.*

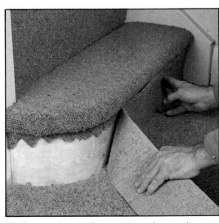

5 *Cut a piece of carpet to size so it fits along the exposed riser under the bullnose tread; then press it round the curve.*

2 *Make zig-zag cuts in the overlap where it fits round the curve. First of all press the carpet under the edge of the tread with your thumb.*

4 *Use a hammer to fix carpet tacks along and under the edge of the bottom tread to hold the carpet neatly and securely in place.*

6 *Nail the width of carpet in place at the sides of the riser and along the top; don't nail along the bottom, where tacks would be visible.*

Ready Reference

COPING WITH HALF-LANDINGS

Where the staircase changes direction at a half landing, treat it as two sets of stairs when you are laying carpet, whether you are fitting carpet edge-to-edge or using a runner.

WINDING STAIRS

Where you are laying carpet on winding stairs, you can use one of two methods to fit the carpet to the winders:

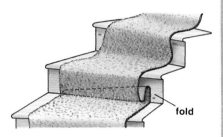

fold

● where you are fitting carpet edge-to-edge, use a separate piece of carpet for each winder. Fix additional gripper strips to the sides of the treads

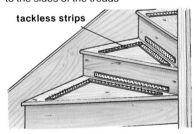

tackless strips

● where there is a carpet runner, leave the gripper strips off the risers of the winders and take up the slack with a series of folds which you can tack in place using 40mm (1½in) non-rusting tacks.

MOVING CARPET RUNNERS

You can move a carpet runner to equalise wear if you allow an extra 500mm (20in) when first laying it. Tack the carpet at the top and bottom with the extra 500mm tucked under the bottom step, to act as an underlay. Move the carpet (*before* signs of wear become obvious) as follows:
● start from the top and remove the tacks carefully so you don't damage the carpet
● gently ease the carpet off the grippers (or remove tacks or stair rods), move it and then fit it back on to them
● as you move the carpet up, insert strips of underlay on the bottom tread and riser.

LAYING VINYL FLOOR TILES

Vinyl tiles are supple, easy to handle and don't take much time to lay. They come in many colours and designs so you should have no trouble finding tiles of the type you want.

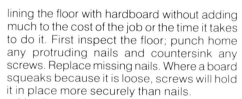

Vinyl tiles are ideal for use on kitchen and bathroom floors because they are waterproof and resistant to oil, grease and most domestic chemicals. They have the advantage over vinyl sheet flooring in that they are easier to handle, and also, if you make any mistakes when cutting, they will be confined to individual tiles. So if you have a room where you will have to carry out quite a lot of intricate cutting to make the floorcovering fit round obstacles or awkwardly shaped areas, it would be well worth considering laying tiles rather than sheet material.

The tiles come in a wide variety of patterns and colours, with a smooth gloss finish or a range of sculptured and embossed designs. They can be bought with or without a cushioned backing. Cushioned tiles are softer and warmer underfoot, but more expensive than uncushioned tiles. However, even among tiles without a cushioned backing there is a wide variation in price. The cost of a tile is usually a fair indication of its quality, so, in general, the dearer the tile the longer it will last. However you don't need to be greatly concerned about this: even the cheapest tiles can have a life of twenty years in average domestic use, and long before then you will probably wish to remove or cover up the tiles. (On average floorcoverings are changed every seven years.) So your choice of tiles will probably be based simply on the fact that you like the colour or pattern and feel it will fit in well with the rest of the decorative scheme in the room.

Preparing the surface

The floor surface on which you intend to lay vinyl tiles should be free of dust and dirt, so you should go over it first of all with a vacuum cleaner. Then check that the subfloor is in sound condition.

If it is a timber floor you will have to repair any damaged boards, and if the floor has been treated in whole or in part with stains and polishes these will stop the tile adhesive from adhering properly, and will have to be removed with a proprietary floor cleaner. There may be gaps between the boards and they could possibly be warped and curling at the edges. You can cure these faults by

lining the floor with hardboard without adding much to the cost of the job or the time it takes to do it. First inspect the floor; punch home any protruding nails and countersink any screws. Replace missing nails. Where a board squeaks because it is loose, screws will hold it in place more securely than nails.

Hardboard sheets 1220mm (4ft) square will be a manageable size for this type of work. To condition them, brush water at the rate of 1/2 litre (2/3 pint) per 1220mm (4ft) square sheet onto the reverse side of the sheets. Then leave them for 48 hours stacked flat back to back in the room where they will be laid so they will become accustomed to its conditions. When fixed they will dry out further and tighten up to present a perfectly flat subfloor.

You can begin fixing the hardboard in one corner of the room. It's not necessary to scribe it to fit irregularities at the walls; small gaps here and there at the edges of the boards will not affect the final look of the floor.

Fix the sheets in place with hardboard pins at 150mm (6in) intervals round the edges and 225mm (9in) apart across the middle of the sheets. Begin nailing in the centre of a convenient edge and work sideways and forwards so the sheet is smoothed down in place. On a floor where there are water pipes below, use pins of a length which will not come out on the underside of the floorboards.

The sheets should normally be fixed with their smooth side down so the adhesive will grip more securely; also the pin heads will be concealed in the mesh.

Nail down the first sheet and work along the wall. When you come to the end of a row of sheets, you will have to cut a sheet to fit. Don't throw the waste away; use it to start the next row so the joins between sheets will not coincide. When you come to the far side of the room you will have to cut the sheets to width. Again, don't worry about scribing them to fit the exact contours of the wall.

On a solid floor, check to see if there are any holes or cracks and whether it is truly level and smooth. Fill in holes and small cracks with a sand/cement mortar. Large cracks could indicate a structural fault and, if in doubt, you should call in an expert. To level an uneven floor, use a self-levelling compound, applying it according to the manufacturer's instructions.

When dealing with a direct-to-earth floor you will have to establish whether it is dry or not. There's no point in attempting to lay the tiles on a damp floor: you will get problems with adhesion and in time the tiles themselves will curl and lift.

One difficulty is that dampness in a floor is not always immediately apparent, especially if there is no floorcovering. (If the floor has a sheet covering you should lift up a corner of the covering and inspect beneath for any signs of damp.) A slight amount of damp can rise up through floors of quarry tiles or concrete and evaporate in a room without being noticed.

To test for damp you can heat up a plate of metal over a gas ring or blowlamp, or heat a brick in the oven for about an hour, then

LAYING SELF-ADHESIVE TILES

1 Sponge primer over the floor and leave it to dry for 24 hours. It will help the tiles to form a secure bond when they are fixed in place.

2 Snap two chalk lines which bisect at the floor's centre. Dry-lay a row of tiles along one line to find out the width of the cut border tiles.

3 Adjust the first (centre) tile if the cut tiles will be too narrow. Fix the tiles in place by peeling off the backing and pressing them down.

4 With the first row in place, continue fixing the tiles, working in sections, until all the whole tiles are laid. You can then lay the cut border tiles.

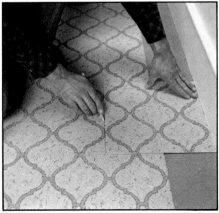

5 Place a tile over the last whole tile in a row and another one over it butted against the wall to use as a guide to mark the cutting line.

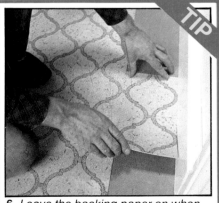

6 Leave the backing paper on when cutting the tile with a sharp knife. Remove the paper and press the cut border tile in place.

Ready Reference

TILE SIZES
Vinyl tiles are sold in packs sufficient to cover 1 square metre (1 square yard). The most common size tile is 300mm (12in) square.

FIXING TILES
Some tiles are self-adhesive; you simply pull off a backing paper, then press the tile down in place. Others require adhesive; this should be special vinyl flooring adhesive.

TIP: MAKE A TRAMMEL
A simple device called a trammel can help you find the centre of a room. Take a batten about 900mm (3ft) long and drive a pin through the batten near each end.

FINDING THE CENTRE OF THE ROOM
In an irregularly-shaped room you can find the room's centre in this way:
● strike a chalk line to form a base line, parallel to and 75mm (3in) away from the wall with the door
● place the centre of your trammel on the centre of the base line (A) and use the trammel to mark points B and C on the chalk line
● with one pin of the trammel placed in turn on points B and C, scribe two arcs, meeting at D
● strike a chalk line through points A and D to the wall opposite (this line will be truly at right angles to the base)
● find the centre of the line through A and D to give the centre point of the room (E), then draw a line across and at right angles to it using the same technique.

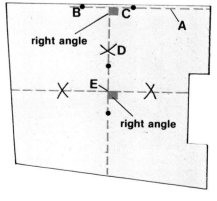

TILING AN L-SHAPE

1 At an external corner, place the tile to be cut over the last whole tile in one of the rows of tiles which adjoin at the corner.

2 Place another tile over the tile to be cut, but butted up against the skirting and use it as a guide to mark the cutting line.

3 Place the tile to be cut over the last whole tile in the other row leading to the corner. Use another tile as a guide for marking off.

4 Cut the tile along the marked lines with the backing paper on. Test if the cut tile fits, then peel off the paper and fix it in place.

TILING ROUND AN ARCHITRAVE

1 Make a template of the area round the architrave. Always test a template out: put it in place before using it on the tile to be cut.

2 When the template fits, use it to mark out the required shape on the tile. Cut the tile, remove the backing paper and press it in place.

place it on the floor. If a damp patch appears on the floor or moisture gathers underneath the metal or brick this indicates that damp is present. Another test is to place a sheet of glass on the floor, seal its edges with putty, then leave it for a couple of days. If moisture appears underneath it is again a sign of damp. These methods are, however, rather hit-and-miss and you may feel it's worth calling in an expert to give a true diagnosis.

Curing a damp floor is a major undertaking which may involve digging up the existing floor and laying a new one with proper precautions taken against damp. You should seek professional advice here.

Existing sheet floorcoverings should be removed before you start laying vinyl tiles. You can, however, lay them over existing vinyl tiles provided these are in sound condition and are securely fixed. If they are not, you will have to remove them before you fix the new tiles. To lever them up, use a paint scraper, or even a garden spade (the long handle will give you plenty of leverage).

Marking up

You should start laying tiles from the middle of the floor. To find the centre of a room which is a reasonably regular shape you should take one wall and, ignoring any bays, alcoves or projections, measure and mark its centre. Go to the wall opposite and do the same. Between these two centre points you should snap a chalked line. Snap a second chalk line from the middle of the other two walls: the point where the lines meet is the centre of the floor.

If you are going to tile an irregularly-shaped room you should strike a chalk line, to form a base line, parallel to and 75mm (3in) away from a wall which has a doorway in it. You can then strike a line at right angles to the base line and stretching to the wall on the other side. The centre of this line will be the centre point of the room; draw a line through this centre point parallel to the base line. (Instead of using a large square to help you draw the lines at true right angles, you can use what's known as a trammel; see *Ready Reference*.)

Laying the tiles

When you come to lay the tiles, the first one is all-important. There are four possible positions for it. It can go centrally on the centre point; neatly inside one of the angles where the centre lines cross; centrally on one line and butting up to the second, or centrally on the second line and butting up to the first.

You should choose the position that gives you the widest border of cut tiles round the room. Very narrow cut strips at the edges will tend to give an unbalanced look, especially if you are laying the tiles in a dual colour or chequerboard pattern. So set out the tiles dry

TILING ROUND A WC

1 Butt a paper template, which is the same size as a tile, against the base of the WC and mark off the shape of the WC on the template.

2 Cut the template to shape, then test to see if it fits exactly round the WC base and between the base and the whole laid tiles.

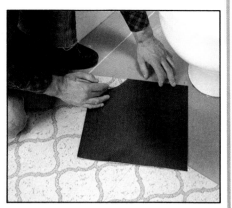

3 Place the template over a whole loose tile (check the tile is the right way round for pattern matching) and mark off the cutting line.

4 Use a sharp knife to cut the tile to shape following the marked line. You can then remove the backing paper and fix the tile.

5 Aim to get the tile position right first time. Tiles can be taken up and restuck, but will lose some of their adhesive in the process.

6 Continue to make templates and fix shaped tiles round the curved WC base. You can then fix the cut border tiles next to the walls.

(that is, not stuck down) to find out which position for the first tile gives you borders with the largest cut tiles. In a regularly-shaped room this will be quite straightforward; a couple of dry runs should make things clear. In an awkwardly shaped room, especially if it has a lot of alcoves or projections, you will have to make several of these practice runs. When you've decided on your final starting position, draw round the outline of the first tile to be placed.

When you've stuck down your first tile you can begin laying the rest. If you are laying tiles which require adhesive, you should apply this to as large an area as you can cope with in one go; possibly a square metre (square yard). Butt all the tiles accurately up against each other, and check that they are precisely aligned. Then apply firm hand (or foot) pressure to bed them firmly in place.

It's normal practice to stick down all the full

tiles, known as the 'field', leaving a border of cut tiles to be fitted round the edges.

If you are laying self-adhesive tiles, you simply peel off the backing paper and press each tile into place. Where you have to cut tiles, don't peel off the backing until the cutting-to-size is completed. Should a tile be misplaced, lift it quickly and relay it correctly; the adhesive 'grabs' quickly and later attempts to lift the tile will probably tear it.

Cutting tiles

Vinyl tiles can be quite easily cut using a sharp knife and a straightedge. For an intricate shape make a template first.

Border tiles can be marked up for cutting in the usual way; that is, you take the tile to be cut, place it on the last complete tile in the row, place another tile over the first one but jammed hard against the wall and use this tile as a guide for marking off the cutting line

on the first tile (see step-by-step photographs). The main thing wrong with this method is that it can leave a narrow border in which it is difficult to apply adhesive, with the consequent risk that the border tiles will not adhere properly.

Another method, which avoids this problem, is to lay the field except for the last full tile in each row. Then take a tile and place it against the last full tile in the field. Place another tile on top of the first one and jammed against the wall. Use this second tile as a guide to cut through the first (and it will itself become the last full tile fixed in the relevant row).

The two tiles can temporarily be placed on top of the field, adjacent to the position they will occupy, while you cut the rest of the border. When you come to stick the border tiles down you will have plenty of room in which to wield your adhesive spreader and ensure adequate coverage.

LAYING CORK TILES

Cork tiles will provide you with a floor surface which is warm, wears well and is quiet to walk on. In addition, they are the easiest of tiles to lay.

You can use cork floor tiles in bathrooms, kitchens, dining rooms and children's rooms; anywhere, in fact, where any other resilient floorcovering (eg, vinyl sheet or tiles, or thermoplastic tiles) could be used. They are warmer and quieter than most other floorcoverings and tend not to 'draw the feet', unlike, for example, ceramic tiles, which are very tiring if you have to stand round on them for long periods. They will look particularly elegant if they are softened with rugs or rush matting and blend equally well with modern or traditional style furniture and décor

Ordinary cork tiles are made from granulated cork, compressed and baked into blocks; the natural resins in the grain bond the particles together, though sometimes synthetic resins are added to improve wearing and other qualities. The tiles are cut from these blocks so they are 5mm (¼in) or more thick. 'Patterned' cork tiles (see below) are made by alternating wafer-thin cork veneers with thicker layers of insulating cork and sealing with a protective PVC surface.

Types of tiles
Cork tiles have an attractive natural look; usually they are a rich honey-gold, although there are some darker browns and smoky tones. Dyed cork tiles are available in many different colours ranging from subtle shades to strident primary colours. There are also 'patterned' tiles which have an interesting textured, rather than a heavily patterned look; these come in natural colours as well as red, soft green and rich dark smoky brown: the colour tends to 'glow' through the top surface of cork. One design gives a subtle miniature checkerboard effect. Other tiles come with designs (such as geometric patterns) imprinted on them.

For floors that are likely to get the occasional flood or where spills and 'accidents' are inevitable, such as in kitchens, bathrooms and children's rooms, it is wiser to use pre-sealed types of tiles (see *Ready Reference*). The cheaper seal-it-yourself types are, however, perfectly adequate for living rooms, bedsitting rooms and halls.

Preparing the surface
As with other types of tiles and resilient floor-coverings the subfloor surface on which you lay cork tiles must be smooth, clean and free from lumps, bumps, protruding nails, tacks or screws. Where floorboards are uneven, it's best to cover them up with flooring-grade chipboard, plywood or flooring quality hardboard, either nailed or screwed down securely. Remember to stagger the sheets of chipboard or other material to avoid continuous joins. Then, if there is any floor movement it will not disturb the tiles fixed on top and cause them to lift or be moved out of alignment.

There must also be adequate ventilation underneath a wooden subfloor. Poor ventilation can cause condensation which could lead to the rotting of the floorboards and the floorcovering above them. If the floor is laid at ground level, or directly to joists or battens on ground level concrete, you should protect the cork from moisture penetration by covering the timber with bituminous felt paper before laying hardboard or plywood. The paper should be fixed with bituminous adhesive; and you should allow a 50mm (2in) overlap at joins and edges.

Solid subfloors, such as concrete or cement and sand screeds, should be thoroughly dry. Make sure the floor incorporates an effective damp-proof membrane before laying the tiles: this can

Ready Reference

TILE SIZES
Cork floor tiles are commonly available 300mm (12in) square. There is also a 450mm (18in) square size and a 'plank-shaped' 900x150mm (36x6in) size in the more unusual colours and textures.

BASIC FINISHES
Tiles come in two basic finishes:
● pre-sealed, with a factory-applied coat of clear vinyl, forming a wear layer on top
● unsealed: you seal these tiles yourself with a transparent clear or coloured polyurethane sealer after laying.

TIP: BUY EXTRA TILES
It's always wise to buy a few extra tiles to allow for replacements in the event of damage. You may not be able to obtain tiles of the same colour or pattern later.

AVOID HEATED FLOORS
It's best not to lay cork tiles over underfloor heating systems because they could dry out, causing the seal to crack. Underfloor hot water plumbing pipes should be adequately insulated for the same reason.

ESTABLISHING THE STARTING POINT

1 *Find the centre points of two opposite walls. Stretch a string line between them, chalk it and snap a line across the floor.*

2 *Repeat the procedure, but this time between the other two walls. Where the two lines intersect is the exact centre of the floor.*

3 *Dry-lay a row of tiles along the longest line from the centre point to one wall. Adjust the other line if necessary (see Ready Reference).*

4 *Lay a row of tiles along the other line from the centre point and again adjust to avoid wastage or very narrow strips at the edges.*

be in polythene sheet form, a cold-poured bitumen solution, or a hot pitch or bitumen solution. If the subfloor is porous or flaky and tends to be very dusty, you can use a latex floor-levelling compound to cover it. This is also practical for very uneven floors. The solution is poured on, left to find its own level and then allowed to dry out before the final floorcovering is laid.

Other floors, such as quarry or ceramic tiles, can have cork laid on top, but they have to be degreased, dewaxed and keyed by rubbing them with wire wool; once again, a floor-levelling compound may be necessary. With flagstones laid directly on the ground there could be damp or condensation problems; it may be best to take up the existing floor and re-lay it, probably a job for a professional to do. Alternatively, the floor could be covered with a layer of rock asphalt at least 16mm (5/8in) thick but you will need to call in professional help for this. (Always seek expert advice if you are worried about the state of the subfloor; the expense incurred will be worth it to get successful results when you are laying the final floorcovering.)

If there is already a linoleum, vinyl sheet, tile or other resilient floorcovering on the floor, you are advised to take this up, then resurface or rescreed it if necessary; alternatively, use a floor-levelling damp-resistant latex powder mix, or an epoxy surface membrane. If it is not possible to remove the old floorcovering, you should use a proprietary floor cleaner to degrease and dewax it and then key the surface by rubbing over it with wire wool.

Planning
Measure the room, at floor level, using a steel tape or wooden measure; don't use a cloth tape as these stretch in use. If the room is irregularly shaped, divide it into rectangles and measure each one separately. If you take these measurements to your supplier, he should be able to help you calculate the quantity of tiles you will require. Or, as many tiles are sold ready-boxed with a guide to quantities printed on the box, you can study the guide to work out the number of tiles you'll need.

If you plan to buy tiles of contrasting colours, and to form a border pattern, or to lay them so you get a checkerboard effect, you should plan out the design on squared paper first. Divide up the floor area so each square represents a tile, and colour the squares in different colours to represent the different colours of the tiles so you can judge the effect. You can then calculate the quantity needed by reference to your plan.

Laying tiles
Whichever type of tile you are laying, it is best to work at room temperature, so don't switch off the central heating. Leave the tiles in the room overnight to condition them.

Make sure you have enough tiles and adhesive on the spot; you don't want to have to stop work halfway through the job and go out and buy extra. Collect together the necessary tools: measure, chalk and string, pencils and ruler or straight edge, notched trowel or spreader, sharp knife, cloth and white spirit. If you are using the seal-later type of tile you will need a sander and brush or roller plus sealer.

As with other types of tiles, cork tiles look best if they are centred on the middle of the room and any narrow or awkwardly shaped tiles come at the edges. So you'll have to establish your starting point (see *Ready Reference*) at the centre of the room. You can then begin laying whole tiles, working from the centre outwards. It's best to work on a quarter of the floor at a time; when all four quarters of whole tiles are laid, you can cut and fix the border tiles. If you are using adhesive, you may have to spread only about one square metre (1 square yard) at a time before it is ready to take the tiles. In other cases it will be best to cover a larger area with adhesive, so you don't have to wait too long to bed the tiles, increasing the length of time it will take to complete the job. Since the length of time needed before the adhesive is ready to take the tiles does vary depending on the type of adhesive, you should follow the manufacturer's instructions.

If tiles have to be cut to fit round obstacles such as door architraves, WC bases, or wash stands you can use a scribing block to mark the outline you require. Make up a paper template or use a special tracing tool (which has little needles which retract to fit the shape) if the shape is particularly complicated.

Ready Reference

MARKING OUT

For a balanced look, aim to cut your edge tiles to equal size on both sides of the room. To do this, establish the centre point of the floor, using chalked string lines (see step-by-step photographs, page 582):
● if, when you've dry-laid a row of tiles from the centre point out to the wall, a gap remains of more than half a tile-width at the wall end (A), adjust your chalked line half a tile-width off-centre (B); this will save undue wastage later when you are cutting the perimeter tiles.

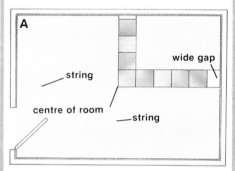

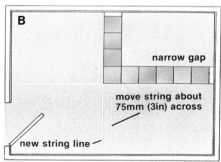

● if, however, by moving the chalked line you are left with very narrow perimeter strips (less than 75mm/3in wide) leave the centre of the floor as your starting point; there will be wastage but narrow cut perimeter tiles won't look very good and should be avoided if possible
● when marking out, avoid narrow strips at door thresholds where they will be subjected to a lot of wear
● adjust your starting point so you don't end up with narrow strips round a feature of the room, such as a chimney breast.

CHECK UNSEALED TILES

Be sure to lay unsealed tiles the right way up. They have a smooth top surface and a bottom surface which is rougher to provide a key for the adhesive. You can judge which surface is which by running your fingers over the tile.

LAYING WHOLE TILES

1 Use a notched spreader to apply adhesive to a quarter of the floor area, using the marked lines as a guide to the area to be covered.

3 Lay a row of tiles following the guidelines, treading each tile down gently but firmly to make sure it is securely bedded.

2 Place the first whole tile in the centre right angle which has been coated with adhesive. Check that it aligns with the guidelines.

4 Work across the floor until that quarter is covered with whole tiles. Then lay tiles on the other quarters of the floor area.

For some awkard shapes (eg, fitting tiles round an L-shape or in an alcove) you can mark out the pieces to be cut by placing a whole tile or tile offcut up against the skirting and the tiles which are already in place and draw the required shape on it. Cork tiles are very simple to cut: all you need is a sharp knife and a straight edge to guide it; there is no risk of breakages as there may be with other tiles which are more difficult to cut, such as ceramic types.

Sealing tiles

If your tiles are the seal-after-laying type, you will have to sand the floor carefully, using a powered sander, to ensure the surface and joins are smooth. Dust carefully; you can wipe the tiles with a slightly damp cloth to remove excess dust but take care not to saturate the tiles. Leave them to dry and then seal them, using a brush or roller to apply the sealer.

If you attach your applicator to a long handle, you can avoid bending or crawling on all fours; work from the furthermost corner, backwards to the door. Leave each coat to dry thoroughly, before applying the next one. There will always be more than one coat of sealer but the exact number will depend on the type of wear to which the floor will be subjected (see Ready Reference).

Ideally, you should leave the sealer to dry for a few days before you walk on the floor, but if you have to use the room, seal half the room at a time. Cover the unsealed part with brown paper so it can be walked on without damaging or marking the cork. When the sealed part is completely dry, you can seal the other half.

Don't wash a new cork floor for at least 48 hours after laying and sealing; ideally it should be left for at least five days. It's worth

LAYING BORDER TILES

1 To cut border tiles accurately to size, place the whole tile to be cut exactly on top of the last whole tile in a particular row.

2 Place a second tile over it, this time butting it up against the skirting. Use its edge as a guide to scribe a line on the first tile.

3 Remove the tile to be cut and make a deeper mark. The tile should then break through cleanly when gentle pressure is applied.

4 Place the cut border tile in position against the skirting. You may need to apply extra adhesive to its back to ensure secure fixing.

TILING AN L-SHAPE

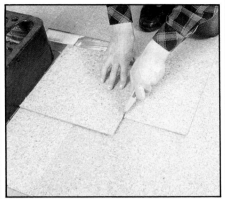

1 As when cutting other border tiles, use a tile as a guide to scribe the outline of one side of the L onto the tile to be cut.

2 Move the tile to be cut and the guide tile to the other side of the L and use the same method to scribe its outline for cutting.

3 Remove the loose tiles, cut through the back of the tile along the scribed lines and then fix the tile in position so it aligns with the whole tiles.

putting up with grubby marks for a few days rather than running the risk of moisture penetrating the flooring and reducing its useful life.

Care and maintenance

Once pre-sealed tiles are laid, or the unsealed type has been properly sealed, it will probably be unnecessary to do more than wipe over the floor with a damp mop or cloth to keep it clean. To remove grease or dirt, add a few drops of liquid detergent to the washing water; wipe over again with a cloth rinsed in clean water to remove any traces of detergent. If there are some particularly stubborn marks, made, for instance, by rubber-soled shoes, or paint or varnish spots, you should be able to remove them by rubbing gently with a little white spirit on a damp cloth.

An important point to remember when you are cleaning your cork floor is that you must take care not to overdampen the floor or the tiles may lift. Also, never use strong abrasive cleaners as these can damage the PVC wear layer.

If you like a fairly glossy surface or are worried about scratches on the floor, you can use an emulsion wax polish on top of the sealed tiles. However, never use a wax floor polish as the surface could become too slippery.

Sometimes a tile can become damaged. If the area which needs repair is small (a cigarette burn hole, for instance) you can fill it with shavings from a cork out of a bottle and reseal the tile. For more extensive damage, you should remove the tile carefully and replace it with a spare one; reseal if this tile is an unsealed type with the number of coats of sealer required to give it adequate protection.

Ready Reference

TIP: STORE TILES FLAT

If you take tiles out of their box, weight them down to keep them flat when you are storing them.

FIXING TILES

Fixing methods and adhesives vary. Some adhesives should be applied to both the back of the tiles and floor, others to the floor only; follow the manufacturer's instructions. Remember:
● pre-sealed tiles are always fixed with adhesive
● unsealed tiles are often fixed by driving in 5 headless pins, one at each corner and one in the centre, a technique which may be combined with adhesive (the pin holes can be filled, if necessary, and will then be covered up by the sealer).

REMOVE EXCESS ADHESIVE

As you lay the tiles, wipe off any adhesive from the front of the tiles with a soft cloth which has been dipped in white spirit.

CUTTING ROUND PIPES

To cut a tile so it fits round a pipe, make a cardboard template of the shape required and trace the shape onto the tile. Then cut a slit from the hole made for the pipe to the skirting board; this line will be almost invisible when the tile is fixed in place.

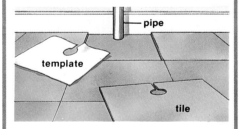

SEAL TILES PROPERLY

Cork is porous and fairly absorbent, so proper sealing is essential; if the tiles get wet, they swell and lift and have to be trimmed and re-stuck. For unsealed tiles, several coats of sealer will be necessary for real protection:
● in areas of ordinary wear, apply two or three coats of sealer
● in heavy wear areas you will need to apply 4 or 5 coats.

TRIM DOORS

To allow doors to open freely after the cork floor has been laid you may have to trim along the bottom of the door to give adequate clearance.

LAYING TILES IN AN ALCOVE

1 *Place a tile over the fixed tiles with its corner butting up against the skirting and make a mark on the 'wrong' side at the correct distance.*

2 *Repeat this procedure, this time to make a mark on the adjacent edge. Transfer the marks to the front of the tile and draw a line between them.*

3 *Cut along the drawn line to give the required shape and then place the cut tile in position so it aligns properly with the whole tiles.*

4 *Use the same techniques to cut the next tile. If there is a pipe against the wall, butt the tile up to it and mark where it's to be cut.*

5 *Cut the triangular-shaped piece required to fill the gap between the two larger shaped pieces and fix this in position so that it butts right up against the skirting.*

6 *To complete the job, cut the corner piece to shape and fix it in place. For economy, you can cut these smaller shaped pieces from any tiled offcuts which you may have available.*

LAYING SHEET VINYL

Vinyl provides a tough, easy-to-clean floor surface which is ideal in kitchens, bathrooms and other areas of the house where floors are likely to be subjected to heavy wear or spillages. It's also straightforward to lay.

Vinyl flooring was developed in the 1960s and revolutionised the smooth (and resilient) flooring market. At first it was a thin and rather unyielding material. But it was something which could be laid fairly easily by the DIY enthusiast; and this was a breakthrough because its predecessor, linoleum, had had to be professionally laid. Since then, vinyl flooring has been greatly improved and there are now several different types available.

Types of vinyl
The cheapest type of vinyl is known as a 'flexible print' and has a clear wear layer on top, with the printed pattern sandwiched between this and the backing. Then there are the cushioned vinyls, which are more bouncy underfoot and have a soft inner bubbly layer between the wear layer and the backing. They are often embossed to give them a texture, which is particularly successful when the embossing enhances the design, as with simulated cork or ceramic tile patterns. Finally, the most expensive type is solid flexible vinyl, made by suspending coloured vinyl chips in transparent vinyl to create colour and design which goes right through the material and consequently wears longer.

All three types come in a wide variety of colours and designs ranging from geometric and floral patterns to simulated cork, wood block, parquet, ceramic tiles, slate and brick. Some ranges include special glossy no-polish surfaces. Also, there is a special 'lay-flat' type which does not have to be stuck down, except on very heavy wear areas or at doorways. Some vinyls can be folded without cracking, but as with carpets, a good guide to durability is price: the more expensive the flooring, the longer-lasting it is likely to be.

Buying vinyl
To work out the amount of vinyl you'll need, measure up the floor using a metal tape; note down the measurements and then double-check them. Draw a scale plan of the room on squared paper, marking in all the obstacles, door openings and so on.

Take the measurements and plan to your supplier, who will help you to work out quantities. Remember to allow for walls which are not quite true and for trimming the overlap (see *Ready Reference*).

Whatever the type, vinyl is available in standard sheet widths (see *Ready Reference* again). Choose one in a wide width for use on a floor where you do not want to have a seam. (A wide sheet can be difficult to lay so make sure you have someone to help you – If you are going to lay sheets of a narrower width which will have to be joined, remember to allow for pattern matching when buying.

Check the manufacturer's instructions for fixing and order the correct adhesive and other sundries. Make sure you get the right amount; there is nothing worse than running out of adhesive halfway through the job.

A roll of vinyl is usually 30 to 40m (100 to 130ft) long and the retailer will cut off the length you want, re-rolling it for you. Take the roll of vinyl home and leave it, loosely rolled, in the room where it is to be laid for about 48 hours. This will allow it to become acclimatised and it should then be easier to lay. Do not stand it on edge as this can crack the material and take care not to damage the ends when you are transporting or storing the roll.

Preparing the sub-floor
Vinyl must be laid on a sound, reasonably smooth and even sub-floor if the best results

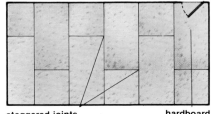

LAYING HARDBOARD SHEETS

1 Fix sheets of hardboard, rough side up, by nailing them to the old floor surface. The nails should be spaced about 100-150mm apart.

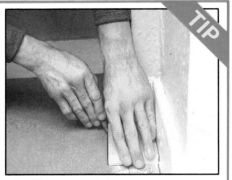

2 Where part of the wall protrudes, use a scribing block to provide a guide when marking off the contour of the wall on the hardboard.

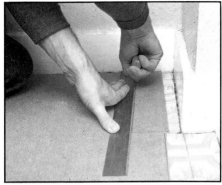

3 Cut along the line you have marked on the hardboard, using a sharp knife and a straight edge to guide the knife.

FITTING AND FIXING VINYL

1 Lay the flooring out fully across the room; with a large width such as this you will probably need help to get it roughly into position.

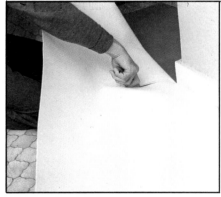

2 Make diagonal cuts at each corner, taking care not to cut too deep, to make accurate positioning much easier.

3 With the vinyl in position, use a sharp knife to trim off the excess, starting at the longest straight wall. Remember to allow an overlap.

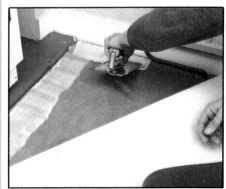

5 With the excess trimmed away from the longest straight wall and the adjacent wall, pull back the vinyl and spread adhesive on the floor.

6 Push the vinyl down onto the adhesive making sure it is firmly stuck down. Smooth out the surface as you go so there are no air bubbles.

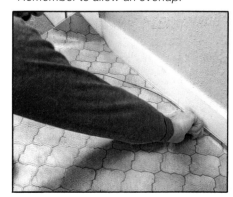

7 Trim off the overlap on the edges where the vinyl has been stuck down. Continue fitting, fixing and trimming round the rest of the room.

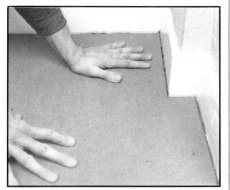

4 *After you have cut out the required shape, push the hardboard into place, making sure it butts up against the bottom edge of the skirting.*

4 *At a doorway, cut into the corners (see* Ready Reference) *and again trim off the excess, allowing for an overlap for later, final trimming.*

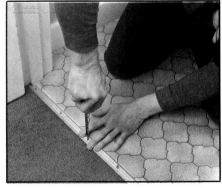

8 *At the entrance to a room, fasten down the fixed vinyl with a threshold strip to cover the join between the vinyl and the carpet.*

are to be achieved and the flooring is to give adequate wear. The floor must also be free from dirt, polish, nibs of plaster or splashes of paint, but above all it must be damp proof, so deal with this first.

In an old property with no damp-proof course (dpc), it may be necessary to install one or to have some other form of damp-proofing carried out. The floor may have to be rescreeded or old floorboards taken up and replaced. But whatever is needed must be done before laying the new flooring. A cover-up job will never be satisfactory and the new material will start to perish from the back.

Remember that screeding a floor will raise its level and so doors will almost certainly have to be taken off their hinges and trimmed at the bottom to accommodate the new floor level.

Where the existing floor covering does not provide a suitable surface for laying vinyl you will have to remove it. You can remove old vinyl by stripping it off from the backing, then soaking any remaining material in cold water, washing-up liquid and household ammonia before scraping it off with a paint scraper.

With a wooden sub-floor you should remove any protruding tacks, nails or screws, or punch them down level with the floor. Any rough or protruding boards should be planed smooth and wide gaps between boards filled with fillets of wood; small holes or gaps can be filled with plastic wood. If the floor is very bumpy it can be covered with man-made boards.

Fitting seamed lengths

Measure for the first length of vinyl along the longest unobstructed wall unless this brings a seam into the wrong position (see *Ready Reference*). After measuring you can cut the first length from the roll. Butt the edge of the vinyl right up to the skirting at one end of the room, tucking the overlap underneath the skirting if possible so you don't have to trim this edge. Then cut the material off across the width, allowing for an overlap at the other end, at doorways and obstacles.

To fit the first doorway you will have to cut slits at the door jambs and then ease the vinyl round the door recess and supports, cutting off a little at a time, until you get a perfect fit. Next, either tuck the overlap of the vinyl under the skirting which runs along the length of the room if you can, or trim along the wall or skirting, allowing for a good (but not too tight) fit. Smooth down the flooring as you work along its length and then cut the vinyl to fit at the other end.

If the wall is uneven you will have to 'scribe' its contour onto the vinyl. You pull the vinyl slightly away from the wall and then run a wooden block, in conjunction with a pencil,

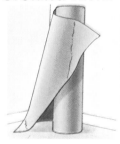
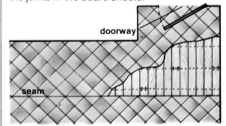

LAYING VINYL IN A RECESS

1 *With the vinyl fixed in place at the straightest edges of the room, deal with awkward areas like a recess. First trim at the corners.*

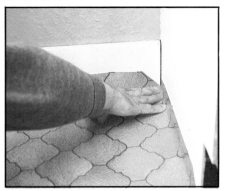

2 *Turn back the vinyl and spread a band of adhesive round the edges of the recess. You can then push the floorcovering firmly into position.*

3 *To complete the job, use a sharp knife to trim off the overlap. Again, make sure there are no bubbles by smoothing the vinyl down.*

along the wall so its profile is marked on the vinyl. To cut along this line you can use a knife and straight edge (with the straight edge on the vinyl which will be used), or if the line is very wobbly, use scissors.

With the first length fitted, you can then place the next length of vinyl parallel to the first, matching the pattern exactly, and cut off the required length, again allowing for extra overlap at the ends and sides. Some people cut all the required lengths first before fitting, but if the room is not perfectly square and several widths are being used, there could be a mismatch.

If the two sheets overlap, the excess will have to be trimmed away. Place one on top of the other, aligning the design carefully, and cut through the two sheets together at the overlap, using a knife and straight edge. Remove the trimmings and then adjust the second sheet to fit doors, skirtings and so on, trimming where necessary.

Where there are more than two sheets, repeat the fitting procedure, making sure the pattern matches.

If you are renewing the skirting, to get a perfect fit you can fit the material first and put the skirting on after the vinyl is laid. Remember, though, that this may make it difficult to take up the floorcovering when you need (or want) to change it.

Fitting extra-wide flooring
The technique is largely the same as for fitting strips of vinyl except there will not be any seams to stick, or pattern matching to do. You should start by laying the flooring out fully – you will probably need help for this – and try to find a long straight wall against which the first edge can be laid. Then make diagonal cuts at each corner to allow the flooring to be positioned roughly, with the

excess material 'climbing up' the skirting board or wall. Trim away the excess, leaving a 50 to 75mm (2 to 3in) overlap all round. Scribe the first wall, if necessary, then trim and ease the flooring back into its exact position. Deal with corners, projections, and obstacles as you work your way round the room, leaving the same overlap; finally trim to a perfect fit.

Fixing vinyl
How you fix vinyl will depend on the type; always follow the manufacturer's instructions. As vinyl can shrink it's wise to stick it down immediately before or after trimming it. To stick the edges you should first turn them back and apply a 75mm (3in) wide band of adhesive to the sub-floor, using a serrated scraper in a criss-cross motion, and then press the vinyl into position immediately. This will usually be at doorways, round the edges of the room, or round obstacles. Where heavy equipment will be pulled across the floor regularly (a washing machine for example) it is worth sticking down the entire area.

At the seams, you should make the width of the spread adhesive generous – 150 to 200mm (6 to 8in). Again, turn back the edges, apply the band of adhesive to the sub-floor and press the vinyl back into position immediately. Wipe away any adhesive which seeps through the seam or round the edges of the vinyl immediately, as this can discolour the flooring if it hardens.

At the entrance to rooms, particularly in heavy traffic areas, or if you have used the 'lay-flat' type of vinyl, you can fasten down the vinyl with a ready-made threshold strip These come in metal, wood or plastic and are also used to cover joins between two different materials, such as vinyl and carpet.

Cleaning and maintenance
Once you have laid your floor you will need to look after it. Always wipe up any spills immediately, particularly hot fat and grease. It is also wise to protect the surface from indentation by putting heavy pieces of furniture on a piece of hardboard, or standing legs and castors in castor cups.

Some of the more expensive vinyls have a built-in gloss, so they do not need polishing. This type can be mopped with a damp cloth.

Never use a harsh abrasive cleaner on any type of vinyl floor as this could damage the surface layer. The glossy surface should not wear away, but if it does become dull in heavy traffic areas, it can be recoated with a special paint-on liquid provided by the manufacturer.

The less glossy vinyls will need regular sweeping or vacuuming and mopping. It also makes sense to use a clear acrylic polish, applied very sparingly according to the manufacturer's instructions and then buffed gently. Wash occasionally with warm water and a mild liquid detergent, and don't apply lots of coats of polish, or you will get a thick discoloured build-up, which spoils the look of the floor; 2-4 coats over a 12-month period is plenty. Always let the floor dry thoroughly before walking on it, after it has been washed or polished.

Once several coats of polish have built up, you will have to strip off the polish and start again. To do this, add a cupful of household ammonia to a bucket of cold water, to which a little washing-up liquid has been added. Scrub the floor with this, taking care not to saturate it too much. When the old surface begins to break down, wipe it with an old soft cloth, rinse thoroughly with warm, clean water and dry before applying a new protective coating.

CUTTING ROUND OBSTACLES

The best way to get a neat floor when fitting vinyl round obstacles such as bathroom fittings is to make a template of paper or cardboard which is slightly larger (by about 25mm/1in) than the obstacle. Place one sheet of paper up against the basin pedestal, WC base or whatever, and tear it round so you have half the obstacle's shape on it. Then repeat the procedure with another sheet of paper for the other half.

Fit the template round the obstacle and use a scribing block and pencil to give the exact profile. Then lay the pattern over the flooring and use the block and pencil to reverse the procedure and transfer the exact outline onto the vinyl by running it round the inside of the line. You can then cut and fit; you will have to make a slit in the edge of the vinyl in some cases to get a snug fit at the skirting. Carefully trim away any excess material round the obstacle once the flooring is placed in position. Fix the vinyl according to the manufacturers' instructions.

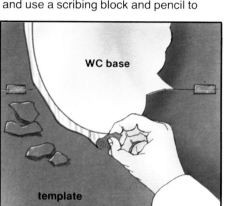

Making a template

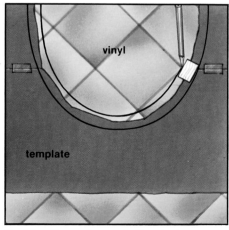

Scribing the contour onto the vinyl

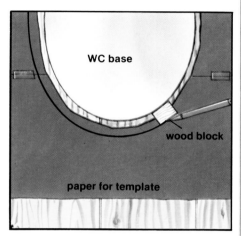

Scribing the contour onto the template

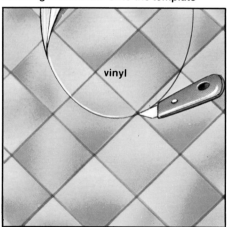

Cutting the vinyl

Ready Reference

FITTING CORNERS
To fit vinyl:
● at internal corners, gently push the vinyl into the corner and cut away the excess, diagonally across the corner, until it fits. Cut a little at a time and pare the edge carefully
● at external corners, press the vinyl into the corner, pull up the excess and cut to allow the vinyl to fall into place round the corner; then trim the excess.

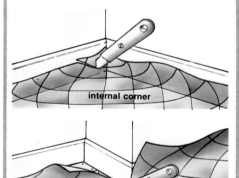

FIXING METHODS
Sheet vinyl can be fixed either by sticking it down all over or only at the edges and seams. Check the manufacturer's instructions.

'Lay-flat' vinyls do not have to be stuck down but they must be firmly fixed at doorways by glueing, or another method. Double-sided tape may be used to secure seams.

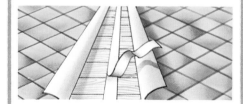

TIP: SMOOTH OUT BUMPS
If there are any bumps in the vinyl after you have laid it fill a pillowcase with sand and drag this round the floor to iron them out.

TIP: HIDING GAPS
If you have an unsightly gap between the skirting and the floor, because the walls are very uneven or your vinyl has shrunk, you can pin painted quadrant beading to the skirting round the room to hide the gap.

If you wipe up spills at once you should not get any stains on vinyl flooring, but sometimes they become marked from tar or grit trodden into the house; some types of shoe can leave black scuff marks, and cigarette burns are not unknown.

If normal cleaning doesn't remove marks rub them very gently with a very fine grade wire wool, used dry. Take care not to rub too much of the surface layer away. Wipe with a damp cloth, and reseal/polish the area if necessary. Some grease marks can be removed with white vinegar, others with petrol or lighter fuel. Always, however, wipe the area immediately with clean water.

Any badly discoloured or damaged area may have to be patched, so save any offcuts of sufficient size for this purpose.

LAYING CERAMIC FLOOR TILES

You can lay ceramic tiles to provide a floor surface which is particularly resistant to wear and tear. If you follow a few basic rules you shouldn't find it too difficult a task and you could at the same time turn the floor into a decorative feature.

Ceramic floor tiles provide a floor-covering which is attractive, extremely hard-wearing and easy to maintain and keep clean. The wide variety of tiles available means you should easily find a pattern which suits your colour scheme.

Floor tiles are usually thicker than ceramic wall tiles (they are generally at least 9mm/3⁄8in thick), very much stronger and have a tough hardwearing surface to withstand knocks as well as wear from the passage of feet.

The backs of the tiles have a brownish appearance caused by the extra firing – done at a higher temperature than for wall tiles, which are often almost white on the back.

Types of tiles

Square tiles are commonest, in sizes from 150 x 150mm (6 x 6in) to 250 x 250mm (10 x 10in). Besides square tiles you can choose oblong ones in several sizes, hexagons or other interlocking shapes. Surfaces are usually glazed but are seldom as shiny as those of wall tiles or scratch marks would inevitably become apparent as grit was trampled in. So most floor tiles are semi-glazed; others have a matt, or unglazed finish.

Patterned ceramic tiles are quite frequently designed in such a way that several tiles can be laid next to one another to complete a larger design. The commonest is built up by laying four identical tiles in a square, each tile being turned at 90° to its neighbours. The full impact will only be achieved if a sufficiently large area of floor is being tiled.

Patterned and plain tiles can also success-fully be intermixed to create unusual designs, but it is essential that the tiles are all supplied by the same manufacturer, and ideally come from compatible ranges, to ensure uniformity of thickness and size.

Some manufacturers supply floor tiles designed to co-ordinate with wall tiles, and in addition make matching panels to act as skirtings between wall and floor tiles.

Types of adhesives

There are several types of adhesives for laying floor tiles. Some come ready-mixed, others in powder form to be mixed with water. A number are waterproof and where the floor will be subjected to frequent soakings (as, for example, in a shower cubicle) or heavy con-densation you will need to use one which is water-resistant. Usually the adhesive does not become waterproof until it has set completely, which means that you can clean tools with water and do not require a special cleaner.

On a solid floor with underfloor heating you should use an adhesive which is also heat-resistant or the adhesive will fail and the tiles will lift necessitating continual re-fixing.

A cement-based floor tile adhesive is suit-able for use on good, level concrete whereas a suspended wooden sub-floor will need an adhesive with some degree of flexibility built in. Combined cement/rubber adhesives are available for this purpose but even these should not be used on suspended wooden floors which are subject to a lot of movement – you will have to add a covering of man-made boards to provide a more stable surface before fixing the tiles.

Manufacturers' instructions give guidance as to the type of adhesive suited to a particular situation and you should study these carefully before making your choice. You should also follow their recommendations as to the thickness of adhesive bed required; most resin-based ready-mixed adhesives are used as thin beds (3 to 6mm/1⁄8 to 1⁄4in), while cement-based powder adhesives may be laid up to 12mm (1⁄2in) thick. Usually a spreader is supplied with the adhesive to make applying it a straightforward job.

Planning

As when tiling a wall, it is well worth planning your layout on paper first, particularly if you intend using a complicated design. For rec-tangular or square tiles make a scale drawing on graph paper; for hexagons or other specially-shaped tiles, draw the shapes to scale on tracing paper, to act as an overlay to a scale floor plan of the room. From your scale drawings you can see if the layout you have in mind is going to work. It will help you set out an attractive design and it will also enable you to work out the number of tiles you will require.

Mark on your plan the position of fixtures such as a WC, wash or sink stand, cupboards or pipes to indicate where cutting will be required – where necessary adjust your plan so you will not have to cut pieces which are too narrow for convenient cutting.

Similarly, your layout should be designed so you avoid having to cut narrow pieces of tile to

MARKING UP

1 *Choose the corner at which you wish to start tiling, and use a tiling gauge to find out how many whole tiles will fit alongside one wall.*

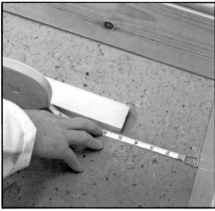

2 *Measure the gap left and halve it to give the width of the cut pieces for each end. Allow one less whole tile in the row to avoid very narrow cut pieces.*

3 *Measure in the width of one cut piece, plus grouting gaps, from the adjacent wall. Mark a line to show where one edge of the first whole tile will be placed.*

4 *Repeat the measuring process along the adjacent wall to establish the position of the other edge of the first whole tile. Mark this line on the floor too.*

5 *Lay a batten on the line drawn in **4** and nail it to the floor alongside the first wall to act as a guide for laying the first complete row of tiles.*

6 *Pin a second batten alongside the other wall, its edge on the line drawn in **3**, and check that the two battens are at right angles to each other.*

Ready Reference

THE RIGHT TILES
Always check that the tiles you buy are suitable for use on floors.
● floor tiles are usually 6mm (¼in) or more thick and have brown backs
● some are flat-backed, others have projecting studs.

TILE SHAPES
Most floor tiles are square or oblong. Common sizes, and the number of each needed to cover 1 sq metre (11 sq ft), are:
● 150 x 150mm (6 x 6in)　：44
● 200 x 200mm (8 x 8in)　：25
● 250 x 250mm (10 x 10in)：16
● 300 x 200mm (12 x 8in)　：17
Hexagons usually measure 150mm (6in) between opposite edges. You need 50 per sq m (11 sq ft).

ADHESIVES AND GROUT
● use a *thin-bed* (3mm/⅛in) adhesive for *flat-backed tiles* – you'll need about 3.5kg (8lb) per sq metre (11 sq ft)
● use a *thick-bed* (6-12mm/¼-½in) adhesive for *tiles with studs* or if the floor is uneven – you'll need double the above quantities
● allow 1.2kg (2½lb) of *grout* per sq metre (11 sq ft) for joints 6mm (¼in) wide.

TILING SPACING
● space tiles that build up to form a larger pattern about 2mm apart. With plain tiles a wider gap looks better. Use a tile on edge as a spacer

● dry-lay a row of tiles along each wall to see how wide an edge piece you will need at each end of the row.

● avoid having to cut thin edge pieces by laying one whole tile less in each row.

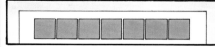

TILE GAUGE TO MAKE
Use a straight 1830mm (6ft) long timber batten and mark its length with tile width and grouting space.

TIP: BUYING TILES
Add on a few extra tiles to allow for breakages during laying and replacements in the future.

LAYING TILES

1 *In the corner framed by the two battens, spread enough tiling adhesive with a notched spreader to cover an area of about 1 sq m (10 sq ft).*

2 *Lay the first tile in position in the angle between the two battens, pushing it tightly up against them, and bed it into place with firm hand pressure.*

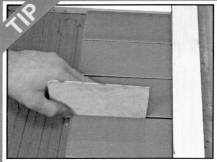

3 *Continue laying tiles along the first row, butting them against the batten to keep the edge straight. Use a cardboard spacer to create even gaps.*

4 *Lay tiles until you have reached the edge of the adhesive, using the spacer as before. Carry on area by area until all whole tiles are laid.*

fit around the perimeter of the room. Floor tiles, being so much tougher, are less easy to cut than wall tiles and attempting to obtain narrow strips is likely to cost you several broken tiles.

Where you are not using a complicated design you can plan your layout directly on the floor. For this you will need a tiling gauge (see *Ready Reference*).

Preparing the floor surface

Surfaces to be tiled should be dry, flat, stable, clean and free from grease, dirt and unsound material. A flat, dry, level concrete floor can be tiled without special preparation. If, however, there are small depressions in the concrete these should be filled with a mortar mix of 3 parts sharp sand and 1 part cement. A more uneven floor should be screeded with a proprietary brand of self-levelling flooring compound.

The screed should be left for two weeks to allow it to dry thoroughly before fixing tiles. If the floor is a new concrete one, it should be left for a minimum of four weeks to allow all moisture to disperse before you begin covering it with tiles.

Existing ceramic floor tiles, quarry tiles or terrazzo surfaces can be tiled over. They should be checked to ensure that there are no loose or hollow-sounding areas. Any defective sections must be made good before you lay new tiles on top.

You can tile on suspended wooden floors, but it is important that the floor should be made as rigid and firm as possible. To achieve this, cover the floorboards with a layer of water-resistant resin-bonded plywood at least 12mm (½in) thick. Alternatively, you can use chipboard of the same thickness.

Before laying tiles over timber floors cover the surface thoroughly with a priming coat – either a special priming agent from the adhesive manufacturer, or else diluted PVA building adhesive.

Finding the starting point

The first whole tile you lay will determine where all the other tiles are laid, so it is important that you get this positioning correct. Choose the corner in which you wish to start tiling and, laying your tile gauge parallel to one of the walls, measure how

many whole tiles will fit along that side of the room. There will almost certainly be a gap left over. Measure this gap, and divide the answer by two to find the width of the cut tiles that will fill the gap at each end of the row. (These should be of equal size.)

If these cut tiles turn out to be less than one quarter of a tile-width across (and therefore tricky to cut), reduce the number of whole tiles in the row by one. The effect of this is to increase the width of each cut tile by half a tile – much easier to cut.

Return to the corner and with your tile gauge parallel to the wall along which you have been measuring, move it so the end of the gauge is the width of one cut tile away from the adjacent wall. Mark this position off on the floor – it indicates where one edge of the first whole tile in that row will fall.

Repeat this same measuring process along the adjacent wall to establish the positioning of the row at right angles to the one you've just set out; you will then be able to mark off where the other edge of this same first tile will fall, and so fix its position precisely. Once that is done, every other tile's position is fixed right across the floor.

You can then place this first tile in position. Mark off and cut the boundary tiles between it and the corner. Remember to allow for the width of the grouting gap when measuring each cut tile.

Each cut tile should be measured individually because the wall may not be perfectly straight. You may then go ahead with laying whole tiles, starting from your original corner.

Laying tiles

In the corner area spread adhesive evenly on the floor over an area of about 1 sq m (11 sq ft) – it is important to work on only a small area at a time, otherwise the adhesive may have begun to dry out by the time you reach it. With a gentle, twisting motion, place the first tile in the corner, and use light hand pressure to bed it firmly in the adhesive. Place the second tile alongside the first, using the same gentle pressure, and placing spacers of cardboard or hardboard between the tiles if they don't have spacer lugs. Continue laying tiles, building up a rectangular area, until you have reached the edge of the adhesive bed.

Use a spirit level to check that the tiles are level; if any are too low, lever them off the bed as quickly as possible with a wide-bladed trowel, add adhesive and re-set them, pressing them down gently.

With the first square metre of tiles laid, you can spread another layer of adhesive over a further area, and lay the next area of tiles.

As you lay the tiles, it is worth checking every now and again that adequate contact with the adhesive is being made and that there are no voids beneath the tiles – any gaps or

FITTING BORDER TILES

1 Mark the width of each border tile in turn, using the spacer to allow for the necessary grouting gap. Kneel on a board so you don't disturb the whole tiles.

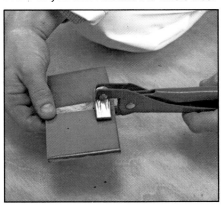

3 Use a tile breaker with V-shaped jaws to break the tile along the scored line. Floor tiles are usually too thick to break over a straight-edge.

5 Finally mark and cut the piece of tile to fit in the corner of the room, lay it and leave the newly-tiled floor for 24 hours to allow the adhesive to set.

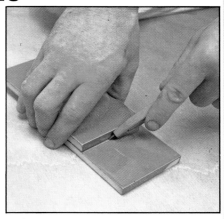

2 Score across the tile surface at the mark with a tile cutter. Press firmly so its tip cuts the glaze cleanly; scoring again may cause a ragged edge.

4 Butter adhesive onto the back of the cut piece, and press it into position. Use the spacer to form an even grouting gap at either side of the cut piece.

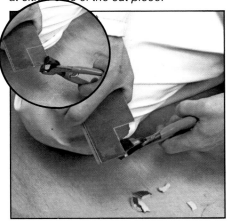

6 To cut an L-shaped piece of tile, score the surface carefully and nibble away the waste with tile pincers. Work from the corner (inset) in to the score lines.

Ready Reference

TIP: CUTTING FLOOR TILES

Because of the high-baked clay back, floor tiles can be hard to snap by hand. Save time and breakages by buying a tile cutter with angled jaws, or hire a special floor tile cutter from a tool hire shop.

TIP: ALLOW 48 HOURS SETTING

● don't walk on the floor for at least 48 hours after tiling
● where access is essential, lay plywood or chipboard sheets over the tiles to spread the load
● avoid washing the floor until the grout and adhesive have set completely (1 to 2 weeks).

DON'T FORGET DOORS

Tiling will raise the floor level. Remove inward-opening doors from their hinges before starting tiling or they will not open when tiling reaches the doorway.

● measure the depth of tile plus adhesive laid
● plane the door bottom down by this amount
● fit a sloping hardwood strip across the door threshold

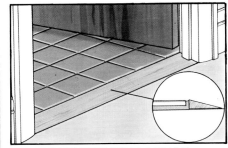

TIP: TILES FOR WET AREAS

Unglazed tiles are less slippery than glazed but ones with a textured surface reduce the chance of accidents in bath and shower rooms.

GROUTING TILES

1 *When the adhesive has set, you can grout the joints. Use a sponge or a rubber squeegee to force the grout into all the gaps.*

2 *Wipe off the excess grout as you work with a damp sponge; if you allow it to set hard it will be very difficult to remove later.*

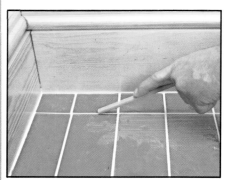

3 *Use a piece of thin dowel with a rounded end to smooth off the joints. Don't be tempted to use a finger as grout could irritate your skin.*

4 *Leave the grout to set for the recommended time, and then polish the surface all over with a clean, dry cloth to remove the last traces of grout.*

PREPARING FLOOR

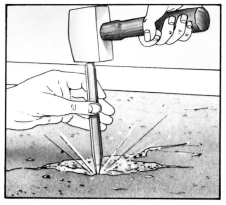

Clean out the small depressions and cracks to be filled with a club hammer and chisel. Beware of flying chippings.

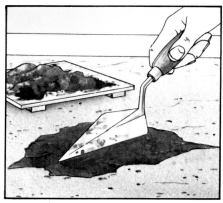

Use a trowel to fill in the depressions with mortar and to level off to provide a suitable surface for the tiles.

hollows under the tiles will become weak points later on.

You can proceed with the tiling in 1 sq m sections until all the tiles are , in place, then leave them for at least 24 hours. The tiles must not be walked on during this time so that any risk of them being knocked out of place or bedded too deeply is avoided. If you have to walk on the tiles, lay a sheet of plywood or chipboard over them first to spread the load. When 24 hours – or longer; check the manufacturer's instructions – are up, you can remove the spacers. Check with the adhesive manufacturer's instructions to see whether you need to allow extra time after this before you begin grouting.

Cutting tiles

You will have to cut each tile individually since you will almost certainly find variations around the room. Place the tile which is going to be cut against the wall and on top of the adjacent whole tile. Mark it off for cutting.

Using a straight edge as a guide, score the tile surface and edges with a scribing tool. You *can* use a hand tile cutter to cut and break the

tile along the scoreline; but its probably worthwhile hiring a special floor tile cutter to make the job easier.

To cut a tile to give an L-shape you will need to use tile nips to nibble away at the waste area. You can use a tile file, carborundum stone or coarse glasspaper to smooth off the rough edge. For curved shapes (eg, to fit round a WC pedestal), you will need to make a template and again use tile nips to nibble away at the tile.

Grouting the tiles

Mix the grout according to the manufacturer's instructions; make up only a small amount at a time and, as with adhesive, work in areas of 1 sq metre (11 sq ft). Apply it with the straight edge of a rubber float, or a sponge or squeegee, making sure the joints are properly filled. Pack the grout firmly into the joints and smooth off using a small rounded stick – don't try using a finger as the grout is likely to irritate your skin.

It's best to remove excess grout (and adhesive) as soon as possible. If it sets it will be difficult to remove.

Filling cracks and hollows

If you have a concrete floor which is flat, dry and level you can go ahead and lay tiles without further preparation. Often, however, the floor is not level or there are cracks and small hollows on the surface. Indentations should be filled with mortar (a 3:1 sand:cement mix is suitable) mixed to a creamy but not too runny consistency. For mortar with a good bond add some PVA bonding solution to the mix. Cut back the holes to a clean shape and brush out any loose material so it doesn't mix in with the mortar making it difficult to get a smooth surface. You can also coat the holes with a PVA bonding solution to help the mortar adhere.

SURFACES FOR TILING

1

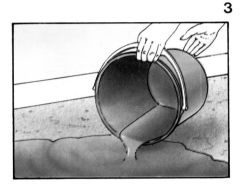

2

Levelling a concrete floor

A concrete floor which is out of true can be levelled using a self-levelling flooring compound so it is suitable for tiling. For the compound to form a smooth, even surface it should only be applied to a floor which is clean and free from dust, oil, grit or grease so you should first sweep the floor and then scrub it thoroughly (1). You may find you have to use a proprietary cleaner to remove stubborn greasy patches. The compound comes in powder form and you will have to mix it up according to the manufacturer's instructions so it forms a runny paste (2).

If you try covering the entire floor in one operation, it's likely the compound will set into large pools which are difficult to join up. It's better to work in small areas; you can delineate your working area by forming a bay using timber battens. Pour the compound onto the floor (3) and then spread it out as evenly as possible using a steel float (4), any marks from the float will disappear quickly. The compound will set within a couple of hours. If you want extra thickness you can apply a second coat once the first is hard.

3

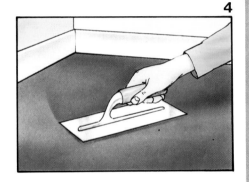

4

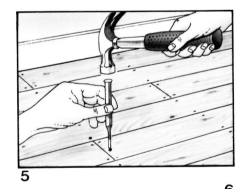

5

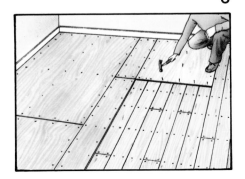

6

Laying plywood over a timber floor

A floor which is subject to movement will disrupt tiles laid over it so if you intend tiling over a suspended wooden floor you will first have to make the surface as firm as possible by covering it with a layer of man-made boards. Water-resistant resin-bonded plywood is a suitable material as it will resist penetration by the damp adhesive you will be spreading over it and you will avoid the problem of rotting boards. The boards should be at least 12mm (1/2in) thick. To prepare the floor to take the plywood you should punch any protruding nails below the surface (5) at the same time checking that the floorboards are firmly secured. You can then go ahead and fix the sheets of plywood to the floor (6) using nails spaced at 225mm (9in) intervals across the middle of the sheets and at 150mm (6in) intervals round their perimeter. You will have to cut the boards to shape round any recess or alcove (7), and where there is a pipe run, fix narrow strips of plywood over the pipes to make access to them easier. Make sure you stagger the joints; this will prevent any floor movement causing the tiles to break up in a run across the floor.

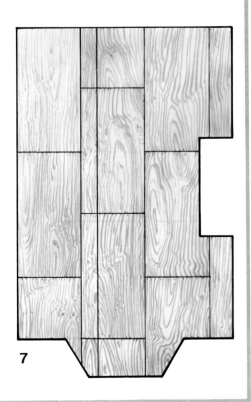

7

LAYING QUARRY TILES

Quarry tiles will provide a highly attractive natural-looking floor surface in kitchens, bathrooms, hallways and other areas which receive hard wear. They can also be used outdoors – as a patio surface, for example.

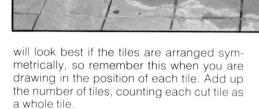

Glazed ceramic floor tiles are ideal as a floorcovering in kitchens, bathrooms, utility areas and WCs, but, whether plain or patterned, they are also expensive. This is where unglazed ceramic tiles, commonly known as quarry tiles, compare well. Like glazed tiles, quarry tiles are hardwearing and easy to clean but they are cheaper and, if you want really good value for money, they're well worth considering. They come in subtle shades of brown, red or yellow and will fit in with almost any décor, whether modern or traditional.

Buying quarry tiles
You'll first have to decide on the type of tiles you want (see *Ready Reference*) and their size. Where thickness is concerned, it's worth asking your supplier for advice. Obviously, the thicker the tile, the more hardwearing it is likely to be, but, in practice, few domestic situations warrant anything more than the thinnest of the range. There's also the question of shape: in addition to ordinary square-edged tiles, you'll find RE and REX tiles – with one and two rounded edges respectively – for use on steps (none of these, by the way, has spacer lugs). And, to complete the job, most manufacturers offer a range of skirting tiles, including those for straight runs, internal and external corners, plus stop ends. You can use these in place of timber skirtings and they are ideal in situations where water is likely to be splashed around, providing protection against moisture penetration.

Measuring up
For a rough estimate of how many tiles you need, measure the length and width of the area to be tiled using the size of a whole tile plus the width of a joint as your unit of measurement. Round each dimension up to the next whole number then multiply the two together to find the number of tiles required to cover the whole floor area.

If the area you're going to tile is an awkward shape, perhaps because of sanitary fittings, built-in units and so on, it's better to work out the number of tiles you need accurately with the aid of a floor plan drawn to scale on graph paper, so long as it's not too large. The floor

will look best if the tiles are arranged symmetrically, so remember this when you are drawing in the position of each tile. Add up the number of tiles, counting each cut tile as a whole tile.

Preparing the surface
Your aim should be to provide a surface which is sound, stable and free from anything likely to stop the tiles sticking, such as dirt, grease, dust, polish and moisture.

With bare concrete you will usually only need to give it a thorough clean, though if the surface is at all powdery you will also have to treat it with a stabilising solution. You may need to give highly polished concrete additional attention, depending on the type of adhesive you intend using. With some adhesives you have to roughen the surface to provide a key. This is not an easy task and you may decide that it's worth looking for an alternative fixing product.

Suspended timber floors require rather more preparation. You should begin by checking that the floor shows no sign of movement when walked on, as any problem of this kind will be increased by the weight of the tiled surface. Loose boards should be refixed with screws and, while you're about it, you should punch all nail heads well below the surface. Overall 'springing' of the floorboards caused by sagging joists presents rather more of a problem for the simple reason that the cure involves virtually rebuilding the floor. In this case it may be better to give up the idea of tiling the floor.

Assuming the floor is sound, the next step is to ensure that the underfloor space is adequately ventilated: in other words that there are sufficient airbricks. You can then level off the surface of the floor with a covering of exterior-grade plywood sheets (see *Ready Reference*). If you intend using adhesive to fix the tiles, check with the manufacturer's instructions to see whether the plywood has to be treated with a special primer before you apply the adhesive.

If you can do so without too much trouble, you should lift existing vinyl sheet or tile floorcoverings and treat the floor surface beneath as already described. You can generally afford to leave existing floor tiles in place. Remove any damaged sections, together with those which have come loose, then fill in any deep depressions that result with mortar. The tiling adhesive should be able to accommodate minor lumps and bumps in the floor. Finish by thoroughly cleaning the floor, making sure you remove all trace of dirt, grease and polish. (Certain tiling adhesives are unsuitable for use over plastic floorcoverings so remember to check for this with the adhesive manufacturer's instructions.)

Depending on the thickness of the floorcovering formed by the tiles plus adhesive or mortar, you may have to remove and refix the skirting boards. If you do remove them, you will have to make good the wall where they were fixed in place, whether you intend to replace them with skirting tiles or to replace the original skirtings when the tiling is finished.

LAYING THE TILES

1 Establish a starting point for the first whole tile and temporarily nail the guide battens in place. Check they are square using a set-square.

2 Use a tiling gauge to work out the position of a third batten, four tiles in from one fixed batten, and temporarily nail it in position.

3 With a spirit level check that the battens are level. If they are not you will have to pack them up (see Ready Reference).

4 Use a trowel to spread a layer of mortar in the bay formed by the battens; aim to get the mortar coverage as even as possible.

5 Draw a notched dragging board over the battens so the mortar is smoothed down to the correct distance below the battens.

6 Using your tiling gauge as a guide, bed the tiles by hand, making sure you leave the correct grouting gap between them.

7 When you've bedded 16 tiles by hand you can go over them again with a block of wood, tamping them down into the mortar bed. Check they're evenly laid with a spirit level.

8 With the first 16 tiles in place, remove the third batten and fix it in place so it forms another bay for fixing the next area of tiles. Fix all the whole tiles in this way.

9 When a section of tiles is laid securely, you can cut tiles for the border areas and fix these in place. Make sure you don't disturb the whole tiles when you are doing this.

CUTTING TILES

1 *Score deeply along the cutting line with a tile cutter. If the tile has ribs on the underside, score in the same direction as the ribs.*

2 *To help the tile break cleanly, hold it carefully and use a pin hammer to tap the tile sharply on its underside just beneath the scored line.*

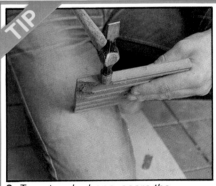

3 *To cut an L-shape, score the shape onto the tile and then tap away at the back of the waste with a hammer so it's thinner and easier to remove.*

4 *Use tile nips or pincers to nibble away at the waste, taking out small pieces at a time so you don't risk breaking the tile.*

Laying the tiles

Whether you are going to lay the tiles on a mortar bed or adhesive you will first need to mark up a tiling gauge. You can make up a gauge rod from a 50x25mm (2x1in) timber batten. Lay a row of tiles on the floor, spacing them the correct distance apart, and then transfer the tile positions on to each batten with a pen or pencil.

It's best to begin tiling next to a long, straight wall, preferably the wall furthest from the door. As when laying glazed floor tiles you will have to establish a right-angled starting point for the first whole tile (see Laying ceramic floor tiles). Temporarily nail timber battens in place to indicate the starting point and to serve as a guide for the rest of the tiling. Where you are laying the tiles on mortar and the mortar is simply used as an adhesive, the battens' thickness should equal twice the thickness of the tiles; where

the mortar is to double as a screed their thickness should equal the thickness of the screed (usually 50mm/2in) plus the thickness of a tile.

Then, if you are tiling on mortar, use the gauge rod to work out the position of another batten four tiles in from one of the battens already in place, and temporarily nail this batten in position. You now have a 'bay' formed by the three battens and it is within such bays that you work across the floor, spreading the mortar and bedding the tiles area by area.

If you are using adhesive, once you have fixed battens to indicate your starting point and to serve as guidelines for the rest of the tiling, you can begin to apply the adhesive, spreading on enough to cover about 1sq m (1sq yd) of floor area at a time. If you are laying the tiles on a 3mm (⅛in) thick bed of adhesive you simply pour some adhesive onto the floor, spread it out as evenly as possible to the required thickness with a trowel or steel float

Ready Reference

TILE TYPES

There are two types of quarry tiles produced by different methods of manufacture:
● those which are smooth and uniform in size, like ordinary ceramic tiles
● those which are rougher in texture; tiles sold as the same size and shade may in fact vary slightly from each other, particularly in terms of thickness and also in colour. This type may be vitrified or only partly vitrified, with the former being slightly harder and more impervious.

TILE SIZES

Quarry tiles for floors range in size between 75 and 150mm (3 and 6in) square with thicknesses ranging from 12 to 30mm (½ to 1¼in).

TIP: ALLOW FOR BREAKAGES

After counting up how many tiles you will need, be on the safe side and remember to add an extra 5 to 10 per cent to allow for any breakages when you are cutting and laying the tiles.

TIP: LET CONCRETE CURE

If you intend laying quarry tiles on a new concrete floor, wait at least 30 days after the new concrete has been laid before you go ahead and fix the tiles over the new concrete surface.

LEVELLING A TIMBER FLOOR

To provide a level surface on a timber sub-floor lay sheets of exterior-grade plywood. When fixing them remember to:
● stagger the joints between the sheets so any floor movement won't cause the sheets to move in a continuous line and break up the floorcovering
● use galvanised screws rather than nails to secure the sheets, driving them in at roughly 300mm (1ft) centres across the face of each sheet and roughly 230mm (9½in) apart round the edges (with nails, you run the risk of them pulling out if the plywood warps)
● take special care there is no change in level across the joins between sheets; if need be, reduce the spacing of the screws round the edges to 150mm (6in) or even 100mm (4in) to prevent this.

TIP: KEEP LAYOUT SIMPLE

Quarry tiles for floors are difficult to cut so it's best to avoid the need for awkwardly shaped or very narrow cut tiles. If you are using tiles which vary slightly in size you will not be able to work with 100 per cent accuracy, so ensure that small errors don't lead to big problems by going for the simplest layout you can.

TILING A SKIRTING

1 When the skirting board has been removed you can proceed to butter the back of the skirting tiles with mortar; aim for an even coverage.

2 Press the skirting tiles carefully into place, leaving a grouting gap between them and making sure they align with the tiles on the floor.

3 Where necessary, you will have to fill in the gap between the skirting tiles and the rest of the tiles with narrow pieces of cut tile.

TILING A STEP

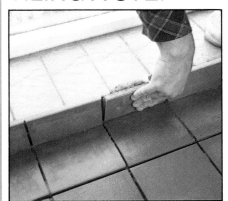

1 Start by covering the riser. Cut the tiles so they will reach 13mm (¹/₂in) above the top of the step, then butter their backs and press them into place.

2 Then spread a layer of mortar onto the step tread so it just reaches the top of the riser tiles. Smooth the mortar so it's even and level.

3 You can then go ahead and fix the lipping tiles on the tread to form a neat nosing at the front of the step. Fill in with cut tiles at the back.

and then lightly rub the surface with a serrated scraper.

If you are applying a 6mm (¹/₄in) bed of adhesive you could apply it in areas delineated by timber bays as when using mortar. However, it is easier to lay a 3mm (¹/₈in) thick bed as described and then to butter the necessary additional adhesive onto the back of each tile just as you are about to lay it. Alternatively, apply the entire 6mm (¹/₄in) of adhesive to the tile.

Once the adhesive is down you can press the first square metre of tiles firmly into place. Take care that the whole of each tile is firmly in contact with the adhesive and that there are no gaps or pockets of trapped air. Once two or three tiles are down, use a spirit level to check that they finish flush with each other, then repeat this test as each subsequent tile is pressed in place. When you have covered one square metre, clean off any adhesive that has strayed on to the surface of the tiles before moving on to put down more adhesive and tiles. It's important to do this before the adhesive sets.

When you are fixing tiles in mortar it's best to work in sections when you are laying the cut tiles. Otherwise you risk disturbing the whole tiles which are already laid.

If you wish, instead of bedding the tiles in a dry, crumbly mortar (see *Ready Reference*) you can use a mix like this as the base and then spread a runnier mix over the top in which to bed the tiles.

Cutting tiles
Quarry tiles are cut in much the same way as any other type of ceramic tile. You score the surface with a tile cutter, or where you are cutting an L-shaped piece you nibble away at the waste with pincers or tile nips. Having said that, it's worth remembering that these floor tiles are thick and it's best to take care to score deeply into the tile. If you tap the underside of the tile sharply with a hammer just beneath the cut line it will break more easily. Nibbling away at waste with pincers may still prove troublesome and in some cases it could be worth resorting to the use of a cold chisel and hammer to chip off the tile to the shape you want. You will have to work with care, resting the tile on a firm bed of newspaper for

GROUTING TILES

1 *Leave the tiles for at least 12 hours without disturbing them and then spread grout over the surface with a sponge or plastic spreader.*

2 *To remove the excess grout, first rub a cloth diagonally across the joins, taking away as much of the excess as possible.*

3 *Then, with most of the hard rubbing done, work along the joins with the cloth to neaten the finish. This saves you removing too much grout from within the joins.*

support, to stop the tile from cracking. Alternatively, you can thin the waste part of the tile to make it easier to nibble it away.

Tiled skirting

According to the traditional method of tiling, tiled skirtings are always laid before the floor is tiled. However, you may find it easier to get a neat result, matching the skirting's joins with those between the floor tiles, if you fix them after tiling the floor; this is perfectly acceptable. In this case, make sure you leave the correct gap between the floor tiles and walls to take the skirting tiles.

If you are working with tiling adhesive, use this to fix the skirting tiles to the wall in exactly the same way as when you are fixing tiles to the floor. If you are using mortar, apply this to the wall using a steel float, aiming for a continuous bed roughly 6mm (¼in) thick. Alternatively, you can butter the back of each tile with mortar, taking care that the whole of the back surface is covered.

Finishing off

Where the tiles have been laid on adhesive, leave them at least 12 hours before you grout them. Where you have laid them on a mortar bed this 'waiting time' should be increased to 24 hours.

In both cases it's worth reducing the risk of disturbing the tiles if you have to walk on them by spreading your weight on 'crawl boards' roughly 900x600mm (3x2ft) made from chipboard or some equally rigid sheet material.

The grouting is done in much the same way as when you are grouting other ceramic floor or wall tiles, in that you rub the grout over the tiles so it fills the joints and then clean off the excess. Do make sure that you are using a grout which is designed for floors and that you don't remove too much grout when cleaning off (see step-by-step photographs). Most grouts which are suitable for use with floor tiles are cement-based and are likely to irritate the skin, so avoid unnecessary contact with the grout by wearing gloves. Remember you can buy coloured grout or add colour to a standard type of grout if you want to match the colour of the tiles or set them off in coloured grout which provides a striking contrast.

After grouting you should leave the floor for a day or two to harden and then wash it thoroughly using water and detergent. You can finish off by applying a proprietary tile sealer or, if you like, floor polish, but tiles which have been laid outdoors must never be polished.

A word of warning: do be careful when you are carrying out this first floor wash. Take care that you don't use too much water. The floor, in particular the grout and adhesive, will not be up to a heavy soaking for at least a fortnight.

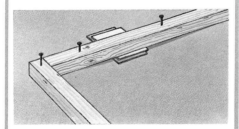
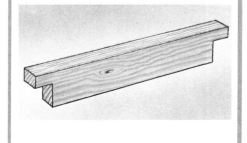

LAYING HARDWOOD FLOORS

Hardwood flooring comes in a variety of types and timbers. It can provide you with a particularly elegant floor without your having to spend a great deal of money.

If you want a wooden floor and have decided that sanding and sealing existing floorboards would be inappropriate, you can simply lay hardwood flooring over the floorboards or, for that matter, over a solid concrete floor. Wood flooring is available in several varieties of hardwoods: oak, teak, iroko, beech, sapele, mahogany, maple and walnut, for example. It can be particularly decorative in terms of grain, figure or colour and with a few rugs scattered over it, a hardwood floor can add real elegance to a room. In addition to its decorative qualities the flooring will be hardwearing, durable and easy to clean and maintain.

Another factor in its favour is cost: you can get an attractive hardwood floor for less than the price of a good quality carpet with underlay. And, besides lasting longer, the timber will stand up better to spills and dirt.

Choosing the flooring

The type of hardwood flooring which is most widely available is mosaic flooring, which comes in panel form (see *Ready Reference*). Normally, mosaics are the most flexible of the various types of flooring and therefore the easiest to lay, though those joined by wire and glued together at the edges are more rigid. If you decide to use mosaic panels, you might choose to have types made from different timber on the same floor, building them up into a pattern.

Traditional solid timber parquet blocks are still available, though most manufacturers and importers restrict themselves to supplying the professional floor layer. One or two varieties are, however, available on the DIY market. The problem with blocks is their rigidity, so that it's all too easy to end up with some that have edges sticking up over which people, especially young children or elderly people, might trip. Furthermore, there's the problem of setting out the patterns. Traditional herringbone can be tricky and the trouble with brick bond is that any expansion of the blocks due to moisture absorption from the atmosphere will be in the same direction. Also, since the blocks must go on a flat, rigid floor you must be painstaking with your preparation.

The advantages of block flooring are that the blocks are usually a high quality material which will last a lifetime and you can choose your own pattern (mosaics, on the other hand, always come in basket-weave form).

Wood strip floorings can be laid on top of existing timber or concrete floors; some varieties can also be fixed direct to joists and so can take the place of floorboards. The latter types are therefore particularly worth considering if you are faced with renewing a timber floor or having a house custom-built for you. Laminated strips are always pre-finished, so if you want to avoid having to sand the floor and finish it you might choose this type of flooring. Mosaic panels and solid strips are sometimes pre-finished, sometimes not. Unfinished types are less expensive to buy than their pre-finished counterparts, but you will have to sand and finish them.

When buying the flooring remember to allow about five per cent extra for wastage when you are cutting to fit or to remove any defect. Also, if you have underfloor heating you should check with your supplier that the type of flooring you have in mind is one which will not be affected by the heating.

Preparation

The floor must be in sound condition and as level as possible before you lay hardwood flooring over it. One point to remember here is that the more level the sub-floor is before

you lay the new flooring, the less sanding you will have to do when finishing.

On a timber floor you will have to punch home protruding nails or countersink screws; knots should be planed down. You may also have to remove any accumulated polish or stains; this is particularly important if you are using adhesive to fix the flooring or it will not stick properly. Instead of going to this trouble, however, you could cover the floor with sheets of hardboard or plywood to ensure a clean level surface. Condition hardboard first, before you lay it, by brushing water into its mesh side and then stack it flat, with the sheets back to back, and leave it in the room where you're going to use it for 48 hours.

It's worth using relatively small sheets of hardboard, say 1220mm x 1220mm (4ft x 4ft) because these are easier to handle than large sheets. Start laying the hardboard in one corner of the room. You don't have to take too much trouble and aim for an absolutely perfect fit; there's no need, for example, to scribe the hardboard so it exactly follows the outline of the skirting. If you are going to use adhesive to fix the hardwood flooring, lay the hardboard mesh side up to help the adhesive to grip properly. Fix the sheets by nailing them at 100mm (4in) centres round the edges and 150mm (6in) centres in the middle. Begin in the middle of one and work forwards and sideways so that the sheet will lie truly flat. When you come to the end of a row, use the

LAYING AND CUTTING PANELS

1 *Snap a chalked line alongside a straight wall. It should be the width of a panel, plus 12mm (1/2in) to allow a gap for expansion, away from the wall.*

2 *Using the chalked line as a guide, spread on the adhesive with a notched spreader. When working, protect your hands and clothing from the adhesive.*

3 *Lay the first row of panels along the wall, 12mm (1/2in) away from it. Butt the panels against each other, making sure they are aligned.*

4 *Continue spreading adhesive and laying the panels; check they're in straight rows. When the whole ones are laid you can lay the cut border panels.*

5 *To mark off a panel to be cut, place it over the last full panel in a row. Place another one over it 12mm (1/2in) away from the wall to use as a guide.*

6 *When you have marked the cutting line you can go ahead and cut the panel. Use a tenon saw and work with the panel face side up.*

offcut from the sheet you've cut to size to start the next row so the joins in the sheets won't coincide; this helps to prevent any movement of the floor occurring in a continuous line down the joins and disturbing the flooring above.

With solid floors there could be a damp problem. If, after you've tested for damp (for example, by heating a metal plate, placing it on the floor and seeing if moisture forms underneath), you are in any doubt at all about the condition of the floor, you should take precautions against damp by laying a damp-proof membrane. The exception to this rule is where you are going to use bituminous adhesive to stick the flooring down, since the adhesive itself will prevent moisture from penetrating the flooring. If you are going to fix the flooring to battens set into or placed on the floor, make sure you use battens which have been preservative-treated.

The other question to consider with a solid floor is how level it is. If it is uneven you should level it using a self-levelling screeding compound (see Laying ceramic floor tiles, pages 122-123, for more details).

Apart from the state of the floor you will also have to examine the door. Your new floor might stop the door from opening properly; test for this by placing a piece of flooring under the door. If necessary, you will have to take the door down, trim the required amount off the bottom and then re-hang it.

You should also condition the flooring. Buy it at least a week before you intend laying it, then unpack it and leave it in the room where it will be laid so it can adjust to the atmosphere; stack it so the air can circulate freely around it.

Setting out

You can start laying mosaic panels, strips and wood blocks alongside the longest uninterrupted wall in a room. You should check first that the position in which you intend to lay your first row won't mean you have to cut very narrow pieces to fit on the other side of the room by dry-laying a row of panels across the room. In the case of strips and blocks it would be easier to work this out on a scale drawing of the floor. Also, check by dry-laying a row of panels alongside the wall that there won't be very narrow cut pieces at the ends of the rows. If necessary, adjust your starting point, then snap a chalked line down the room to serve as a guide when you are fixing the first row. A tip here: if you want, instead of snapping a chalked line you can make a mark at each end of the room in the relevant position, drive in a nail at each mark and then tie a length of string so it's tightly stretched between them. Unlike a chalked line this can't be prematurely rubbed out.

If you are laying wood blocks in an intricate pattern, you would be better off starting from

LAYING PANELS IN AN ALCOVE

1 *At the corner leading into the alcove, place the panel to be cut to fit round it on the last full panel in one of the rows which meet at the corner.*

2 *Place another panel over the panel to be cut, 12mm (¹/₂in) away from the wall and use this as a guide to mark off one side of the required L-shape.*

3 *Repeat this procedure at the end of the other row of panels leading to the corner, to mark off the other side of the L-shape on the panel to be cut.*

4 *Cut the panel, spread on adhesive and lay the L-shaped panel. Take care to wipe off any adhesive from the front of the panels before it dries.*

5 *You can now fit the cut border panels at the back of the alcove. Mark them up for cutting in the usual manner before spreading the adhesive.*

6 *Lay the cut panels so they align with the full-size panels, and make sure there is an expansion gap of 12mm (¹/₂in) between them and the wall.*

Ready Reference

TYPES OF WOOD FLOORING

There are different types of hardwood flooring available. They include:

● mosaic flooring which consists of thin fingers of wood (generally only 8mm/⁵/₁₆in thick) fixed together in a series of squares on a panel to form a basket-weave pattern and stuck to a backing pad of bituminous felt. (Some are, however, wired together and glued at the edges; some are also tongued-and-grooved.) Usually there are 5 fingers per square and 16 squares per panel

● traditional parquet wood blocks which can be laid in different patterns. They must be laid on a flat, rigid base and are usually laid on a solid floor though they can be fixed to suspended timber floors. They are stuck down and are sometimes interlocked by tongues and grooves

● strip flooring, ie, a series of strips rather like very narrow short floorboards. They may be solid and thin (9.5mm/³/₈in) or quite thick (19 to 23mm/³/₄ to ⁷/₈in). Other types are laminated, either coming in pieces designed to look like a solid strip of wood or having a veneer which is split up into strips. They are longer than wood blocks and are usually laid side by side in straight runs. They can be 'secret nailed' to wood floors, joists or battens or glued together along the tongued-and-grooved joints and laid 'floating' on solid floors.

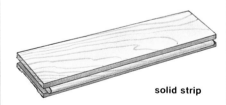

solid strip

FLOORING PATTERNS

Apart from the figure and colour of the wood, the patterns in which wood block flooring is arranged are also a source of interest. Arrangements include various types of basket-weave patterns, brick bond and herringbone patterns.

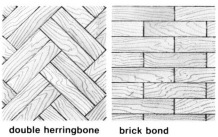

double herringbone   **brick bond**

131

FIXING MOULDING

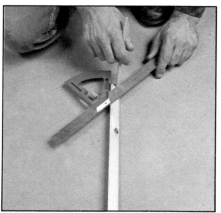

1 *Use a combination square to mark off 45° angles on lengths of moulding which will meet at a corner. When cut they should form a neat mitre join.*

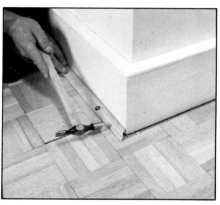

2 *Use the moulding to cover the gap left for expansion round the perimeter of the room. Fix it by driving panel pins through it into the skirting.*

3 *At a corner, nail two lengths of moulding so they form a mitre join. You can seal the moulding later at the same time as you are sealing the floor.*

DOORWAYS

1 *Where a panel will have to be cut to shape to fit round an architrave, trace the outline of the architrave from a template onto the block.*

2 *Cut the panel to the required shape; a jigsaw is ideal for this sort of work. You don't need to allow for an expansion gap in the doorway.*

3 *To finish off the job, fix a length of moulding so it fits just over the edge of the shaped panel and covers the expansion gap along the wall.*

the middle of the room, as the effect will be much neater this way.

For a herringbone pattern you should first mark a line or stretch string tightly between the mid-points of two opposite walls. Then, starting at the centre of that line, dry-lay the blocks at an angle of 45° to the line. Once the rows on each side of it are in place the rest are positioned automatically. With other patterns, begin from the middle, setting out your blocks dry first to make sure you get the edge cuts equal and not too small. To prevent them from moving during the setting out, you can pin the odd one here and there on a timber floor.

Laying and cutting flooring

Having worked out your starting point and set up guidelines to help you get it straight, you can go ahead and lay the flooring. If you are using a bitumen-based adhesive, spread it on the floor so it covers an area only slightly larger than the piece of flooring you are laying, then very carefully place the flooring in position. This type of adhesive is very messy to work with and you should aim to avoid getting any on the face of the flooring as it can be difficult to remove; if any does adhere to the flooring surface, scrape it off immediately before it has a chance to set. Also, it's worth wearing gloves when you're applying it and clothes that you don't mind getting possibly permanently marked.

To get tongued-and-grooved boards to slot together fully, you can knock them in using an offcut to protect the exposed tongue. Secret nailing (see *Ready Reference*) will provide a professional-looking fixing. If you're laying strip flooring over joists you should make sure than no two joints between strips are within 150mm (6in) of each other, in any direction to ensure a sound and stable floor surface. (Before you begin laying the flooring check also that the joists are in reasonable condition; you might need to add a splint to an uneven joist to provide adequate support for the flooring.)

In some cases, it is recommended that besides allowing a gap for expansion round the perimeter of the flooring that you leave small gaps (of about 1mm) between the individual units of flooring. Check with the manufacturer's instructions.

The normal procedure is to lay all the whole pieces of flooring first, however you happen to be fixing them, and then to fill in with the cut pieces at the borders. Cutting should be done with a fine-toothed saw; check that it's sharp before you start cutting. Where you have to cut out an intricate shape, for example to fit round an architrave or a WC, a jig saw will make the job much easier and will reduce the risk of splintering the wood so it has to be recut, thus lessening the likelihood of wastage. Make a template of the area where

SEALING

1 *Sand the floor to provide a clean, even surface, removing any high spots between the panels. To make the job go more quickly, use an orbital sander.*

2 *Remove dust arising from the sanding, and then brush on a thin coat of special wood flooring sealer over the panels (and the moulding).*

3 *For a good finish, wait until the sealer dries, then buff it gently with worn, fine sandpaper or steel wool to provide a key for the second coat.*

intricate cutting will be required, and test the template by placing it on the floor in the relevant position before you trace its outline onto the flooring. It makes more sense to remake an inaccurate template than to waste flooring by cutting it to the wrong shape.

If you are using cork strips (see *Ready Reference*) to fill in the gaps you've left for expansion at the perimeter of the room, you may find that some of the intricate cutting which would otherwise be required will not be needed. Round a fluted architrave in a doorway, for example, you can simply cut the flooring as if it were a square corner and then fill in with the flexible cork strip.

Finishing the floor

If you have laid flooring which is not pre-finished, you will have to give it a sanding first to smooth it over. In fact, one of the advantages of using an unfinished type of flooring is that sanding may in any event be necessary to remove the odd high spot here and there.

You can tackle the floor in a small room by hand or with a portable powered orbital sander, but on larger rooms you'll need a heavy-duty floor sander (which you can hire) and an edging sander for the borders. Since these sanders are powerful you should take care when using them; many of the wooden flooring materials have thin surface veneers and you run the risk of going right through them. It's best to use only a fine abrasive belt for this reason.

Seal off the room in which you're using the sanders, and wear a dust mask because they generate an enormous amount of dust. Remember too to wear ear protectors as they're also very noisy to work with. Sharp edges or nail heads can rip the abrasive belt, causing bits to fly around; this can be dangerous so make sure you've punched home nails and removed splinters from the flooring before you start.

Aim to be very careful not to scratch the floor surface. To avoid this you should always sand along the grain, never across it. Even when you're using the edge sander, move it along the grain only. In patterns where the grain is going in all directions (such as basket-weave) the trick is to approach such patterns at a 45° angle.

Finally, you'll have to seal the floor. Floor sealers come in matt and gloss versions and you will need two or three coats, according to how fine a finish you want. For a good-looking result, it's worth sanding each coat (except the final one) lightly with very fine glasspaper to provide a key for the following coat. If you do this, wipe the floor surface with a cloth moistened with white spirit to pick up any dust. If you wish, you can apply a little polish to the flooring once the sealer is properly dry.

Ready Reference

FIXING FLOORING
Some brands of hardwood flooring are self-adhesive. Others are stuck in place with a bitumen-based adhesive. Sometimes they are nailed down (on timber floors only). A few just lock together. In some cases both nailing and adhesive are recommended. Follow the manufacturer's instructions, whatever type of flooring you are fixing.

TIP: ALLOW FOR EXPANSION
When laying the flooring, allow a gap at the perimeter next to the wall to take account of expansion when the timber absorbs moisture. The gap should be about 12mm/1/2in wide (check with the manufacturer's instructions) and can be covered later by lengths of quandrant moulding nailed to the skirting, or else fitted with special cork strips (see below).

TIP: SECRET NAILING
Tongued-and-grooved floorings can be fixed by secret nailing: the nail is driven through the top of the tongue at an angle and punched home through the main body of the block or strip so it becomes invisible in the finished result. (If you use a punch with a hollowed end you're less likely to damage the flooring.)

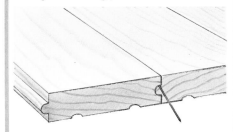

CORK EDGING STRIPS
Instead of using strips of quadrant moulding to cover the gaps left for expansion at the perimeter of the flooring (see step-by-step photographs) you can fill the gaps with special cork edging strips (about 7mm/1/4in thick and 12mm/1/2in wide). These strips are ideal for filling in round curves or awkward areas such as a fluted architrave in a doorway.

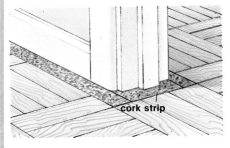
cork strip

LAYING WOODSTRIP FLOORING

Hardwood strip flooring can be laid over an existing floor or, provided it's a suitable type, directly over the joists. In either case, it should prove extremely durable.

The various types of hardwood flooring can be divided into three main types: mosaic panels, wood block and hardwood strip. Of the three, wood blocks require the most skill to lay and with these, unless you're feeling really confident, you may decide to leave the job to a professional. Mosaics were specifically developed for the DIY market; the techniques required for laying them have been explained in Laying hardwood floors. Laying strip flooring can be more or less complicated depending on the type of flooring selected and where it is going to be laid. The general skills you will require for this are described here, and how to lay one particular type of strip flooring is shown in detail in the step-by-step photographs.

Preparation

First of all you must get the existing floor ready to receive the flooring. Preparation is particularly important with floors, since safety, as well as appearance, is involved. An uneven floor could cause someone to trip, and this could be serious, especially in the case of an elderly person.

Floorboards will often be unsuitable as a base for applying hardwood flooring, as shrinkage will probably have caused gaps to appear between them. Some, or all, may have curled up at the edges because of warping. You can, however, use a relatively simple and inexpensive method of correcting this: by lining the floor with hardboard.

A chipboard or plywood floor in good condition presents the perfect base for a hardwood floor. Suspended concrete floors, such as one finds in very modern houses and high-rise buildings, also make a good base. However such a floor may have 'ripples' caused during the 'tamping-off' of the top screed and may be slightly uneven here and there. In that case, it should be treated with a self-levelling compound (see pages 122-123 for more details).

Modern direct-to-earth floors are usually in concrete and these make superb sub-floors, although they, too, may need to be treated with a self-levelling compound. Older solid floors, in quarry tiles and flag-stones, are not suitable, and even an older concrete floor may be subject to damp. In this case a new damp-proof membrane will have to be laid.

Once you've got the sub-floor into a suitable condition you may still have to carry out some preparatory work before you can begin laying the flooring. For example, some manufacturers recommend that you put down a layer of polythene sheeting or polystyrene first, others supply a special underlay. On floorboards one manufacturer recommends that you put down layers of newspaper. The question of an underlay will arise when you plan to install a so-called 'floating floor' – that is, one which gets its stability by the strips being fixed to each other, but not to the sub-floor itself.

Methods of laying

If you wish, you can remove the skirting before you lay the flooring; when it's replaced (slightly higher up than its original position) it will conceal the gap you've allowed for expansion at the perimeter of the floor area. Otherwise you will have to fill the gap with special cork strips designed for this purpose, or else nail quadrant moulding or similar to the skirting in order to hide the gap.

It's usually recommended that you begin laying strip flooring along the longest wall you will be laying parallel to, starting in one corner. Remember that with a timber sub-floor you should lay the strips so that they run at right angles to the floorboards. You should lay complete rows, starting with the tongue outwards in the case of tongued-and-grooved flooring. Make sure you get the first run straight; don't rely on your walls being perfectly square and an accurate guide. Instead stretch a taut string line, or snap a chalked line which you have ensured is true by the standard methods (see photograph 1 on page 130), alongside the wall. Use this to help you get a straight run of strips. In order to protect the tongues and the edges of the strips of wood, use a wooden block when you are knocking the strips together. An offcut of the flooring will be suitable.

The manufacturer may recommend 'secret nailing' – that is, where the nail is driven through the top of the tongue at an angle and punched home through the main body of the strip so that it is invisible in the finished flooring. If, instead, you nail straight through the face of the strips you will have to fill all the nail holes with matching stopper. With the clip-type system no nails are necessary; the longitudinal joints of the strips are secured by the clips. You will, with this system, need to use a woodworking adhesive to fix the ends of the strips together. By glueing the header joints you'll stop them dislodging.

PREPARATION

1 *It's usual to remove the skirting before you lay the flooring. You'll also have to cut away the bottom of any architrave to match the thickness of the new flooring.*

2 *Remove any debris and chippings from the floor surface and make sure it's level. Then lay down polythene sheeting over the entire floor area.*

3 *The polythene will help protect the new flooring against moisture. Cut it so there's an overlap of about 100mm (4in) at the floor's perimeter.*

4 *Roll out the foam underlay supplied with the flooring and cut it to length. It should reach to within about 25mm (1in) of the walls all round the room.*

If you are using adhesive, you should follow the manufacturer's instructions as to which type to use and where to apply it. For example, one manufacturer specifically states that the adhesive should be spread on the top side of the groove and not just squirted in so it lies on the groove bottom.

With the strip system which has interlocking 'ears', the individual strips can either be secret-nailed or glued together.

Where you are laying tongued-and-grooved flooring over the joists rather than over an existing floor, (obviously you should use a thick type of strip flooring for this), then so long as the ends of the strips are tongued-and grooved it's not necessary to make the joints fall over the joists. However, the joints should not be closer than 150mm (6in) to each other in any direction.

You will have to cut flooring to fit the ends of the room and go round obstructions.

Finishing the surface

Obviously, if you have chosen a pre-finished flooring you will save yourself the time and trouble of finishing the surface. If you have bought an unfinished type of strip it may be necessary to sand the surface after you've laid the flooring, and you can hire a floor sander for this. You should normally require only fine grades of belt, but a coarse grade may be necessary in some instances. Sand the floor with the coarsest grade first and then sand using progressively finer grades. Take care as you work; you don't want to gouge out the surface so that all the effort you have spent laying the flooring is wasted. (For fuller information on sanding floors see Stripping floors, page 85.) When all the dust from the sanding has been removed you can apply the recommended number of coats of varnish or seal according to the manufacturer's instructions.

(For fuller information on sanding floors see Stripping floors, page 85.)

Ready Reference

TIP: LET FLOORING ACCLIMATISE

Whichever type of strip flooring you choose you should leave it for at least a week, unpacked from any wrapping, in the room where it will be fitted in order to allow it to acclimatise to the atmosphere.

STORING FLOORING

Some laminated strips come with backs which are not perfectly smooth. You should store these strips with the hardwood veneers facing each other so that the roughness of the backs does not damage the decorative sides.

TIP: REMOVE DOORS

You'll find it easier to lay the flooring if you remove doors first. You may find that you have to trim a little off the bottom of the doors before you re-hang them so that the flooring will fit beneath them.

LAYING PATTERNS

Strip flooring can be laid according to various patterns. For example:
● some strip flooring is available with long and short lengths mingled in a design
● some come with short lengths of strip at right angles to the main run. These form what's known as a 'Dutch' pattern
● oblong tile-type strips can be used to build up into a herringbone pattern.

'Dutch' pattern

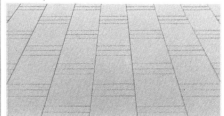

EASE OF REMOVAL

If you think you are likely to want to take the flooring up later, take account of this when choosing your fixing method. Gluing the flooring down all over will make it difficult to remove. The type of flooring which is fixed by the clip system is one of the easiest to take up again.

ALLOW FOR EXPANSION

You will have to allow an expansion gap – the recommendation ranges from 10mm (⅜in) upwards – all round the room. To maintain it, insert small wood wedges at the edges of the flooring when laying. In very large rooms, it's sometimes recommended that you allow a slight gap at intervals across the flooring too.

LAYING THE FLOORING

1 Laying begins alongside the longest straight wall, or failing that, the one with the least obstructions. Mark where the first straight run of timber will go.

2 In this case, you will also have to cut the flooring which runs next to the wall to shape. Scribe onto the timber the profile to be cut.

3 Cut the timber as required. Before you cut flooring to length, make sure the strips which make up the flooring will end up with the joints staggered.

6 You will need to leave an expansion gap of about 10mm (³/₈in) round the room, so cut timber wedges of this size and insert them at the perimeter.

7 Drive fixing clips into the adjacent lengths of flooring. They should be arranged so they will be no closer than 75mm (3in) to any other clips.

8 To interlock the tongues and grooves of adjacent lengths, drive them together using a hammer and an offcut of the flooring to protect the edges.

11 With the end groove glued, position the next length so it will align with the neighbouring lengths of flooring at its end and side.

12 You can then drive the length of flooring into place at the header and side joints, again protecting the tongue with an offcut of the flooring.

13 Continue in this way until all the floor is covered. You work back and forth down the length of the room, clipping and glueing as required.

A MAT WELL

1 It's unlikely that the walls will be perfectly square, so use a sliding bevel to measure the angle. Transfer this measurement to the flooring.

4 Turn the first length of flooring so its back is facing you, then drive in the toothed end of a clip into the groove channelled in the timber.

5 Fix other clips in the same way; they should be spaced about 750mm (30in) apart along the length of the flooring. You can then lay the first lengths.

9 As these offcuts show, you fix a clip in one length and the pressure of the floor drives the untoothed end into the groove on the neighbouring length.

10 You will have to glue the header joints. Apply woodworking adhesive along the bottom inside of the groove on the piece to be joined.

2 You can use the mat itself to mark off on the flooring the rest of the shape which will need to be cut. Use an ordinary saw or jig saw to cut the timber.

14 Where you won't be fixing a skirting at the outer edge you will need to insert special flexible cork strips to keep the flooring in place.

15 For a neat effect trim the polythene overlap. Replace the skirting, insert cork strips or fix beading to cover the gap you've left.

3 Cut the other strips which will fit round the mat to size and shape, and fix them in place, clipping and driving the lengths together in the normal manner.

LAYING CARPET TILES

Like fitted carpet, carpet tiles can provide warmth and softness underfoot, but they don't require anything like the same sort of skill to lay them.

Carpet tiles are small squares of carpet which you can lay side by side to create a fitted carpet look. You could of course choose to lay ordinary fitted carpet but carpet tiles have advantages that make them well worth considering. For example, since the majority are loose-laid (carpet tiles which require sticking down are available, but only in heavy 'contract' ranges for industrial and commercial use), laying carpet tiles is extremely simple. You certainly won't need to call in a professional carpet fitter for the job. You don't even need an underlay. What's more, they are just as easy to take up again (though some may stick to the floor beneath in heavy traffic areas) which means that, normally, you can remove badly-stained examples for cleaning or else simply move the tiles around to even out wear.

You can also remove the tiles completely if you are redecorating the room, though it's worth pointing out here that you may have a little trouble in achieving the same neat fit as you had before as the tiles may have spread with use. And finally there is the financial aspect. Although not exactly cheap, allowing for the savings you will make on fitting them, carpet tiles tend to be a good deal less expensive than fitted carpet.

What's available
In spite of their advantages, carpet tiles are not very widely available so you should expect to do a fair amount of shopping around before you find exactly what you want.

Basically, the choice is between carpet tiles designed specifically for heavy-duty areas where looks and feel aren't terribly important, and those designed as a straight-forward carpet substitute. In the former category, you'll find versions that look rather like needlecord, as well as quite a few very rugged examples made by embedding synthetic fibres, which are often quite coarse in texture, in a fibrous reinforced base. In the second category, you can expect the tiles to have a proper pile, though quality varies considerably with price. At the lower end of the price scale the 'pile' may amount to nothing more than synthetic fibres embedded vertically in a rubber backing. If you pay a little more you will begin to be offered tiles that approach the quality of normal carpet, with a more luxurious feel.

Calculating quantities
If you simply want to create a plain fitted carpet look, measure the length and breadth of the room using the length of a tile as your unit of measurement. Round each dimension up to the nearest whole number and multiply them together to get the total number of tiles.

If you intend to create a pattern, you will have to work out the quantities of each colour more carefully. It's best to draw up a scale floor plan of the room; then, on this draw a grid to represent the positions of the individual tiles. Colour in the grid to produce the design you want and count up the number of tiles required. Count cut tiles as whole tiles.

Preparation
As with most floorings, the surface on which the tiles are laid must be clean, level and free from damp. So take special care over preparation, levelling concrete floors with a self-levelling compound and floorboards with sheets of plywood or hardboard pinned down all over (see pages 122-123 for more details).

Setting out
Although with carpet tiles which have a thick pile the joins between tiles should in theory be invisible, they nearly always show to some extent in practice, so it's worth going to the trouble of laying the tiles symmetrically.

This is done in exactly the same way as for vinyl and cork floor tiles (see pages 104-107 and 108-112 respectively). You stretch a chalked string line between the mid-points of opposite walls and snap it down onto the floor to leave a cross at the centre of the room. Then lay two rows of tiles in an L-shape, starting at the cross and lining up the edges of the tiles with the chalk lines, working out towards the walls until cut tiles are needed to fill the gaps. If your first layout means that you would have cut tiles which are too narrow (see *Ready Reference*) restrike the guide-lines in a slightly different position, up to half the length of a tile away from the first set of lines, and try again. Keep trying until you have achieved the required layout.

Laying and cutting tiles
Once you've found a suitable arrangement you can begin laying the whole tiles, starting with one which goes in the angle of the guide-lines where they meet at the centre of the room (see step-by-step photographs).

You will eventually have to cut tiles to fill the gaps at the edges. Most tiles can be cut with ordinary scissors; scissors with contoured plastic handles are best, allowing you to apply the pressure needed to cut thick tiles without too much discomfort. Alternatively, you can use a sharp knife. The only thing you have to watch, apart from the obvious need to cut a straight, true line is that when cutting tiles which have a pile, you don't shave off the pile at the edge of the piece you want to use. Although the cut edge will be up against the wall, the bald line sometimes spreads and can look quite unsightly after a short time.

To work out where you make the cut you can, with tiles which have no pile, use the same trick as you would with cork, vinyl or ceramic tiles. That is, you lay the tile to be cut over the whole tile which will be its neighbour, then lay another whole tile on top with its edge butted against the wall to serve as a guide to mark the cutting line on the tile to be cut. The snag with this method is that because there is a certain amount of 'give' in the tiles, it tends not to be very accurate.

A more sensible approach, therefore, is simply to measure the width of the cut tile required. To allow for the fact that the walls may not be exactly straight or out of square, take three readings, one at each end and one in the middle of the gap to be filled and transfer these measurements to the back of the tile you are going to cut using a very soft pencil. Don't use a felt-tipped pen; on rubber-backed tiles in particular, the ink may not dry, with the result that it transfers itself to the pile of the tile you are cutting via the scissor blades, or it may stain tiles you have already laid when you throw aside the offcut. If you feel fairly confident you can, in fact, cut down on the measuring and marking part of the process when it comes to cutting tiles. You can take the tile to be cut, and with its back side facing you, place it so it butts against the wall and exactly over the gap to be filled, then make nicks on the back with a sharp knife to indicate where it should be cut and, finally, cut it to size (see step-by-step photographs).

Finishing off

With all the tiles in place, it's worth leaving them for a few days to settle down under normal use. If they spread it may be necessary to re-trim the edges around the walls.

You can then carefully lift the tiles round the edge of the room and re-lay them, sticking them down with a single strip of heavy duty double-sided sticky tape, positioned close to the edge of the tiles which faces into the room. If you have been unable to avoid narrow cut tiles you should use 'tramlines' of adhesive tape, with an extra line of tape running close to the wall. Sticking down tiles on the perimeter is not essential but it helps to stabilise the tile arrangement and prevents further movement. On very large floors in heavy traffic areas it may even be desirable to fix perhaps one in three rows of whole tiles right across the floor.

You should fit ordinary carpet threshold strip to protect the edges of the tiles at doorways and eliminate the risk of them lifting and forming a ridge which you could trip over. Do remember to vacuum the floor thoroughly to remove any surplus lint.

LAYING THE FLOORING

1 Snap chalk lines which cross at the room's midpoint. Adjust this point if it means you'll have narrow cut tiles. Use the lines to get the tiles straight.

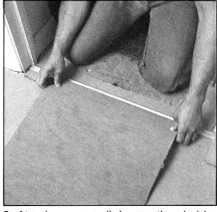

2 At a doorway, nail down a threshold strip. This will give you something to work against when the tile edge is pressed into it.

3 Lay the whole tiles. When you reach the outer edge, take the tile which will fill the edge gap and nick it slightly at either end to mark where to cut it.

4 Still working on the back of the tile, join up the nicks with a sharp knife using a straightedge to guide you. Then slice right through the tile.

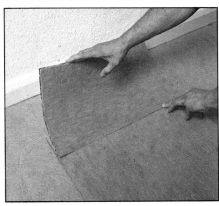

5 The cut tile is now ready to be fitted in place. If it's the right size it should stay in place in much the same way that a complete tile does.

6 It's best if you work in a quarter of the floor area at a time. Check that the tiles are straight as you work and cut them to fit at the perimeter.

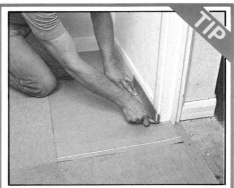

7 Where there is an awkward shape for the tiles to be fitted round, such as the base of a WC or an architrave, make a cardboard template of the shaped area.

8 Place the template on the back of the tile to be cut and trace round it with a pencil. You can then cut out the shape with a sharp knife.

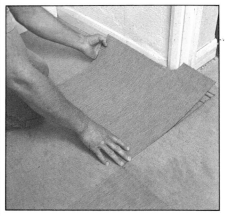

9 Fit the shaped tile in the same way as you would any other, butting it against adjacent tiles and, in this case, press it under the threshold strip.

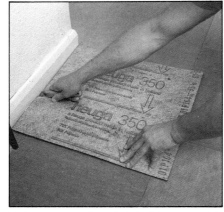

10 When cutting a tile to fit round the angle formed by an alcove, nick on the back on two adjacent sides to indicate where it should be cut.

11 Cut the tile to the required shape and then lay it in place. Here, another tile will have to be cut to fill the gap near the alcove back wall.

12 Vacuum the flooring to remove surplus lint. The tiles shown here have been laid with the pile directions at right angles for a chequerboard look.

Ready Reference

TILE SIZES
Carpet tiles are commonly available in the following sizes: 300, 400 or 500mm (12, 16 and 20in) square.

CREATE YOUR OWN PATTERN
Patterned tiles are not commonly available (though many heavy-duty tiles have a flecked effect). You could, however, create your own pattern by:
● using tiles of different colours and arranging them in either a simple chequer-board pattern or some sort of geometric design, or

chequerboard pattern

● for a more subtle effect, choosing tiles with a distinct pile direction (normally indicated by an arrow on the backing) and laying alternate tiles with the pile directions at right angles.

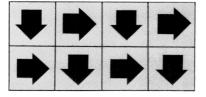

TIP: ALLOW A FEW TILES EXTRA
When you are buying the tiles, buy two or three more than the number required to cover the floor area to allow for mistakes (this is particularly worthwhile if the shape of the room damands awkward cutting). You may in fact be compelled to buy extras where the tiles are sold in packs rather than singly. But don't buy too many extras as it's too expensive.

TIP: AVOID NARROW CUT TILES
If possible you should avoid having cut tiles which are less than 100-150mm (4-6in) wide. Apart from the difficulty of cutting narrow strips of carpet tile, such small areas tend not to lay flat.

CHECK PILE DIRECTION
For a normal carpet effect the arrows on the back of the tiles should all point in the same direction.

CHAPTER 6

UNUSUAL WALLCOVERINGS

Once you've mastered the basic paperhanging techniques,
you can tackle some of the more exotic wallcoverings now on the
market, and add the final touches to any room by putting
up friezes, decorative borders and cornices to match
its architectural style.

HANGING FABRICS ON WALLS

Hessian and other fabric wallcoverings are ideal as a cover-up for less-than-perfect walls. They can give a softer, richer look to a room and provide an ideal backing for prints, pictures or other items on display.

There are many fabric wallcoverings available. Some are nubbly and tweedy; others have a delicate silky or moiré (watered silk) surface; some are like damask: woven figured material. There are wallcoverings with wool and linen strands stretched across a backing to give an overall effect of striped, half-woven cloth; fragile grasscloths (strands of natural grasses bound lightly into a mat on a paper backing); and other coverings with an Oriental effect such as raw silk and split bamboo. There are thick sound-deadening felts; wallcoverings with a leather look, including crushed and brushed velvety suedes; ones with cork slivers on a coloured, or foil, background (which glints through the cork 'skin') and last, but by no means least, ever-popular hessian which comes in a natural oatmeal colour, various dyed colours and also in a special 'sized' version intended for over-painting.

Most of these wallcoverings are paper-backed, which makes hanging easy and straightforward. Some, however, are not. Ordinary upholsterers' hessian, for example, which is only about one-third of the price of the paper-backed version, can be hung on walls; but a different hanging technique is required (see *Ready Reference*). A point to bear in mind, if you are considering hanging one of the more expensive speciality wallcoverings like silk, grasscloth or cork, is that while they come with a paper backing, which prevents stretching and wrinkling, you cannot afford to make any mistakes in measuring and cutting; also these types of wallcovering stain very easily if any paste gets onto the surface.

Real fabric of almost any type can also be hung to cover walls, so long as it is firmly woven, but usually it is not stuck into place; instead, one of two other fixing methods are used. With one method, a staple gun is used to staple the fabric to battens which are in turn stapled to the wall. With the other, special plastic fabric-fixing track is fixed to the wall and the fabric tucked into this. Either way, the fabric can be removed fairly easily for cleaning, or when you are ready to change it again.

Choosing and buying wallcoverings

While taste is obviously an individual matter and you will choose the type of wallcovering according to the look you want (and the amount you are prepared to pay), the different textures of the various fabric wallcoverings do tend to make them appropriate for use in particular settings. The silks, moirés and grasscloths tend to look better in a more traditional setting whereas corks, suedes, wool weaves and tweedy effects complement a modern décor and blend particularly well with exposed brickwork, timber cladding, slate and stone. Hessian usually looks right in both modern and traditional settings, is a perfect foil for pictures, prints or other exhibits and is frequently used on one specific wall area to back a prized collection.

Quite a few fabric wallcoverings have a 'random' match, which means you don't have to allow for pattern-matching when buying. However, where there is a very heavy texture or a definite striped effect running horizontally across the material, some pattern matching may be necessary if the results are not to be disappointing. Some speciality wallcoverings, like grasscloth, can have a rather untidy look when hung, but this is characteristic of the material and it is supposed to have a random-match effect. If you think this is likely to worry you, buy something a little less defined in texture.

When buying, try to see as large a sample as possible before making up your mind. If you can, see two rolls unwrapped and placed side by side and also try to see them arranged vertically as they'll be seen when hung. The more expensive wallcoverings must usually be ordered in advance from specialist decoration shops, and you may only be able to select from smallish samples. In which case, try to have an arrangement with the supplier so you can return the material for a credit if it does not match the sample to your satisfaction.

Check the width and length of roll before ordering; many fabric wallcoverings are imported and may not conform to standard sizes. So if you don't check you risk ordering too much or little.

Also remember to check carefully for colour variations between rolls. Colour differences will be only too apparent when the wallcovering is in place.

HANGING LINING PAPER

1 *Measure and cut the paper, allowing for an overlap at both ends of the room. Paste the back, folding the paper into concertina folds.*

2 *Hang the first length horizontally across the wall. Then hang the second length so it butts against it, pulling the concertina folds out.*

3 *Use a wallpaper brush to smooth the paper into place and ensure an unwrinkled surface; if right-handed, you should work from right to left.*

4 *At the corners of the room, you will have to trim off the overlap. As a guide for the knife you can use the edge of a scraper to get a clean cut.*

Preparing the surface

As with any wallcovering, the wall must be properly prepared first. This means old wallpaper should be stripped off and the wall washed clean of any old paste and size. Cracks, holes and indentations should be filled, any crumbling, or otherwise faulty plaster should be cut and filled, and the whole area should be smoothed down and then sized with a weak coat of size.

Newly-plastered surfaces must have dried out throughly; cracks should be filled, 'nibs' of plaster smoothed down and any efflorescence rubbed off with a cloth or brush. It is wise to apply a diluted coat of alkali-resisting primer, brushed well into the plaster.

Previously-painted surfaces should be washed down to remove grease and dirt and then rubbed down with glasspaper to provide a good 'key'; this is particularly important with a gloss-painted surface. Again, fill any cracks and holes and sand them down after filling.

Lining the wall

Before fixing a fabric wallcovering you should first line the wall with lining paper. The need for this is obvious with unbacked fabrics but it is equally important with other types of fabric wallcoverings since it will greatly improve the appearance of the finished result.

The lining paper should be hung horizontally (starting from the top of the wall) so there is no risk of the joins coinciding with those in the wallcovering. The edges of the paper should be butt-joined and surplus paper trimmed neatly into the corners of the room at each end. For the final length on a wall, you should trim the length roughly to size before pasting it and carry out final

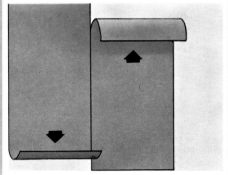

HANGING UNBACKED HESSIAN

1 Measure and cut the hessian to the required length, allowing about 100mm (4in) top and bottom. Cut enough for most of the room.

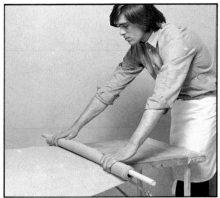

2 Roll the first length round a stout tube or a strong stick (a piece of old broom handle is suitable) with the right side of the hessian facing in.

3 Using a plumbline as a guide, mark the wall vertically into strips which will be the width of the overlap narrower than the hessian width.

4 Spread the adhesive on the wall with a brush, using feathered strokes, but don't apply it too thickly. Stop short of the drawn line on each side.

5 While the paste is still wet, start unrolling the hessian onto the wall from the roll you've made, using the lines on the wall as a guide.

6 To smooth the hessian into place and ensure it is securely fixed, run a clean paint roller over it when it is in place between the guidelines.

7 Hang the next length in the same way as you hung the first; make sure that you leave an overlap of at least 25mm (1in) between the lengths to allow enough material for trimming.

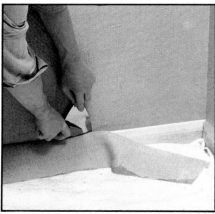

8 Hang hessian round the room. Before you carry out any trimming, leave the adhesive to dry to allow for shrinkage. Then trim to size at the top, bottom, and at joins.

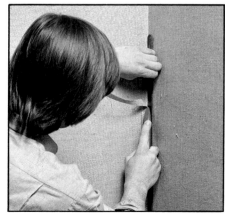

9 At an internal corner, you will have to trim one length neatly into the corner, then fix the adjoining piece and trim the overlap to ensure you form a neat butt join.

MAKING A NEAT BUTT JOIN

1 *Place a straight edge over the middle of the overlap between two lengths of hessian and then run a sharp knife through both lengths.*

2 *You can then peel off the surplus hessian; with the top waste piece removed you will be able to see and remove the piece underneath.*

3 *Paste the wall underneath the hessian on both sides of the join. Use a small brush and work carefully to ensure no adhesive gets on the front.*

4 *With a seam roller, gently run over the two edges to make a neat butt join. Make sure you don't press too hard or you risk a shiny surface.*

Ready Reference

JOINING LENGTHS
Fabric wallcoverings should be hung with butt joins. This is straightforward where the edges are straight, but if they are ragged you will have to allow an overlap that measures at least 25mm (1in) wide between lengths during hanging and trim later (see step-by-step photographs).

REMOVE EXCESS ADHESIVE
Any adhesive which gets onto the front of the fabric should be wiped off at once. With delicate finishes (silk, cork, grasscloth) paste must not get onto the front or it will be spoiled. So with these types:
● paste only one length at a time
● wipe the pasting table to remove surplus adhesive after pasting each length
● remove instantly any adhesive oozing out at seams during hanging.

SMOOTHING DOWN
To smooth down most fabric wallcoverings use a foam or felt-covered roller over the entire area:
● with very coarsely-woven fabrics, simply press firmly with your hand so the material is not squashed and adhesive is not squeezed up through the weave
● never use a seam roller on a heavy texture as this flattens the joins and makes them look more obvious.

HANGING FELT
Felt is sold in extra-wide widths and is very heavy. To support a length when hanging it, bottom upwards, on a pasted wall:
● roll the length round a long batten with the wrong side facing out
● support the roll between the tops of two stepladders.

Use the adhesive recommended by the manufacturer (some make their own brand).

trimming above the skirting board when it has been brushed into place.

If you are hanging an open-weave fabric, such as furnishing hessian, it's worth painting the lining paper in the same colours as the hessian so it won't be conspicuous if it shows through the fabric.

Hanging wallcoverings
Depending on the type of wallcovering, you may be cutting and pasting several lengths or one length at a time. Or you may use the paste-the-wall technique.

If the material is to be reverse hung (see *Ready Reference*), mark the back of each length with an arrow to indicate which way each piece is to go.

If you are using paper-backed hessian, you can trim off the overlap at the top and bottom as you go along, but for an unbacked type you should leave the adhesive to dry to

allow for shinkage before you start to trim.

Turn hessian well round external angles as you do not want a raw edge on an exposed wall area. On inside angles, cut the corner length material into two strips and butt-join them in the angle (use the overlap technique – see step-by-step photographs – if appropriate).

Looking after fabric wallcoverings
For fabric wallcoverings to look their best, they will have to be dusted every few months. Gently run the upholstery attachment of a vacuum cleaner over the wallcovering (alternatively, you can brush it down with a soft brush). If there are any stains on the fabric, use dry-cleaning fluid to remove them (after testing the fluid on an inconspicuous area like behind a picture – to make sure it doesn't cause discolouration). Loose seams should be pasted down again.

DECORATING WALLS WITH CORK

Cork in tile, panel or sheet form provides an easy-to-fix wallcovering which is highly decorative and warm to the touch. It will also add to your peace and quiet by insulating against noise.

You may decide to decorate one or more walls of a room in your house with cork simply because you like the look of it. But there are practical advantages in doing this as well. You will also be providing extra insulation as, apart from its decorative qualities, cork deadens sound, is warm to the touch and keeps heat in and cold out. Also, it doesn't cause condensation and will absorb a certain amount of moisture. It can be quite hardwearing, taking its share of knocks and bumps without bruising, and many of the ranges of cork tiles, panels, sheets and rolls available are treated to be fully washable and steam-proof.

Where to use cork

Because of its highly decorative quality and natural texture, cork usually looks best as a feature wall, or forming a focal point on a chimney breast, or in an alcove, or behind some display shelves. But because of its insulating quality it is ideal on the inside of walls which face away from the sun, particularly if a bedhead or seating is placed next to them. Cork tiles on a ceiling can help reduce noise and also add warmth; in children's rooms, teenage bedsitting rooms, family living rooms, hobby areas, even the kitchen, a panel of cork can also provide a place to pin pictures, posters and memos. Pre-sealed cork is practical for kitchens and bathrooms so long as it does not come in direct contact with the bath, sink or basin edge (you can isolate it with a row of ceramic tiles). It can also be used to face doors, cover window seats and ottomans, or cover screens and bath panels – so long as you select the right product.

Types of cork

Cork for walls comes in several different types. Some is made by pressing the cork into layers, or mixing cork chippings with a binder, and then cutting it into sheets, tiles or panels of various sizes, thicknesses and textures. Sometimes, to get a rougher home-spun look, the actual bark of the cork tree is peeled, mounted on a backing and sold for decorative purposes. The backing may be coloured, and if the cork is slivered thinly

enough, this backing will show through, giving a hint of colour to the cork. This type may be sold as panels or sheets.

Another attractive cork wallcovering is made by shaving the cork so thinly that it is almost transparent and because of the natural uneven texture, the effect is like hand-crocheted lace. This is then mounted onto a foil backing which glints through the layer of cork. This type is usually sold in sheets or by the roll, as wallpaper.

A new development is a wallcork which is laminated to crêpe paper so it is extremely flexible and can be bent round curved surfaces. This type comes in a natural finish, which can be painted, and also in several colours. It is sold by the linear metre, off the roll.

Most wallcorks are presealed, either waxed or treated with a sealant, which makes them washable; some come unsealed including some of the heavily textured types and the very open granular tiles.

Buying and planning

Cork tiles, panels and sheet come in various sizes. When you have decided on the type you want to use you will have to work out how much you will need to order from your supplier. Remember the cardinal rule that you should always order more than will be exactly required to cover the wall, to allow for any mistakes, accidents or errors when you are putting the cork up.

You may decide to fix tiles or panels in a particular pattern, for example, so they create a diamond or herringbone design. If so, it's best to work out the design on paper

first; then, after you've prepared the surface, you can square up the wall and mark the position of each tile or panel on it. (Remember you can also create interesting effects by using light and dark tiles to form a chequerboard pattern or to form a border or 'framed' effect; but you shouldn't need to mark up the wall for this.)

Preparing the surface

As with any other form of decoration, cork must be hung on a properly prepared surface. If you are going to cover a wall with cork which has already been decorated you should strip off old wallpaper, scrape off any flaking paint and fill any deep holes; cut and re-plaster any crumbling 'live' areas. If the plaster is porous, prime with PVA primer diluted 1:5 with water.

Gloss or emulsion-painted walls can be keyed by rubbing over them with glasspaper to roughen the surface, but as the paint can sometimes cause the adhesive to break down, most cork suppliers recommend lining a painted wall with heavy lining paper before fixing the cork in position. Follow the instructions supplied with the particular product you intend using. If you are going to use lining paper, remember to cross-line the walls, that is, hang the paper horizontally just as you would before hanging a good quality wallpaper or fabric wallcovering to avoid the risk of joins coinciding.

If you are hanging sheet cork wallcovering and using a heavy-duty wallpaper paste to fix it, it may be necessary to prime the wall surface first with a coat of size or diluted wallpaper paste.

FIXING THE FIRST TILE

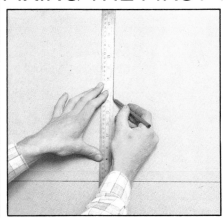

1 *Work out how the tile pattern will fall on the wall by drawing central horizontal and vertical lines. Adjust these to avoid awkward cuts.*

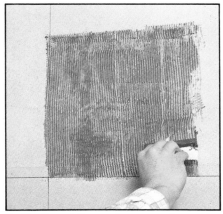

2 *Starting at the centre, spread adhesive in one of the angles formed by the lines. (With contact adhesive apply it to the back of the tile as well.)*

3 *Cover an area slightly larger than a tile, then align the first tile using the horizontal and vertical lines as a guide to the exact position.*

4 *Press the tile into place flat against the wall, taking care not to let it slip out of line as you do this. It's crucial you get the tile correctly positioned.*

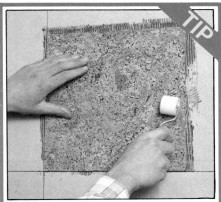

5 *Roll the tile with a wallpaper seam roller to get a better bond particularly at the edges. Be careful not to get adhesive on the roller.*

6 *If any adhesive gets onto the face of the tile wipe it off with a damp cloth before it sets. With some adhesives you may need to use white spirit (turps).*

Ready Reference

CHOOSING THE RIGHT CORK

Cork swells when it gets wet and could become distorted and start peeling off the wall. It therefore makes sense to
● use a pre-sealed type for kitchens, bathrooms and areas where you are going to have to wipe off sticky finger marks, or
● use a type of cork which can be sealed after hanging in these areas.

TIP: CONCEAL CUT TILES

When you are planning the layout of the tiles you are going to use on a wall, aim to place cut tiles where they won't draw attention. For example:
● it's best to have cut tiles at the skirting rather than at the ceiling
● on a chimney breast, butt cut tiles up to the junction between the chimney breast and wall rather than to the outer corner of the chimney breast.

TIP: MAKE DEMOUNTABLE PANELS

Because of the adhesive used to fix them, cork tiles can be difficult to remove once they are up; if you try to scrape them off you may either have large lumps of cork left stuck to the wall or large holes left in the plaster. To help you make it easier to have a change of decor later:
● fix the cork to panels of plasterboard, hardboard, partition board, chipboard, plywood or other dry lining
● fix the panels to battens which are screwed to the wall; these can be unscrewed and removed when you choose.

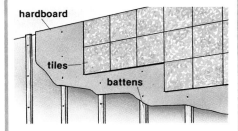

TILES IN HOT SPOTS

If you are fixing cork tiles to a chimney breast where a fire will be used, behind a radiator or other 'hot spot', it is best to put adhesive down the edges of the tiles as well as on the back to make extra sure of a secure bond.

PREVENT FIRE RISK

Many adhesives suitable for use with cork are highly inflammable. Therefore, when using them, make sure all pilot lights are switched off and turn off any electric or gas fires. Don't smoke or work near a naked light, and provide adequate ventilation.

FIXING OTHER TILES

1 *Apply more adhesive then butt the second tile into place using hand pressure and a roller. Then continue to fix all the whole tiles.*

2 *Where the tile has to be cut, for example, to fit at the edge of a chimney breast, you should first place it over the last whole tile in the row.*

3 *Butt another tile up against the corner so that it overlaps the tile to be cut; use this as a guide to mark off a cutting line with chalk or pencil.*

4 *To cut the tile, place it on a firm surface then use a sharp kife to cut along the marked line. Use a straightedge as a guide.*

5 *Coat the exposed wall with adhesive and fix the cut tile in the same way you've fixed the whole tiles. Continue marking up, cutting and fixing the tiles.*

6 *When you've completed the front of a chimney breast you can tile the sides. Work so the cut edges go into the junction with the wall.*

Tools and equipment

You are already likely to have most of the tools and equipment required for covering walls with cork, particularly if you have hung some other type of wallcovering before. You will need a sharp knife to trim the cork, a straightedge, a notched adhesive spreader (sometimes supplied with the adhesive) or a pasting brush, a plumbline and chalk or pencil, a T-square or set square, a wallpaper seam roller and (for sheet cork) a wallpaper hanger's roller (which is wider than a seam roller). You will also require a tape measure and, to cut bark-type cork, a fine-toothed tenon saw. A pasting table (or some other suitable surface) may be needed; put this in a good light so you can see that the back surface of the tile or sheet (where these are pasted on the back rather than pasting the wall for fixing) is completely covered. As you'll be working at a height for part of the fixing process you'll need a stepladder. Make sure this is in sound condition so it will provide you with safe, secure access.

Fixing the cork

When you are fixing cork tiles or panels, as with all tiling, the setting-out is vitally important. The tiles should always be centred on a focal point or wall, so you end up with cut tiles or panels of equal width in the corners or at the edge of a chimney breast. Once you have established your central point and squared up the wall for the first line of tiles, tiling should be quite straightforward; the tiles are fixed with contact adhesive applied to the back of the tile and the wall or with an adhesive which is applied to the wall only.

Sheet cork is hung in different ways (see *Ready Reference*). The crucial thing here is to hang the lengths of cork to a true vertical and to plan the layout so cork which has to be cut to fit in width will come at the corners where any unevenness (due to the walls being out of square) will be least likely to be noticed.

Finishing touches and maintenance

If you put up cork tiles, panels, or sheet cork which are not sealed you can seal them with a transparent polyurethane varnish (a matt finish looks best). Dust the surface thoroughly and apply two or three coats of varnish; you may find a spray-on type is easier to apply than one which you brush on but this is only economical if you don't have too large an area to cover.

Most wall corks (whether sealed or unsealed) can be cleaned by dusting them down (use a cloth or the soft brush attachment on your vacuum cleaner). Most of the sealed corks and the crêpe-backed cork can be wiped with a damp cloth. The paper and foil-backed corks may not be wipable, so check before you buy, and don't hang them in a place where they will get dirty quickly.

HANGING SHEET CORK

1 Use a plumb line to mark off a guide line for fixing the first length. It should be less than the width of the cork sheet away from the corner.

3 Trim the first length to size at the ends and then fix it in place; work down the wall and use a wide roller to help you smooth the cork in place.

5 At a corner, measure the width at several places down the wall. Transfer these measurements to the cork and cut it to fit exactly.

2 Mark off more lines the width of the cork sheet apart along the wall. You can then apply the adhesive; in this case with a notched spreader.

4 Fix the next length by applying adhesive and then butting the cork up against the first length. Continue to fix cork lengths along the wall.

6 Fix the corner length in place. It should have been cut to fit an out of square wall. The other adjacent (cut) corner length butts up to it.

Ready Reference

FINISHING RAW EDGES

If you will get a 'raw' edge down the side where you are fixing tiles to the face of a chimney breast only or where thick, soft types of tiles will meet at an exposed corner, protect the tile edges with a wooden lipping or moulding. For this you:
● attach the lipping (of the same thickness as the tiles) with pins or adhesive down each vertical angle before you start tiling
● tile up to the liping as if it were an internal angle
● stain the lipping the same colour as the tiles so it will be barely noticeable or coat it with clear varnish to make it more of a feature in the decorative scheme.

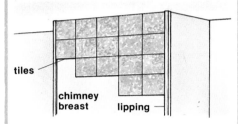

tiles

chimney breast   lipping

TIP: REMOVE EXCESS ADHESIVE

If you inadvertently get adhesive on the front of the cork you may be able to remove it by rubbing with your finger when the adhesive is partly set. If it dries before you notice it, rub it gently with a cloth moistened with white spirit (turps). You may need to reseal or touch up the surface with wax polish when the cork is dry in order to hide the marks.

FIXING CORK SHEET

Cork in sheet form can be fixed in various ways. When you are fixing it, remember that
● with some types you use a special cork adhesive, applied to the wall
● with others you apply a heavy-duty wallpaper adhesive to the back of the cork or to the wall (check with the manufacturer's instructions)
● unlike wallpaper, which you trim after fixing, each length of cork should be cut exactly to fit before you hang it
● the joins between the lengths of cork shouldn't be rolled with a seam roller, as this will simply make the joins more obvious and spoil the overall look.

BARK-TEXTURED CORK

It's a pity to seal a really heavily textured bark cork, as part of its appeal lies in the matt, almost crumbly surface. Another point is that this type of cork should not be hung where it gets constantly knocked or touched, nor used as a noticeboard or pinboard or it will show signs of wear.

PUTTING UP FRIEZES & BORDERS

Patterned friezes and borders can help give a room a touch of style, and they can be used to hide cracks or make a tall room seem smaller – while adding very little to your decorating costs.

Friezes and borders, narrow strips of paper patterned to match the wallpaper in a room, are a traditional form of decoration. They were often either stuck below the picture rail or at the top of the wallpaper to hide the trimmed edges. Sometimes they were used below or above a dado rail, or to 'trim' an attic ceiling by hiding the join between sloping and flat areas.

Their popularity faded for some time but they are now making a comeback. Many of the co-ordinated ranges of wallcoverings, fabrics and beddings now available include border designs, and a definite 'bordered' look is commonly seen in upholstery and curtains. As well as being used with painted walls, borders can be teamed with a papered area, with either a simple texture or a co-ordinating design. There are also some heavily embossed friezes, which can be painted to contrast or tone with the scheme before they are hung, and a border or frieze effect can be created with painted bands of colour or with stencilled designs (see pages 164-167 for details).

Using friezes and borders

Of course, a border can still be used to bridge the gap between ceiling and wall or to hide any unevenness, or for that matter to cover decorating mistakes such as paint drips from the ceiling, the smudges and splodges of an inexperienced decorator, or to hide badly trimmed paper at the top or bottom of the wall. But they are intended to be an integral part of the decorative scheme and should not be thought of simply as a cover-up device. They can be used for various decorative purposes and it's worth taking some time to study the wide range available to see which would suit your requirements.

You can use a bright border to enhance a dull colour scheme, to introduce an 'accent' colour to a monochromatic scheme, or to tie several colours in a room together (the border could link carpet, curtain and wall colours, for example). Alternatively, you could use a quiet frieze to tone down a vivid scheme. Friezes and borders can be used to carry colour through from one room to another, creating a sense of continuity. For instance,

in a 'through' room with an arch or doorway between, one half might be decorated with patterned walls and the other half plain-painted but trimmed with the companion border design. In the hall you could have a dado rail with paint below, paper above and the rail emphasised with a border and the same pattern echoed at cornice or picture rail. You could then hang a companion design wallpaper with a co-ordinating pattern in an adjoining bedroom or sitting room.

You can use borders to play eye-deceiving tricks to improve the proportions of a room. In a hall which is too tall, you could use a deep border below the cornice or coving at ceiling level, and hang a matching or companion border at dado height or to emphasise the dado rail, then decorate below and above to contrast. In a sitting or dining room which looks too tall and where you wish to lower its apparent height, you could hang a very deep frieze (or two rows of a narrower one) just below the coving; or if there is none, leave a strip about twice the width of the border between the ceiling and the top edge, painted to match the ceiling. A very long room can be made to seem shorter if you use borders to form panels on the longest wall, or to outline the two shorter end walls. In an uninteresting box-like room, you can add interest by creating a focal point with a border design or, in a clinical bathroom, add a border design above the tiles to give warmth and character. Borders can also link with a fabric braid used to trim curtains or bedcovers and upholstery.

Trimming your own border

If you want a particularly bold border and have difficulty in finding just the right design, you can trim your own from wallpaper or a vinyl wallcovering which has a positive stripe in the pattern or a definite shape which will give an emphatic silhouette.

You may want to create a dado effect for a hall or breakfast area behind bench seating, to protect the lower part of the wall, or to give a splashback effect behind a dressing table, basin or kitchen worktop. Tile-type designs or definite geometric patterns are particularly suitable; you cut the top, following the pattern to form a castellated, scalloped, or serrated effect. In a bathroom or kitchen, and in children's rooms, you can even use offcuts of sheet vinyl flooring to form a border or splashback.

Suitable surfaces

Borders are applied right at the end of decorating; in fact, sometimes they may be added some time later. They need to be applied to a smooth, clean, dry wall area and if the walls are covered with heavily embossed paper which has been painted over it may not be possible to apply a border because it won't adhere securely to the surface. If a border is not well stuck it is likely to peel at the edges, which looks unsightly. If you want to apply a border to a textured wallcovering, it's well worth doing a trial run on a small area of wall first, to make sure it will stick, rather than risking wasting time and money on doing the whole room.

FIXING A PASTED FRIEZE

1 *Measure down the wall and mark off where the base line of the frieze will come; the top should be a few millimetres below the picture rail.*

2 *Lightly pin a batten to the wall to serve as a guide for marking off the base line. Check that it's truly horizontal with a spirit level.*

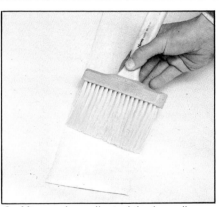

3 *After you've adjusted the base line where necessary you can go ahead and paste the back of the frieze, applying an even coat of adhesive.*

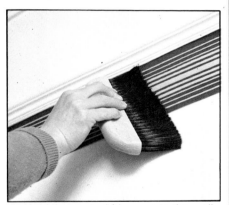

4 *Hold the pasted frieze up to the wall and then smooth it into place. If it's a long length you may need to fold it into concertina folds first.*

5 *Continue working along the wall in this way. Where you need to join lengths of frieze, butt the cut ends, taking care that the pattern matches.*

6 *Remove any excess adhesive and then, unless the frieze is an embossed type, run over it with a seam roller to make sure it is well stuck down.*

Ready Reference

BORDER SIZES
Friezes and borders come in a variety of widths from 18mm (3/4in) up to about 450mm (18in), and also in different lengths (though many are available in 9m/29 1/4ft lengths). They are available from wallpaper stockists; some may have to be ordered from a pattern book where small samples are shown.

CHOOSING THE RIGHT DEPTH
When deciding on the depth of your border you'll get best results if you:
● choose a narrower width (and smaller design) border for small areas
● choose big, bold ones for larger rooms
● when in doubt, cut a template from paper and try the effect first before ordering; (if you are going to make a panel or outline, make a template the same size as the panel and fix it to the wall with sticky tape, to see how you like it.

FIXING METHODS
With many friezes and borders you can buy (or those you've trimmed yourself), you fix them by applying adhesive to the back and then applying them to wall. (Or you can paste the wall instead). Some types are ready-pasted and you use water to activate the paste before fixing them as with ready-pasted wallpaper.

TYPES OF ADHESIVE
The type of adhesive you should use depends on the material from which the border is made:
● for paper friezes, use ordinary wallpaper adhesive
● if the frieze is vinyl or you are sticking a frieze or border to a vinyl wallcovering, use a heavy-duty or ready-mix tub paste
● if you are using sheet vinyl flooring to form a border or splashback, use the recommended flooring adhesive.

TIP: THE SIZE OF BRUSH
To apply adhesive you'll need a brush of a suitable width; use a small one for a narrow border and a wide one for a deeper frieze. A clean paintbrush or an artist's brush is often most suitable.

TIP: MARK UP CAREFULLY
For a professional-looking result it's essential that the frieze or border is fixed (or appears to be fixed) in a straight, horizontal line. You will have to mark up a true horizontal and then adjust slightly where necessary so the picture rail, dado or cornice does not appear to be askew. Use chalk or pencil to make the guideline so rubbing it out is simple.

Tools and equipment

It's important that you don't end up with your frieze or border askew, so you'll need the appropriate items of equipment to ensure this: a plumbline, try-square, spirit-level and a length of batten to serve as a straightedge. You'll need a brush of suitable size (see *Ready Reference*) to apply the paste – unless you're using a ready-pasted decoration – and scissors for cutting the frieze or border to the correct length and for mitring the corners. Unless the decoration is an embossed type, you'll also require a seam roller to smooth down the top and flatten the seams for a neat result.

Hanging borders

The important thing to remember when you are hanging borders is that you need to establish a true horizontal line. However, if you are following a cornice, picture rail or dado rail you may find that the original is not actually horizontal. In that case, try to follow the line with the edge of the border just a few millimetres below or above the edge of the rail or cornice and rely on your eye, adjusting the width between the edge of the border and line you are following, so the border appears to be straight but the rail does not look too obviously at an angle.

To get a horizontal line to follow, use your plumb line, and try-square or spirit level and the batten to help you draw a straight line in chalk or soft pencil (see step-by-step photographs). If you have someone to help you, you won't need to pin the batten to the wall, since one person can position and check for accuracy while the second person draws the line.

If you are hanging a ready-pasted trimming you treat it in the same way as you would if you were hanging ready-pasted wallpaper. If has to be cut to size, immersed in water until the paste is activated and then stuck in place; you smooth it out with a sponge or clean cloth.

Where you will be pasting the back of the trimming, you cut it to length and apply the paste, taking care not to get paste on the front of the paper. Hang it, following the line you've drawn on the wall, and smooth it out carefully with a sponge or clean brush (a conventional paperhanger's brush may be too wide).

A final tip: if you find paperhanging difficult and messy you could cheat and cut a border or frieze from self-adhesive material. Materials of this type are not very wide, but to get a sufficiently long length you could cut down the length instead of across the width. If you do use this type of material, you will need another person to help you; otherwise work in short lengths so you get it in exactly the right position first time, as the adhesive will stick firmly once it touches the wall surface.

FIXING BY PASTING THE WALL

1 *Measure the width of the frieze, then draw two horizontal lines this width apart across the wall to mark where you want the frieze to be fixed.*

2 *Load a brush or roller with adhesive and then spread a fairly generous even coat on the wall between and up to the lines you have marked.*

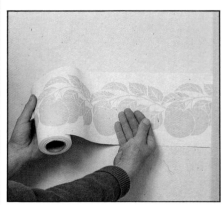

3 *Holding the rolled-up frieze in one hand, apply the loose end at the end of the wall, gently pressing it onto the pasted surface.*

4 *Unroll the frieze and work your way across the wall, smoothing the frieze into place by pressing it all over with a clean, damp sponge.*

5 *When you reach the end of the wall you can cut off the frieze with a sharp knife or scissors to form a neatly finished edge. Press this in place.*

6 *Clean off excess adhesive from the face of the frieze and surrounding wall using a clean damp sponge. Then run a seam roller over the frieze.*

FORMING A PANEL

1 *To use a border to make a panel on the wall, first draw in the outline in pencil, using your spirit level and plumbline to get the lines true.*

2 *Smooth a pasted length of border vertically on the wall so it overlaps the horizontal line by at least the depth of the border you are using.*

3 *Cut another length of border and smooth it into place, following the horizontal line so it overlaps the vertical length you've fixed.*

4 *Take a straightedge and place it diagonally between the inner and outer edges of the corner; then cut along it using a sharp knife.*

5 *Peel off the trimmed overlap on top, then lift back the horizontal length and peel off the trimmed overlap which is underneath it.*

6 *You will now have a neatly mitred corner which you can smooth back into place. Repeat the process to form the other edges and corners of the panel.*

Ready Reference

READY-PASTED TRIMMINGS

Where you intend hanging a narrow trimming which is a ready-pasted type, it may be more practical to activate the adhesive by laying the trimming face down on the pasting table and brushing the back with tepid water (use a clean brush) rather than immersing the narrow strip in a bowl or trough of water.

PANELS AND OUTLINES

If you plan to hang a border paper to form a panel or to outline a wall area, you will have to mitre the corners. You will find some designs, with a definite directional pattern, may not be suitable for this type of treatment, so check before you buy.

MAKING YOUR OWN BORDER

To make your own border from wallpaper or a vinyl wallcovering, you cut the top out to shape and leave the bottom flush.

TIP: LONG FRIEZES

If the area where you are going to apply the frieze is a very long one it may be impossible to hang the frieze in one go without difficulty. In this case:
● if you decide to cut it, do so where the join will not be obvious, and follow either a line or shape in the design (cutting round the edge of a flower shape, for example)
● you can also use this technique if you have to join the material because you are starting another roll.

TIP: REMOVE SURPLUS ADHESIVE

Wipe off immediately any surplus paste which oozes out from the edge of the border. The same applies to any water/paste which may trickle down the wall when you are applying a ready-pasted trimming. Otherwise you risk ruining the trimming and the rest of the wall decoration.

USING A SEAM ROLLER

When you have applied the border you can run a seam roller over it to make sure that it adheres securely. But never use a seam roller if the border is of an embossed type or you will spoil the raised pattern.

PUTTING UP COVING

You can enhance the decorative effect of a room – and hide defects – by adding coving and a complementary centre to the ceiling. Installation is quite straightforward and it should be no trouble to find a variety which suits your room.

When you are planning your decoration scheme, don't forget the ceiling. Often this simply ends up being painted white and without ornament. Sometimes this may be the right solution but at others a more imaginative treatment can enhance the overall appearance of a room.

You can use colour on the ceiling to make a very tall room appear lower; or change the proportions of a box-like room to make the shape seem more interesting; or even increase the apparent size of a small room. Alternatively, you can add some form of ornament to the ceiling surface. In bathrooms and bedrooms where you will be aware of the ceiling much more often than in other rooms – when you are lying in the bath or in bed – it's particularly worth making the view more interesting.

Ornamental ceilings can be created either by using cornices – mouldings fixed in the angle between the wall and the ceiling – or more simple coving which links the two surfaces. (There is a clear distinction architecturally, but here both will be referred to as coving.) Ceiling centres – ornamental mouldings fixed in the middle of the ceiling – will provide an attractive focal point.

In practical terms, a nice, neat coving between wall and ceiling, apart from looking more elegant and 'finished', will hide the joints between ceiling and wall decorations or hide cracks, wires or pipes; sometimes it may be continued to form a pelmet for curtains or blinds, or to conceal strip lighting. Ceiling centres, used to complement coving, will also disguise a poorly plastered ceiling, hide joins, bumps and electrics and are a perfect foil to attractive light fittings like chandeliers.

Types of ceiling ornaments

It is still possible to find a craftsman who will 'sculpt' a decorative coving or ceiling centre for you but this is likely to be prohibitively expensive. It is cheaper to use some form of prepared, preformed coving or ceiling centre.

These come in various materials which break down into four categories: fibrous plaster, plasterboard or gypsum, plastic and wood. Fibrous plaster covings and ceiling centres are available in different styles, mostly traditional. Plasterboard or gypsum covings are streamlined and simple to install. Of the various plastic types there are covings and ceiling centres made from glass fibre and also ones made from cellular plastics such as polyurethane and expanded polystyrene: these are all light and easy to handle. There are also covings and ceiling centres made from a new plastic resin product that looks like genuine plasterwork and can be sawn, drilled and sanded like wood; and, unlike the other plastics, it is fire-resistant.

Wood covings – a final variant – are particularly effective in a room with walls completely or partly covered in wood cladding where they will provide a feature in keeping with the rest of the room.

Types of adhesives

Manufacturers usually recommend a suitable adhesive – always check with their instructions when buying the coving or ceiling centre. Adhesives come ready-mixed or, for fixing plasterboard or gypsum coving, in powder form – you mix the adhesive with water.

As a guideline, fibrous plaster ornaments should be stuck with a wall panel adhesive or a contact adhesive – it will be easier to manage if an application gun is used. Plasterboard or gypsum coving is fixed with plaster – you can use this to fill any gaps as well. Glass fibre is fixed with the same types of adhesive as fibrous plaster. For polyurethane you will need a ready-mixed paste adhesive which again can be used to fill gaps. Polystyrene should be stuck with a special expanded polystyrene adhesive of

PREPARING THE SURFACE

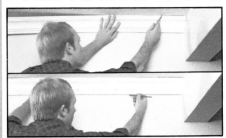

1 *Using a length of coving as a guide, mark guidelines on the ceiling and on the wall. Continue the lines so they go right round the room.*

2 *Score along the guidelines with a handyman's knife or other sharp instrument as a first step to removing the wallpaper from the ceiling and wall.*

3 *Scrape off wallpaper and flaky paint in the area between the guidelines. Soak paper if necessary, taking care to protect wallpaper lower down the wall.*

4 *Provide a key so the adhesive grips properly by slightly roughening the surface, gently scoring the area where the coving will be fixed.*

the type used to fix ceiling tiles. Plastic resin ornaments are fixed in a similar way to wood. Choose a wood adhesive such as PVA, synthetic resin adhesive, a multi-purpose type, or even a wall panel adhesive in an easy-to-apply gun. For wooden covings you will need a wood adhesive – this is often used in conjunction with nails or screws.

Any adhesive is only really effective if it is applied to a clean, dust-free surface. New plaster should be allowed to dry out before multi-purpose, wood, or expanded polystyrene adhesives are used, although the plaster/gypsum filler type can be used on damp plaster.

Always follow the manufacturer's instructions carefully when using any type of adhesive. If you are using an adhesive which is likely to 'go off', or harden quickly, work on manageable lengths of coving at a time. With powder adhesives, don't guess how much water to add, follow the instructions.

CUTTING A MITRE

1 *When using a mitre box, place the coving so the 'ceiling' edge is at the bottom of the box and use the slots in the box to provide a saw guide.*

2 *Where a paper template is provided, mark the cutting line using the template as a guide and then carefully saw along the marked line.*

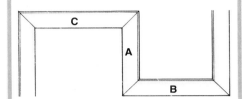
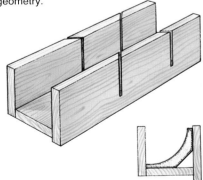

Planning

As with all decorating operations, time and care spent on planning will pay off later, helping you make sure of a successful result. To judge the optimum coving depth before buying, cut a paper template to a likely depth and a length of 1.5 to 1.8m (5 to 6ft) and pin it in the angle between the wall and ceiling where the coving will go. This should be long enough for you to gain an idea of the finished effect. If it seems wrong, (ie, too shallow or too deep), repeat the operation with a template of a different depth until you have the right size.

Having decided on the depth of the coving, the next step is to measure up the ceiling accurately. If it is going to be a difficult shape to deal with – for example, if there is a chimney breast or corners which are out of square – make a scale plan of the ceiling on squared paper. This way you will be able to work out exactly where the joins will come in the lengths of coving and where you will need to cut or mitre the coving for the corners. Use your plan or measurements as a guide for ordering the correct amount of coving.

A ceiling centre is going to be a focal point of interest, and it is essential therefore to choose one which is the right size for the room. They range in size from 150mm (6in) to 685mm (2ft 3in) in diameter; smaller ones suit smaller rooms and larger ones large rooms. To help you decide on the size of the ceiling centre, you can again make a paper template to gain an impression of the finished effect.

Marking up and preparation

You will need to mark guidelines for fixing the coving. You can use a piece of coving to indicate where lines should be drawn at the correct level on wall and ceiling.

The surface must be properly prepared. You will need to make sure all old wallpaper, flaking paint or distemper is removed from between the guidelines. It is also advisable to fill any cracks. Leave the filler to harden and then, if necessary, sand smooth. Bumpily filled cracks could throw the coving out of alignment, making it look distorted. With some types of adhesive you will also have to provide a key, so the adhesive grips properly, by slightly roughening the surface of the wall and ceiling where the coving will be fixed.

For a ceiling centre you can cut a paper or cardboard template round which to draw a guideline before preparing the surface in the same way as preparing for fixing coving. Make the template slightly smaller – by about 6mm (¼in) – than the actual ceiling centre so areas where paper or paint have been removed will not show when the ceiling centre is in place.

Cutting coving

Measure the coving for length. Remember that corners will have to be mitred and that there is a different technique for internal and external angles (see *Ready Reference*). Some preformed coving comes with a special template provided in the pack to make cutting and mitring easier – you place the template on the coving and trace the required mitre shape with a pencil. If you are using coving which does not have such a template provided, you will need to make up a mitre box which you can use to hold the coving while you cut it at the correct angle (see *Ready Reference*). For cutting you will need a fine tooth saw and you should cut from the face of the coving to ensure you get a clean edge.

Fixing coving

A plaster/gypsum adhesive will have to be mixed according to the manufacturer's instructions. If the job is likely to take a while, mix up only part of the adhesive at a time so you don't waste any if it dries out too soon. With some types of adhesive you will need to dampen the surface to be coved with water. If the surface is very porous you will have to seal it with a coat of diluted emulsion or PVA adhesive first.

You can then spread out the adhesive onto the back edges of the coving. Push each length firmly into position and hold it in place until it sticks. If you are using a contact adhesive, spread it on the back of the coving. Press the coving in position, then pull it away immediately and leave for about 10-20 minutes – the honeycomb structure of the adhesive will be on coving, wall and ceiling surfaces. Then fix the coving back in position and adjust its positioning at once as the adhesive will harden quickly and will be firmly bonded within an hour.

Heavier covings may have to be nailed or screwed, as well as stuck, into position. You should use galvanized nails or rustproof screws spaced 500mm (20in) apart, and, so they won't be visible on the finished surface, punch the nails below the surface with a nail punch, or countersink screws and fill the holes you have created with surplus adhesive or with cellulose filler.

Scrape off surplus adhesive which squeezes out from under the coving. (Sometimes this can be used to fill nail holes and gaps. Otherwise, you will have to use a cellulose filler).

Fixing ceiling centres

Ceiling centres are fixed in the same way as coving. Heavier types may need extra support from nails or screws: make sure the heads are countersunk or punched home and fill the gaps with adhesive or other filler.

If the ceiling surface is bad and you want

FIXING COVING

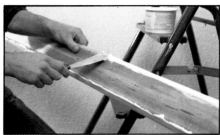

1 *Butter the adhesive on the back edges of the coving with a filling knife – try to avoid getting adhesive on the front of the coving.*

5 *Where coving is to fill a gap between lengths already fixed, hold a piece up so it rests against one fixed length and mark a cutting line on the other end.*

to use a textured paper to help disguise this, it is easier to paper the ceiling first and then cut out the area to be covered with the ornament rather than fixing the ceiling centre and then papering round it.

Where a ceiling centre is to be used to enhance a central light fitting, you will also have to cope with the electrics. As a first step, you will have to remove the existing bulb and lampholder. Where the ceiling centre has a hollow in the middle, it may be possible to leave the existing ceiling rose in place and fit the new ceiling centre over it. Simply pull down the flex through the hole in the middle of the new centrepiece (some already have holes bored; with others you may have to make the hole).

With other types of ceiling centres, which are flatter in the middle, you may have to remove the existing rose and replace it with a terminal connector strip which will fit in the space available before fixing the new ornament into position to conceal it. Both these solutions have the disadvantage that if at a later date you wish to gain access to the wiring, you will have to remove the ceiling centre. As an alternative, you can rewire the light so access can be gained from above (see *Ready Reference*).

If you have a very heavy chandelier, it may be necessary to have a hook to support it –

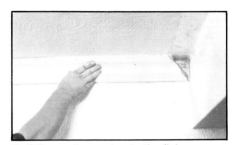

2 Offer up the coving to the fixing area and, when you are sure it is in the right position, press it firmly into place. The adhesive will squeeze out of the edges:

3 To provide support till the adhesive sets, drive nails into the edges of the coving. These can be punched home or removed and the holes filled later.

4 At a corner, place coving so mitred edges meet and fix it in position. You can then use a filling knife to smooth adhesive down for a neat joint.

6 After you have cut the filler piece and applied adhesive, offer it up and install it so it butts against the lengths of coving already fixed

7 Remove excess adhesive by running a filling knife along the edges of the coving. This can be used to fill in any gaps, joins or nail holes.

8 For final cleaning up, use a sponge which has been soaked in clean water to remove any adhesive from the coving face, the wall and ceiling.

coming through the hole in the middle of the decorative centre – and this will have to be fixed to a beam or joist to take the weight. This may also determine the position of the fitting, since there may not be a conveniently placed central support.

Decoration

If you intend painting the ceiling, emulsion paint, which can be applied without silting up any of the more decorative mouldings, is particularly suitable. A matt or eggshell lustre-finish oil-based paint can also be used, but this is not very suitable for delicate mouldings. Lastly, you can use multi-purpose paint (ie one which can be used on walls, ceilings and woodwork). Gloss and other solvent-based paints should never be used on plastic.

Colour is a matter of personal choice but usually the 'bed' – the flat part of the ceiling – looks best in a colour which can be dark, rich or strong if the room is fairly tall and paler if it is low. The relief decorations can be picked out in white or any other contrasting neutral shade, or in a pale, toning or contrasting colour. Give the ceiling decorations their first coat, then paint the ceiling itself with two coats, taking particular care at the edges and where it meets the ornaments. Apply a final coat to the decorations.

FIXING A CEILING CENTRE

1 Draw round a paper template which is slightly smaller than the ceiling centre. You can then prepare the surface within the marked area.

2 Spread adhesive on the outer rim at the back of the ceiling centre, feed the flex down through the hole in the middle and fix the centre in place.

3 Run a filling knife round the edge of the ceiling centre to remove excess adhesive between the centre and ceiling.

4 Use a damp sponge to wipe off traces of adhesive left on the surface of the centre and ceiling.

CHAPTER 7

UNUSUAL EFFECTS WITH PAINT

Walls and ceilings can be painted in a variety of attractive ways
using techniques like stippling and rag-rolling. The finished
effect is unique, and you need only a few simple tools
to achieve it. If you prefer a bolder effect, stencils and murals
offer a striking alternative.

CREATING COLOURED WALL FINISHES

If you fancy a change from the usual expanse of emulsion painted walls, you could try one of these broken colour finishes. They're quick and easy to do.

Painted walls will always be popular because they're quick and easy to decorate and paint manufacturers offer hundreds of colours to choose from. Walls, however, are usually the largest surface in a room and if you're not careful they can look very bare and uninteresting. Professional decorators have always known this and they use many different methods, some of them centuries old, to give a painted surface more texture. These methods – including stippling, sponging, rag-rolling and dragging – all involve 'breaking up' or 'distressing' the paint in some way so that two or more colours mingle together to give a wonderful depth to the wall.

For all these finishes a base coat is first painted on the wall in the usual way; then other coats are applied using one of the special techniques. The effects can be varied depending on the colours chosen for the two coats. You can use two slightly different shades of the same colour for a subtle, gentle effect, or use dark or contrasting colours – deep reds on white for instance – for a bold, rich finish. You can also afford to experiment with bolder colours than you would normally dare to choose because the 'distressing' techniques will always tone down the colour depth.

Preparation
With all these techniques you will get the best effect if you prepare the surface well before you start.

Old wallpaper must be stripped off and any remaining paste should be washed off thoroughly. Painted surfaces will just need a good wash down with a cleaning solution. Start at the bottom of a wall and work your way upwards; then, with clean water and a soft cloth, go over the wall again, this time starting at the top. Walls painted in gloss must be rubbed down with medium-grade glasspaper to provide a good key for the base coat.

Cracks should be filled with an interior-grade filler. Undercut the edges of the crack a little and damp the area slightly. Leave the filler a little proud of the surface, and then sand it down level when it's dry.

Walls that are just plain shabby would benefit from being lined with a good-quality lining paper. Hang the lengths vertically, not horizontally as you would if you were going to hang wallpaper on top, and butt-join the edges for a near-invisible seam. That said, though, a few of these techniques, such as sponging and ragging-on, will actually disguise slightly shabby plasterwork as they will distract your eye from any unevenness. But, ideally, you should always aim to provide a perfectly flat, even wall surface – and for dragging, this is essential.

What you do next depends on the paint finish you intend to use. If the finish needs a base coat of an oil-based eggshell, then first apply an oil-based primer/sealer or undercoat. An emulsion base needs no primer or undercoat, but you may need two coats for good coverage, especially on new plaster.

Tinting paint
The most economical way of buying paint is to buy a large tin of the correct type – matt, silk, undercoat or eggshell – and then to mix your own shades by adding small amounts of universal stainers or even artists' paints

(see *Ready Reference*). This way you can get exactly the shade you want – to match curtains or carpets for instance. But, if you don't feel up to this, several of the paint manufacturers offer a large range of colours that they'll mix up for you. This will save you the uncertainty of mixing your own but they are rather more expensive.

Use the right paint
Traditionally, professional decorators have always used a special paint called a transparent oil glaze or 'scumble' glaze for these special finishes. The glaze is colourless or white and has to be tinted to the right colour and thinned at the rate of two parts glaze to one, two or even three parts of solvent. A glaze has the advantage of being very slow drying, so the distressing techniques can be carried out without panic. Oil paints tend to dry out more quickly.

However, many professional decorators are now using a paint 'glaze' which is simply thinned oil paint. The best type of oil paint to use is trade flat white which gives a nice matt finish. But this is rather difficult to find and you can work quite well with ordinary comm-

SPONGE STIPPLING

1 *Pour a little paint into a shallow dish or onto a board and spread it around with the back of a spoon or a palette knife to give a thin even layer.*

2 *It's essential to use a real marine sponge for this technique. Dip it into water until it expands to its full size and then squeeze it out well.*

3 *Grip the sponge firmly and dab it lightly into the paint. A quick dab is all you need as you don't want it to soak up a lot of paint.*

4 *Keep a sheet of scrap paper handy – lining paper is ideal – and test the print, dabbing until you get the right density of paint.*

5 *Now work lightly over the whole wall, refilling the sponge as necessary. Aim for an even coverage and a regular speckled effect.*

6 *Leave the wall to dry and then repeat the process with the second colour. The base will always dominate, but will be changed by the sponged colours.*

ercial eggshell paint. If you do want a matt finish with an oil-based paint you can always use an oil-based undercoat. Buy one as near to the right colour as possible and then tint it to the right shade. Don't use gloss, as this would be far too shiny for walls.

Of course, you don't have to use oil-based paints for all these techniques. Many of them work equally well with emulsion paint – whether silk or matt – and, in fact, this would be the first choice for techniques such as sponge stippling, ragging-on, colour washing and, possibly, bag-graining.

The techniques

Most of the paint finishes described here can be divided into two basic categories. The first covers all the techniques where a top coat of paint is dabbed or sponged onto a base coat that has dried. This includes sponge stippling and ragging-on. Both these methods work well with a base and top coat of ordinary matt emulsion. But you can use an eggshell base and a thinned eggshell or glaze for the top coat if you wish.

The second method includes bag-graining, rag-rolling, dragging and stippling. With all these techniques the top coat is painted on and then treated in some way while it is still wet to break up the colour. These methods generally work best with oil-based paints – eggshell for the base and thinned eggshell or glaze for the top coat. You *can* use a thinned emulsion paint for the top coat but you would have less time to work on it before it dried.

The technique for this last category is to paint a narrow strip of wall – 600mm (2ft) wide is best – then go over it with the rag, bag or whatever and paint the next strip of wall before the first has dried. It is essential to keep a wet edge to the paint or you'll end up with a patchy result. If you can get someone else to paint on the top coat while you follow closely behind with your chosen technique, so much the better. The work will go much more smoothly this way.

Finally, for a long-lasting finish, coat the walls with a clear, matt, polyurethane varnish.

Sponge stippling

This gives a very pretty informal finish, and is quick and easy to do. Emulsion paint is picked up on a sponge and dabbed onto the wall in an irregular pattern. It's left to dry and the wall is gone over again with another colour. Sponge stippling works best with a soft pastel shade for the base coat and slightly darker shades of the same colour family for the top coats. You can also use contrasting colours, but in this case it's best to keep them all fairly pale. You can vary the effect by sponging on dark colours for a stronger speckled effect, or use lighter or diluted paint for a soft, marbled look.

RAGGING ON

1 Spread a thin layer of paint round a shallow dish, bunch up the rag and dip it lightly in the paint. Test the print on some scrap paper.

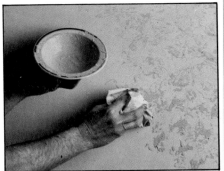

2 Dab the rag on the wall with a light touch, refilling the rag as necessary. Keep refolding the rag, leaving even spaces between each print.

RAG-ROLLING

1 Use an oil-based eggshell paint or scumble glaze for the top coat; dilute it with equal parts of white spirit (turps) and mix well.

2 Soak a fine cotton rag in white spirit (turps) first, then squeeze it out well. This will prevent it clogging with paint too quickly.

3 Brush on the paint next, but don't cover too large an area or the paint will dry before you get to it. A strip 600mm (24in) wide is about right

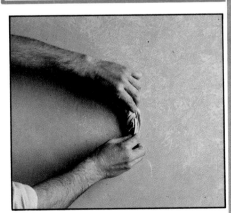

4 Bunch up the rag into a sausage shape and roll it over the wet paint glaze. Keep changing direction but take care not to skid over the surface.

Ready Reference

QUANTITIES OF PAINT

Most techniques use thinned paint so you'll need less paint than usual.
● sponge stippling: one litre of each colour is sufficient for an average room
● ragging-on: one third the quantity required for one coat of base colour
● bag-graining: half the quantity needed for one coat of base colour
● rag-rolling: half quantity needed for one coat of base colour
● dragging: half quantity needed for one coat of base colour
● colour washing: one litre is sufficient for an average room.
For more information on how much paint you need for walls see pages 12-15.

TIP: MIX ENOUGH PAINT

If the technique you're using needs diluted paint, try and mix up enough for the whole room. If you do seem to be running out of paint, finish the wall you're on and mix up another batch adding any paint you've got left. That way, any slight change of colour from one wall to the next won't be noticeable.

MAKE A TEST FIRST

Before starting on the wall it's advisable to practise the technique first. Do this on an out-of-the-way patch of wall or, better still, prop up a board and pin a length of prepainted lining paper to it.

For **sponge stippling** test:
● spacing of the prints
● pressure on the sponge
● thick and diluted paint

For **ragging-on** test:
● different types of material
● different folds and spacing of prints
● thick and diluted paint

For **bag-graining** test:
● thickness of the top coat – if you apply too much paint it will run so brush it out more. It will also run if you've diluted it too much so add more paint and try again

For **rag-rolling** test:
● different folds and method of rolling
● thickness of the paint (see bag-graining)

For **dragging** test:
● different brushes
● thickness of the paint (see bag-graining)

For **colour washing** test:
● brushing technique
● different dilutions of the colour wash.

BAG-GRAINING

1 *You'll need an ordinary polythene bag and some rags. Half-fill the bag with the rags, push them well in and tie or secure the neck of the bag.*

2 *If you're using emulsion paint for the graining coat, dilute it with an equal amount of water. Eggshell paint should be diluted with white spirit (turps).*

3 *Using a wide brush, paint a section of wall about 600mm (24in) wide. Apply a thin coat of paint which covers the ground colour evenly.*

4 *Press the bag lightly over the wet paint and overlap the prints slightly for an even, crinkled finish. Continue painting and graining the wall, a section at a time.*

Bag-graining

Here the texture is produced by going over the wet paint with a graining bag – that is, a polythene bag filled with rags. It gives a much finer texture than rag-rolling, looking rather like crushed velvet. It's easy to do; you just press the bag over the wall and, from time to time, wipe off the excess paint that builds up on the bag. It works best on a white background – either eggshell or silk. Any colour can be used for the top coat, with the darker colours giving a bold effect.

Dragging

Dragging is one of the more difficult techniques to master, since the object is to drag a dry brush over the wet paint to produce regular vertical lines down the wall. Here's where proper glaze works best; if you use oil paint the stripes will tend to merge together a little – though you may prefer this. The trick is to drag the brush in a relaxed way with the bristles only lightly touching the surface. If you're tense, your arm is sure to shake and the stripes will wobble. You can buy special dragging brushes which have extra-long bristles but these are difficult to find and very expensive. As an alternative, a wide paperhanging brush will do quite well.

Stippling

Stippling is easy to do and produces a beautiful finely textured finish. All you do is paint on diluted eggshell or glaze over an eggshell base and then go over the wet paint with a special stippling brush. You must hit the wall square on to stop the brush skidding over the surface.

Stippling is often used to obliterate any brush marks on the top coat before doing other techniques like dragging and rag-rolling.

Real stippling brushes are rectangular, about 100 x 75mm (4 x 3in) and are made of fine bristle. Their only drawback is that they are difficult to find and very expensive. But you can experiment with an old clothes brush or a soft-bristled hairbrush.

Colour washing

This is a splashy technique best suited to country rooms, kitchens and playrooms. The top coat – of emulsion – is thinned much more than usual – as much as 8 parts water to 1 part of paint. This is then slapped onto the wall in haphazard strokes using a wide brush, leaving lots of the base colour showing through. When this is dry the process is repeated using the same colour, but this time brushing over the bare patches to give a dappled variation of colour. It's a messy business and you'll need plenty of protection for the floor as the paint is liable to run off at first. Don't worry though; enough paint will stick on eventually and the second coat of paint will cover up any unevenness.

It is essential to use a real marine sponge for this technique. A man-made one just won't work as the pattern it produces will be too hard-edged and regular.

Ragging-on

This is very similar to sponge stippling, except that a small piece of bunched up rag is used to apply the paint. You can experiment with different materials to get the effect you want – try net, muslin, cotton sheet and sacking. The finished effect also depends on the size and fold of the rag. If you want a regular, repeating pattern, keep the same rag with the same folds for the whole wall. This however, is difficult to do and it's best to keep refolding or changing the rag and aim for an irregular pattern. The most convenient size for the rag is about 300mm (12in) square, but again, experiment to find the size that suits you best.

Like sponging, ragging-on works well with a slightly darker colour ragged over a lighter one, but it looks equally good with the colours reversed. For a softer print you can dilute the top coat with up to 50 per cent of the solvent.

Rag-rolling

In contrast to ragging-on, this method uses a bunched up rag which is rolled over still wet, diluted eggshell paint or glaze.

Soft, fine cotton rags cut into 300mm (12in) squares are best, and you'll need a good supply of these as they soon get soaked with paint. It's best to keep refolding the rag from time to time and altering the directions of the rolling movements, since otherwise the pattern may become annoying and insistent. You should aim for an even and uniform coverage. The pattern produced is similar to soft crumpled silk and is well suited to formal rooms such as some dining rooms.

DRAGGING

1 Here, a scumble glaze is being used. Thin the glaze with an equal amount of white spirit (turps) and then pour it into a paint kettle.

2 To tint the glaze, take a small amount of artists' oil paint (or universal stainer) and mix it with some glaze. Then add this to the glaze and mix well.

3 Paint on the glaze in a smooth, even layer. Finish off with vertical strokes of the brush to prevent a criss-cross finish when you start dragging.

4 Use a dragging brush or, as here, a paperhanging brush and drag it smoothly down the wall. Overlap each strip for a regular striped effect.

STIPPLING

1 A proper stippling brush is very expensive so it's worth experimenting – with an old clothes brush, for example. It must have a level surface like this.

2 Simply hit the wall square on with the brush – hard at first to even out the paint and then more softly for a fine stippled finish.

Ready Reference

TIP: STOP AT A CORNER
If for any reason you can't do the whole room in one session, stop at a corner and do the next wall when the first is dry.

COVERING UP MISTAKES
Apart from dragging, all the other techniques produce a broken finish and any slight irregularities in the pattern or thickness of paint won't be too noticeable. But mistakes can happen so here's what to do:
● if you sponge or rag on a thick blob of paint, let it dry; then go over it again, this time with the sponge or rag dipped in the *base* colour
● if you're rag-rolling or bag-graining and the paint is too thick, simply go over it again with a clean rag or bag
● keep a clean cloth handy soaked in water or white spirit (turps) as appropriate to wipe off any paint from skirtings or ceiling
● if you're rag-rolling and the paint starts to dry out before you get to it, go over the paint surface with a new rag soaked in white spirit (turps).

MIX YOUR OWN COLOURS
If you're using a scumble glaze you'll have to mix your own colours, but you can do so with paint as well. Universal stainers are available for oil and emulsion paints. You can also use artists' oil colours for oil-based paints, and artists' gouache, acrylic or poster paints for emulsion paints.
   For oil paints take a small amount of colour in a dish or on a palette and add paint gradually, mixing until the colour is dispersed. You can then add this mixture to the main body of the paint. Repeat with more colour until you get the right shade. For emulsion paints, dissolve the colour in water first.

USING SCUMBLE GLAZE
Transparent oil glaze or 'scumble' glaze has the advantage of being very slow drying and will stay put rather than run out into a smooth layer. It is therefore ideal for many of these techniques as you'll have more time to work on the finish – up to two hours – before it starts to go off. The glaze will need thinning and colouring before use. It is available from specialists decorating suppliers.

TAKE CARE WITH SOLVENTS
When you've finished rag-rolling you'll be left with a pile of rags soaked in paint and solvent. Let these dry out before throwing them away. They are highly inflammable and could even catch fire spontaneously if left bunched up in a confined space.

STENCILLING WALLS AND FURNITURE

If you want to give walls, furniture or even floors a unique decorative finish, stencilling offers plenty of opportunities. This method of applying a painted pattern is easily mastered.

The art of stencilling can be learned quickly and is an effective way of giving a personal touch to all manner of fixtures and fittings in the home. Anything from a simple frieze design around a wall to an intricate pattern on a piece of furniture can be achieved with stencils, and they are an inexpensive way of brightening up what would otherwise be plain surfaces.

Stencilled designs should be simple, but two or more basic patterns can be combined to create a more intricate effect. Some traditional stencil designs incorporate many different shapes and colours, but usually two or three of each, on a natural or plain coloured background, make the most satisfactory combination.

Make or buy?

Ready-made stencils are available from craft, art or graphic design shops and other specialist suppliers; some are pre-cut in acetate and others are made from the traditional material, oiled card. Acetate is the most expensive, but the surface is easily wiped clean, and such stencils may be used again and again. Oiled card is also easy to clean and does not absorb paint, preventing smudges unless you move the stencil carelessly. However, it eventually deteriorates. These ready-cut designs come in a wide range of sizes, shapes and motifs.

There is nothing to stop you cutting your own stencils, as both acetate and oiled card should be available from the same source as the pre-cut stencils. It is possible to buy books of patterns which may be traced on to the stencil material; some patterns are printed on stiff paper and could be used for stencilling themselves, if only a short life is required. If you have some artistic skills you might even draw up your own design, or adapt a wallpaper, fabric or tile pattern.

Deciding size and colour

You may have to adjust the size of the pattern, particularly if you intend using the same design on several different surfaces for a co-ordinated effect. A delicate floral pattern might look delightful on a small chest of drawers, but would be quite lost on a large area of wall. It is not too difficult to scale any design up or down, using squared paper (see *Ready Reference*).

Once you have worked out the size and shape of the basic stencil design, and the area you plan to cover, think about the colours you want. Colours that contrast with the background are best, dark colours over pale backgrounds looking good if simple bold motifs are chosen. Lighter colours over dark backgrounds are better suited to more delicate designs.

If you plan to use two or more colours to make up a single pattern, test the effect first to see how they look together. The best way to judge the finished job is to cut out a few of the motifs from thick paper, colouring them with the paints you intend using. Hold these coloured shapes against the surface you want to stencil and move them around until you achieve a satisfactory balance. Then, stick them in place with adhesive tape until you are ready to mark out the guide lines for the stencil itself.

As an alternative, you could paint a length of lining paper with the intended background and stencil the design on to it in the chosen colours. Pin or tape this into position and leave it there for a few days to make sure you are completely happy with the result. Different types of light can change the appearance of colours quite dramatically, so look at your patterns carefully under both natural daylight and the artificial lighting you will use in the room to be decorated.

Materials and tools you will need

Apart from the actual stencils you are using, or the sheets for cutting your own, you will need a selection of basic materials and hand tools.

The type of paint you choose will depend on the surface you are treating. Ideally, it should be quick-drying. Apply a gloss or coloured wood stain to floors and furniture, and emulsion paint to walls. The latter is particularly good because it is easily removed if you make a mistake. You will need a solvent suitable for whatever type of paint you use, and some masking tape.

A black felt-tip pen is adequate for marking out the pattern on the stencil material, unless you are using acetate, in which case a special drawing pen will be needed. The latter will mark the acetate permanently, whereas other types of ink will simply rub off.

For cutting stencils, use a sharp craft knife, or possibly an artist's scalpel if the pattern is intricate. A piece of chipboard, blockboard, or even a sheet of thick glass with its edges taped, will serve as a cutting board.

Stencil brushes are specially made for the purpose and have short, stiff bristles which give a characteristic stippled look to the finished pattern. They come in various sizes and you should select them to match the size of the job. If you prefer, you can use paint pads, which are particularly useful when covering large areas. Even normal paint brushes will suffice, providing care is taken not to force paint under the stencil around the edges of the cut-outs.

MAKING A STENCIL

1 *You can draw out your own designs or copy something else, such as a tile. Tape a piece of tracing paper over the design and trace it out with a pencil.*

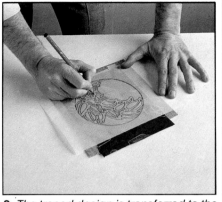

2 *The traced design is transferred to the stencil card by placing a sheet of carbon paper over the card and then drawing over the traced outline again.*

3 *Place the stencil card onto a suitable cutting board and carefully cut out the various shapes. Using a scalpel with a round handle will aid accurate cutting.*

4 *After cutting the stencil, compare it with the original design, and check that you have made all the cut-outs. Trim any rough edges so that you get a fluid line.*

Ready Reference

SCALING PATTERNS

If you intend using the same pattern on a number of different surfaces, you may want to increase or reduce its size to suit its position. To do this:
● draw or trace the original design on to squared graph paper
● then, if you want to increase the size, draw up another grid on a clean sheet of paper, making the squares larger. If, for example, you wanted to double the size you would make the squares twice as large, and so on
● copy the design on to the second grid, square for square, and you will achieve the necessary enlargement automatically
● to reduce the size of the pattern, draw it on a grid of smaller squares.

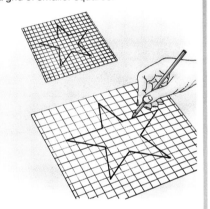

TIP: TRY OUT THE DESIGN

Before you start stencilling, make a series of 'proofs' from tissue paper. Trace through the stencilled motif, using coloured crayons or pencils to fill in the shapes with solid colour. Fix these roughs to the area to be stencilled and move them around until you achieve the effect you want. Tissue paper is particularly useful if you have to superimpose several designs or colours on top of each other. It will allow the background colour to show through, as well so you can more accurately judge the effect than you could if using an opaque material.

BRUSHES FOR STENCILLING

Stencil brushes are unlike normal paint brushes in that they have short, stiff bristles. Various sizes are available.

One or two sponges will be useful for wiping off any smudges but these, too, can be used for applying paint if the design lends itself to this treatment.

You should never apply paint direct from the can as you may overload the brush, so equip yourself with some old saucers or a palette made from a piece of board.

Careful marking out of the surface to be painted is essential if the pattern is to look right. Therefore, you will also need a plumb-line, some chalk, a T-square or set square, a spirit level and a straightedge.

Cutting your own stencils

To cut your own stencils, first transfer the design on to the acetate or oiled card. If using the former, simply lay it over the chosen design and trace over this with the drawing pen. In the latter case, you can use carbon paper to transfer the design. Place the carbon over the card and then put the design on top, making sure that all three layers are aligned. Trace over the outline of the design with a pointed instrument like a ballpoint pen or a knitting needle. Mark out a separate stencil for each colour you intend using.

Hold the acetate or card firmly on the cutting board with drawing pins or masking tape, and carefully cut out the shape. Make the cut line as fluid as possible, and if you do find a slightly ragged edge, smooth it gently with flour-grade glasspaper after removing the stencil from the board.

Keep the original design, storing it flat, so that you can make further tracings if necessary. In fact, if you plan to stencil a large area where the same shape will be repeated frequently, it is a wise move to cut more than one stencil in the first place. Lay them on top of each other to make sure the design is exactly the same on each. Also do this if

MARKING OUT

1 Mark the wall carefully to provide a guide for placing the stencil. Use a chalked line to mark a horizontal guide, checking with a spirit level if necessary.

2 Vertical guide lines can be made with the aid of a set square placed with its base edge against the horizontal line. Use white chalk as this won't stain the paint.

3 Finally, offer up the stencil to ensure that you have achieved the right spacing of the marks. Pencil guide lines and notches in the stencil will help you to align the pattern.

STENCILLING A FRIEZE

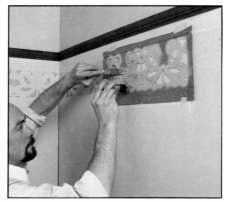

1 When more than one colour is used, apply one at a time. Use the brush with a stippling action, building up several layers of paint.

3 At corners, you can bend the stencil so the design is continuous. Score the stencil lightly with a knife and bend it round a straight edge.

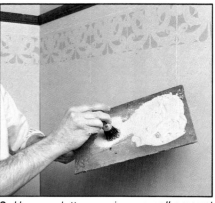

2 Use a palette, pouring a small amount of paint on to it at a time. Dip the brush in and tap it out on the palette until almost dry. Excess paint causes runs.

4 Apply the second colour when the first has dried, taking extra care to align the stencil so that the colours register. Hold the stencil flat with a bladed tool.

several different stencils form part of the same pattern. When all are aligned correctly, punch holes or cut notches through them so that perfect alignment is possible each time they are used.

Preparing the surface

As with all forms of decorating, the secret of a successful stencilling job lies in sound preparation of the surface. Make sure it is clean, dry and dust-free. Repair damaged plasterwork, sanding, painting or sealing walls and woodwork. If treating a floor, sand it smooth and punch any nail heads below the surface. New furniture will need sealing with clear polyurethane varnish if it is un-painted, and old furniture may need stripping before resealing or painting.

A stencilled pattern can even be applied to a textured surface, so uneven walls can be lined with a textured paper first. However, if the surface undulates too much, the pattern will make this more obvious.

To ensure correct placing of the stencil each time, mark out the surface with horizontal base line marks and vertical divisions to match the stencil edges. Use the plumbline, chalk, square and spirit level as necessary to achieve this.

Applying the pattern

Place the first stencil in position, fixing it with masking tape; other types of self-adhesive tape may damage the painted surface. Pour some paint on to your palette and dip the tip of the brush into it. Don't overload the brush with paint; check for this by trying it on a piece of scrap paper or board first. Then dab the colour firmly on to the background through the cut-out in the stencil. Take care not to dislodge the edges of the cut-out or you will smudge the pattern. Work from the

STENCILLING FURNITURE

The techniques you use for stencilling a design on a piece of furniture are much the same as you would use for stencilling a wall. You must, for example, make sure you have the stencil correctly positioned (one thing to watch out for on furniture is mouldings; it's best to arrange things so you won't be trying to paint a stencil over them). Also, you should take care not to smudge the edges of the pattern, so don't overload the brush or use a paint which is too watery. Proper preparation is a must: with old furniture you might have to strip off the existing finish and reseal with new paint or varnish; new furniture may also require sealing with paint or varnish before you apply the new decoration.

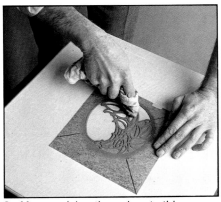

2 *After applying the colour to this central design, most of the paint was wiped off with white spirit to leave an unusual 'faded' finish.*

1 *To position a design in the centre of the top, mark the diagonals in chalk and put similar pencil marks through the stencil design.*

3 *Finally, a decorative border was applied to the top. Taping the stencil in place with masking tape prevents it moving and smudging the pattern.*

edges to the middle, and when all the cut-outs have been filled with colour leave the paint to harden off for a few moments. Then, peel off the stencil, replace it in the next position and repeat the stippling process. Work right across the surface to be stencilled, using one colour at a time. If you would have to place the stencil on top of wet paint to tackle the next area, do alternate areas instead – pattern repeats 1, 3, 5 and so on – and return to do 2, 4, 6 etc when the paint has dried and you can quite safely place the stencil over it.

If the stencil cut-outs become clogged, or there is paint on the surface, wipe it clean each time you reposition it.

It is a good idea to try out the stencil and your stencilling technique on a piece of paper before trying the job in earnest. This is particularly important if you intend stencilling furniture, where mistakes are difficult to rectify.

Finishing off

Proper care will mean you can use the same equipment again. There is little point in saving money by decorating with a stencil, only to waste the money you have spent on equipment by failing to take the few simple measures required for its maintenance. So, when the job is finished, remove any chalk marks from the surface, thoroughly clean all tools and the stencils, storing everything away carefully. Keep the stencils flat in a dry place, separating one from another by a layer of tissue or greaseproof paper.

On furniture and floors, apply a coat of clear polyurethane varnish to protect the pattern. A matt finish will suit most surfaces. However, heavy-wear areas, like floors, may need several coats, and you might prefer to use a semi-gloss or gloss finish for these. Make sure the stencilled pattern is absolutely dry before applying any protective finish.

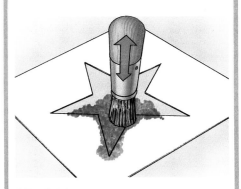

PAINTING MURALS

While the idea of painting a picture on a wall may seem daunting you'll find that a mural is surprisingly easy to execute. You don't need special artistic abilities to achieve a successful result.

Paint is not just for plain walls; it can be used to produce any pattern in any colour. And painting a wall with a mural or wall-pattern will give you a personalised form of decoration which is also inexpensive. You can use this technique to change the visual impression which a room gives; a mural will add an extra dimension to a blank wall or a really tiny room, can reduce the apparent size and give a more homely, cosy look to a vast wall area, or transform a dull, dark corridor, providing colour and interest where there was none before. In a tiny hall, with little light source, you might try painting an imaginary window on the blank stair well wall, complete with curtains, window box and view. In a narrow corridor you could use the trompe l'oeil (literally 'deceive the eye') technique, with, for example, pillars and a vista all down one side, or paint an imaginary doorway (it could be a French door with a view beyond) with trees to each side. In a bathroom or WC, a simple design of colours, waves, rolling hills or a permanent herbaceous border can be used to good effect.

Remember too that if you find a doorway or awkwardly placed pipe, projection or alcove gets in the way of your design you can turn them into an integral part of the mural. You can even include a piece of old furniture in the overall design by 'painting' it into the background; in fact this is a good way of hiding ugly architectural features, or making a junk shop buy blend in with its surroundings.

Proper preparation

Acting on impulse may result in a fine free-style mural, but it could be a waste of artistic effort if the wall surface is in poor condition, or you are painting over wall (or lining) paper which has started to peel, or old, porous, greasy emulsion paint.

So you should start out by providing yourself with a smooth, clean, non-absorbent surface. You will, where necessary, have to smooth down old plaster, fill any cracks and rub the filled areas down with glasspaper afterwards. If the plaster is in good condition, you can paint the wall in a suitable background colour; a standard mid-sheen or matt oil-based finish makes a perfect background for mural painting. Poor plaster can be lined; for this, you should choose as smooth a type of paper as possible and one which is of fairly heavy quality. If the walls are already covered in smooth wallpaper which is in good condition, you can give them a couple of coats of oil-based or emulsion paint, but don't choose a shiny finish (you can, of course, paint over lining paper in the same way). One point here: woodchips and other embossed or relief wallcoverings are not really suitable for mural-painting as it's difficult to get a straight or clearly defined line on the bumpy surface they provide; so if you've set your heart on painting a wall pattern you should remove wallcoverings of these types (and smooth and clean the surface) before you begin.

Materials you'll need

You can use emulsion or resin-based paints (painting murals is an attractive way of using up paint leftovers; you can intermix different colours of the same type of paint together to produce a wider colour range if you wish). You can also tint your own paints using artists' gouache or acrylic colours; these are expensive and can be used neat or thinned with a suitable medium, but though they are fine for small details their cost makes them impractical for large areas. Coloured stains can also be used neat (some of the woodstains now available come in a wide range of colours to give you a fairly reasonable amount of choice) or to tint, and you can even add fine details to your mural with felt pens or crayons.

You will also need an assortment of brushes: artists' brushes with fine points for details (a 'lining fitch' is a suitable type) and outlining the area to be painted, and ordinary decorators' 12 or 25mm (½ or 1in) brushes (or you could use artists' wedge-shaped oil brushes instead) for filling in the outlined areas. Larger brushes or rollers may also be necessary, depending on the design. Paint pads are also useful if you want to create texture interest, or a sponge can be used to create a stippled effect.

A mahl stick, on which you can rest your arm when painting, will help keep your hand steady and reduce the risk of smudging.

Suitable thinner (white spirit/turps or whatever) will depend on the type of paint you are using, as will the paint brush cleanser. You'll also require chalk or charcoal to transfer the design to the wall, and a plumb-line and spirit level to make sure you get the design square onto the surface. You may well need masking tape to get clean lines and perfectly straight edges, or you could use low-tack

THE FIRST STAGES

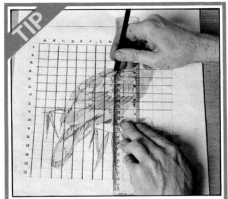

1 Divide your original drawing up into squares and label the grid. Later the labels are transferred to the wall to make referring to the drawing easier.

2 Measure the wall area to be covered by the mural to find out where the grid lines will come. Then use a plumbline to mark off a true vertical with chalk.

3 Then use chalk to mark off the first horizontal at right angles to the vertical lines. Check with a spirit level to make sure it's absolutely true.

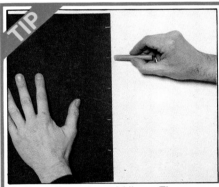

4 Draw the outer grid lines. Then use a marked piece of paper as a guide to mark the rest, which you can draw or snap onto the wall with chalked string.

5 Referring back to your original drawing with its numbered or lettered grid, begin to fill in each square on the wall with the design (in chalk).

6 Continue filling in the squares until the whole design has been transferred to the wall. Then check to see if you've made any mistakes.

Ready Reference

CHOOSING THE GRID SIZE

When you are dividing your original design into a grid to help you transfer it accurately to the wall, the size of the squares will depend on the complexity of the design:
● if the design is intricate, divide it into small 12mm (½in) squares
● if it is simple you can get away with larger squares of say, 50mm (2in).

TIP: PAINT THE WALL

Before you sketch the outline of the mural on the wall, first paint the area to be covered by the mural white. This provides a good base and may save you using two coats of colour.

TIP: OUTLINE AREAS FIRST

Even where you are attempting a free-hand design it's best to first draw its outline in chalk (preferably light-coloured so it won't show through the paint).

USE MASKING TAPE

When a straight line is required, rule the line in pencil first and then apply masking tape. Don't press it into place too hard or it may pull off the freshly applied paint when you remove it.

AIDS FOR DESIGN

There are a number of aids you can use to help you draw designs on the wall:
● diamonds, hexagons, or shaped bands of colour can be transferred to the wall by means of a template, cut from stout card
● triangular shapes can be made by drawing round a set square
● for circles you can use a compass, or draw round household objects like a bowl or glass; if you plan a large circle you can use a drawing pin, length of string and a pencil; pull the string taut and move the pencil round to draw the circle.

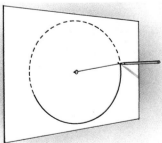

● for small intricate details you can buy a plastic or cardboard stencil (from artists' supply shops) and draw the outline with a pencil through the hole pierced in the stencil.

PAINTING THE MURAL

1 Mix up the paints where necessary and then pour them into containers which will be easy to hold. Assemble a range of brushes of different sizes.

2 Work from the top down. A mahl stick, which you can buy or make from a length of dowel with cloth tied to the end, will make painting easier.

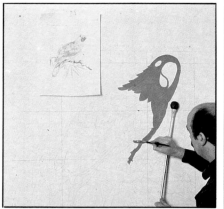

3 Continue to fill in the first area of colour. Try to work outwards from a wet edge, so you don't get a band of dried paint that could cause ugly ridges.

4 Begin painting the next colour. Where it will adjoin the previous colour, check that the first one is thoroughly dry or you will risk smudging it.

5 Continue painting with the other colours. When the larger areas have been completed you can go back and fill in the finer details.

6 Let the paint dry. You may then find, particularly with paler colours, that you need to apply a second coat to cover up the lines of the grid.

7 Again wait until the paint is thoroughly dry. Then clean the chalked grid off the wall by rubbing over it carefully with a damp cloth or sponge.

8 If you wish you can make the outline sharper and its details more obvious by drawing a black line exactly over it using a felt-tipped pen.

9 When the ink has dried, seal and protect the mural by applying polyurethane varnish; if you worked with emulsion paint, use emulsion glaze.

draughtsman's tape (available from good stationers) instead.

Where you will be working at a height you will need a stepladder, or some other form of working platform; make sure, whatever you use, that it is securely positioned. Painting can be a messy job and you should protect your clothing and also the furniture and floor (a dustsheet or old newspaper will suffice) and don't forget to have a plentiful supply of rags available for wiping off brushes and your hands.

Finally you'll need varnish (a clear, matt polyurethane type is best) to protect your finished masterpiece, so it can be wiped down occasionally and won't fade away.

Deciding on the design
The choice of design, is of course entirely up to you; this is the chief reason why painting a mural can be one of the most satisfying forms of decoration to carry out, in that it gives you the freedom to express individual ideas. Having said that, if you are artistic then the sky can be the limit but if you are not, a word of warning: choose a relatively simple design – one you feel confident of handling – for your first attempt.

For inspiration you could look at classical murals, browse through a few books on cave paintings, the art of Pompeii, old tapestries or ethnic or folk art. You can look at landscapes and views, you might even have a photograph of an outdoor scene which you have taken yourself which would transfer to a mural. If the picture is in slide form, and you have a projector, it is sometimes possible to project the design directly onto the blank wall and to sketch in the outline.

Putting the idea on the wall
Once you have decided on the design you should sketch it out on paper and colour it in (with a photograph or picture you've cut out this may not be necessary). Your next step is to transfer this design to the wall, and so that you can get as accurate a representation as possible, the best way to do this (unless you are particularly skilled at freehand drawing) is to use the grid technique. With this you divide the original design up into a grid and then draw a larger grid on the same scale on the wall to provide guidelines for drawing the outline of the mural and for painting it later (see step-by-step photographs). So that your final picture will not end up askew it's essential that you get the grid squarely drawn onto the wall, so make plentiful use of your plumbline, spirit level and try square when you are marking it out.

You can then carefully work your way down the wall filling in one square of the grid at a time with the outline of the design; use your original drawing as a guide.

If you are using the projection technique mentioned earlier you will not need a grid, but it would be wise to establish a true horizontal and vertical and make sure the projected design is correctly positioned before drawing round it.

Another situation where you can dispense with the grid technique is if you decide to use geometric patterns; here there are all sorts of aids available for making sure you get the shape you want clearly and accurately outlined on the wall (see *Ready Reference*). You could, in some circumstances, find that a combination of the grid technique and drawing aids will give you the result you want.

Applying the paint
With the design transferred to the wall you should stand back and look at it carefully and critically, for this is the moment in which you should make any alterations and adjustments necessary. It's a simple matter to rub out any offending chalk or charcoal lines with a cloth, and then redraw them correctly.

When you've got your design exactly how you want it you can begin the painting. Make sure the paint is thoroughly mixed, with the appropriate amount of thinners added, where necessary, and that your brushes are clean, dry and ready for use.

It's best, if possible, to work from the top of the wall downwards as you paint, and to start on the large flat areas of colour.

Use your fine brush to draw in the outline and for filling in on a fairly intricate design; on an uncomplicated job fill in with a larger one to complete the job faster.

When the main, flat painting is completed, you can add shading, modelling, special details or highlights. Sometimes a textured effect can improve a design; you can, for example, stipple the side of a treetrunk by dabbing the paint with a sponge for a more natural effect. Or you might decide to highlight fruit or flower petals with off-white or pale-coloured glaze. Another technique to use when you have completed the mural is to improve the definition of the shapes it contains by outlining them with a thin black line. You could use paint and an artist's brush for this where the design is very simple, but on a more complicated wall-pattern it's much easier and quicker to use a spirit-type felt-tip pen (and you're probably less likely to make mistakes as well).

Finally, however satisfying you've found the process of creating your own wall picture or design, it will have taken you some time to produce. You will want it to last and so you will need to provide it with a protective coating. When the mural is thoroughly dry, you should brush on polyurethane varnish or other suitable sealant so the surface will stand up to wear and tear and so you will be able to clean off any grubby marks without fear of impairing your carefully-wrought design.

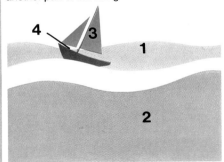

INDEX